Commendations for
The Explorer's Guide to Christianity

'I am inspired by this brilliant book – part history, part anthology, part analysis and wholly inspirational exploration – which will be invaluable to those who wish to know more about Christianity's heritage, and should also confirm believers in the joy of their faith.'

Bel Mooney

'Marcus Braybrooke takes the reader on a tour of Christian beliefs, Christian history and Christian social involvement. Whilst fascinated, I never once felt I was being proselytised – this is a time guide for those who want to know more, with no pressure to join. A *tour de force*.'

Rabbi Julia Neuberger

THE EXPLORER'S GUIDE TO

CHRISTIANITY

MARCUS BRAYBROOKE

Hodder & Stoughton
LONDON SYDNEY AUCKLAND

This book is dedicated to my fourth granddaughter

Anna Clare Hobin

This book's and her gestation took place at the same time

and also to my friends in

The Modern Churchpeople's Union
25 Birch Grove, London W3 9PS

which celebrates its centenary in 1998
and which encourages both commitment
to Christ and intellectual integrity

Copyright © 1998 Marcus Braybrooke

First published in Great Britain in 1998

The right of Marcus Braybrooke to be identified as the Author
of the Work has been asserted by him in accordance with the
Copyright, Designs and Patents Act 1988.

10 9 8 7 6 5 4 3 2 1

British Library Cataloguing in Publication Data
A record for this book is available from the British Library

ISBN 0 340 71005 5

Typeset by Avon Dataset Ltd, Bidford-on-Avon, Warks

Printed and bound in Great Britain by
Clays Ltd, St Ives plc

Hodder and Stoughton Ltd
A Division of Hodder Headline PLC
338 Euston Road
London NW1 3BH

Contents

Acknowledgements

Every effort has been made to obtain permission to use copyright material in this book. Apologies are offered for any oversight in this matter and full acknowledgement will gladly be made in future editions.

Gratitude is expressed for permission to quote the following:

George Appleton's prayer 'O Lord, let the Church . . .' to his daughter Rachel Bennett

From *Saint Augustine's Confessions*, translated by Henry Chadwick (Oxford University Press, 1991)

From John Betjeman's 'Christmas', taken from his *Collected Poems* (© John Murray Publishers Ltd)

From Marcus Braybrooke's *Dialogue with a Difference* (SCM Press Ltd, 1992); *The Global Ethic* (SCM Press Ltd, 1993) and *Yes to the Global Ethic* (SCM Press Ltd, 1996)

Sydney Carter's *Catch the Bird of Heaven* (© Stainer and Bell Ltd, 1969) and *Said to Judas to Mary* (© Stainer and Bell Ltd, 1964)

Chandra Devanesen's prayer 'O Thou, who hast given me eyes', taken from John Carden's *Morning, Noon and Night* (The Church Missionary Society)

From *The Fourth R: Durham Report on Religious Education* (National Society and SPCK, 1990; © Ian T. Ramsey, Bishop of Durham, 1970). Reproduced with permission of the publishers

From Bob Gillman's song 'Bind Us Together' (© 1977 Kingsway's Thankyou Music, PO Box 75, Eastbourne, East

Sussex BN23 6NW, UK). Used by kind permission of Kingsway's Thankyou Music

From Charlene Spretnak's *States of Grace* (HarperCollins Publishers, Inc, New York)

The Third Eucharistic Prayer from 'The Order for Holy Communion, Rite A', taken from *The Alternative Service Book 1980* (© The Central Board of Finance of the Church of England, 1980). Reproduced by permission

Timothy Rees' hymn 'O Crucified Redeemer' (© The Community of the Resurrection)

William Vanstone's *Love's Endeavour, Love's Expense* (© Darton, Longman and Todd)

From Keith Ward's *God, Chance and Necessity* (Oneworld Publications)

Elie Wiesel's *Night* (Hill and Wang, New York, 1958; © 1958 by Editions de Minuit). Reprinted by permission of Georges Borchardt, Inc

Preface

I hope this book will help people of other religions and none to
appreciate Christianity. I also hope that Christians will learn
more about the rich heritage which is theirs.

It is difficult to convey the devotional heart of a faith. This is
why I have included several quotations from hymns and
prayers. Christians, over the centuries, have pictured Jesus in
many different ways and have expressed their beliefs in a
variety of doctrines. Theological debate is as intense today as it
has been in the past. We are, however, beginning to recognize
that truth is multi-faceted and that the True and Living God
transcends all human description and language. Instead of
thinking in rigid terms that one view is right and another wrong
or one belief is orthodox and another heretical, we are learning
that different theologies, be they feminist, classical, black or
liberation, can add to the fullness of our understanding of God's
revelation in Christ.

Christians have also practised their religion in a variety of
ways and the expression of their service to the community has
depended on particular historical, political and geographical
situations. As we learn to live as citizens of one world, the
history of the whole world-wide church becomes the
inheritance of all Christians and a rich resource for the future.
I write from the standpoint of a Church of England parish priest
and many of my examples are from that tradition, but I
recognise that the Church of England is one church amongst
many churches, just as Christianity is one religion amongst
many world religions which are slowly learning to share with

each other their spiritual treasures and to work together for peace, the relief of human need and the preservation of the planet.

It is hard to know what to include in a short book and I am conscious of many omissions. I hope that the suggestions for further reading, at the end of each chapter, will enable readers to follow up topics in which they are interested. The available literature is, of course, enormous.

Those who wish to pursue biblical issues will find *Peake's Commentary on the Bible*, ed. Matthew Black and H. H. Rowley (Thomas Nelson and Sons, 1962), although dated, very useful.

Hans Küng's *On Being A Christian* (Collins, 1977) and *Christianity, The Religious Situation of Our Time* (SCM Press, 1995) are a mine of information.

Various dictionaries are very useful, such as *The Concise Oxford Dictionary of the Christian Church*, ed. E. A. Livingstone (Oxford University Press, 1977); *A New Dictionary of Liturgy and Worship*, ed. J. G. Davies (1986); *A New Dictionary of Christian Theology*, eds. Alan Richardson and John Bowden (1983); *A Dictionary of Christian Spirituality*, ed. Gordon S. Wakefield (1983) and *A New Dictionary of Christian Ethics*, eds. John Macquarrie and James Childress (1986); all of which are published by SCM Press. *The Oxford Dictionary of World Religions*, ed. John Bowker (Oxford University Press, 1997); *Dictionary of Beliefs and Religions*, eds. Rosemary Goring and Frank Whaling (Chambers, 1992) are invaluable, as are the relevant articles in the *Encyclopaedia Britannica*.

Quotations from the Bible, unless otherwise stated, are from the New International Version. Other versions used are the Jerusalem Bible (JB), the New English Bible (NEB) and the Authorised Version (AV).

I would like to thank Judith Longman, Religious Editorial Director of Hodder and Stoughton, for her encouragement, and Mary, my wife, for her enthusiastic support and forbearance, and my teachers, colleagues and parishioners for all that I have learned from them.

Marcus Braybrooke

1

A Life-Changing Encounter

'O great God, who art thou? Where art thou? Show thyself to me.'[1] This was the prayer which Venkayya used to say every morning. Venkayya was one of the first Dalits or outcastes to be converted to Christianity in India in the nineteenth century. The same longing for an experience of God's presence is expressed in a prayer by a twentieth-century Indian Christian leader, Chandra Devanesen, who was the first Indian to be head of Madras Christian College – a missionary college dating back to the mid-nineteenth century, at which I studied for a year in the 1960s:

> *O Thou,*
> *who hast given me eyes*
> *to see the light*
> *that fills my room*
> *give me the inward vision*
> *to behold thee in this place.*
>
> *O Thou*
> *who hast made me to feel*
> *the morning wind upon my limbs*
> *help me to feel thy Presence*
> *as I bow in worship of thee.*[2]

St Augustine, in the fourth century, who said that our heart is restless until it rests in God, had the same yearning for God. 'I tasted Thee, and now hunger and thirst for Thee: Thou didst

1

touch me, and I have burned for Thy peace.'[3]

Indeed, throughout the centuries, famous and unknown Christians have longed for the presence of God and found it in Jesus Christ.

At the heart of the Christian faith is a living relationship to God through Jesus Christ. This can be obscured as one looks at a library full of volumes on Christian doctrine or looks back at the history of Christendom with its arguments and bloody wars. Yet whether in the emphasis on Bible reading or the sacrament of Holy Communion or the Pentecostal experience of the Spirit, there is to be found this same longing for the nearness of God in Christ.

Meeting with Jesus Christ

Christians of every tradition would agree that in Jesus they have been met by God. Their pictures of Jesus may be very different as can be seen from the varied ways in which artists have painted Jesus. How Jesus is one with God is a question that has been much discussed. Yet in different ways they would say that their life had been turned around by Jesus. Illustrations of this, partly in their own words, from the lives of some of those whose influence has profoundly shaped Christianity may be helpful.

Paul

The conversion of St Paul (d. *c.*65), who first spread the gospel of Jesus across the Mediterranean world, was amongst the most dramatic. There are three accounts of it in the Acts of the Apostles and Paul himself briefly described what happened in his letter to the Galatians.

Paul, or Saul as he was then known, like many Jews at the time was not born in the Holy Land, but in Asia Minor at Tarsus, which was an important trading and cultural city. He was brought up in the Pharisaic school of Judaism and was most earnest in his observance of the Torah or Jewish Law. He actively persecuted the early Christian community and was on his way to Damascus to arrest the Christians there, when 'suddenly a light from heaven flashed around him'. Paul fell to the ground and heard a voice saying, 'Saul, Saul, why do you persecute me?' 'Who are you, Lord?', Paul replied. 'I am Jesus, whom you are persecuting,' said the voice (Acts 9:4–5). Paul describes how his life was changed:

> Circumcised on the eighth day, of the people of Israel, of the tribe of Benjamin, a Hebrew of the Hebrews; in regard to the law, a Pharisee; as for zeal, persecuting the church; as for legalistic righteousness, faultless. But whatever was to my profit I now consider loss for the sake of Christ. What is more, I consider everything a loss compared to the surpassing greatness of knowing Christ Jesus my Lord, for whose sake I have lost all things. I consider them rubbish, that I may gain Christ and be found in him. (Phil. 3:5–9)

Instead of persecuting those who believed in Jesus, Paul began to preach the gospel, not only to Jews but also to gentiles. We can almost hear him pleading with his audience. God 'reconciled us to himself through Christ and gave us the ministry of reconciliation ... We are therefore Christ's ambassadors, as though God were making his appeal through us. We implore you on Christ's behalf: Be reconciled to God' (2 Cor. 5:18–20).

Paul in his eagerness to proclaim the gospel travelled, often in great hardship, across much of the Mediterranean world. His letters, extracts from which are read in churches across the world on almost every Sunday, have profoundly influenced the church in every century.

Augustine

It was a verse from Paul's letter to the Romans that had a crucial impact on Augustine (354–430). Augustine longed for God's love, but was unable to control his sexuality. 'Where was I when I was seeking for you?' he asks in his *Confessions*. 'You were there before me, but I had departed from myself. I could not

3

even find myself, much less you.'[4] He despaired at his own weakness. One day, sitting in a garden in Milan in the late summer of 386, as he wrote later:

> I accused myself even more bitterly than usual . . . Weeping in the bitter agony of my heart I heard a voice from the nearby house as if it might be a boy or a girl . . . saying and repeating over and over again, 'Pick up and read', 'Pick up and read' . . . I checked the flood of tears and stood up. I interpreted it solely as a divine command . . . I seized [the book I had been reading], opened it and in silence read the first passage on which my eyes lit: 'Not in riots and drunken parties, not in eroticism and indecencies, not in strife and rivalry, but put on the Lord Jesus Christ and make no provision for the flesh in its lusts' (Rom. 13:14).' I neither wished nor needed to read further. At once, with the last word of this sentence, it was as if a light of relief from all anxiety flooded into my heart. All the shadows of doubt were dispelled.[5]

It was late summer. The vacation was near. Augustine resigned his teaching chair and in the spring of 387 was baptised by Ambrose, the Bishop of Milan. Augustine's writing was prolific and he has exercised a continuing influence on the Christian church. This may best be explained in his own words: 'The true philosopher is the lover of God.'

Luther

Paul's letter to the Romans was also to have a decisive influence on the Reformer Martin Luther (1483–1546). He was born at Eisleben in Germany, the eldest son of seven children. After completing his master's degree at Erfurt, the most famous German university at that time, he began to study law, but after only a couple of months, while out walking on a thundery summer's day, he was felled by lightning. He called on St Anne for help and vowed to become a monk if he survived.

A Life-Changing Encounter

Luther joined an Augustinian monastery but continued to be troubled by the bouts of depression that he had known as a student. In 1507 he was ordained, but was overcome by a sense of terror that he, a sinner, was addressing the Living God. The anguish continued and he found no help in his scholastic studies. He started to do some teaching at the newly founded University of Wittenberg and there got to know Johann von Staupitz (c.1469–1524), who encouraged him to concentrate on the study of the Scriptures.

Luther's inner turmoil was resolved by the verse 'The just shall live by faith' (Rom. 1:17), which led him to an understanding of 'justification by faith alone', which he claimed was a rediscovery of the gospel. Some years later, in 1545, Luther recalled that moment.

> However irreproachably I lived as a monk, I felt myself in the presence of God to be a sinner with a most unquiet conscience . . . I did not love, indeed I hated this just God . . . I raged with a fierce and most agitated conscience and yet I continued to knock away at Paul in this place, thirsting ardently to know what he really meant . . . At last I began to understand the justice of God as that by which the just man lives by the gift of God, that is to say by faith . . . At this I felt myself to have been born again and to have entered through open gates into paradise itself.[6]

John Wesley

Paul's letter to the Romans, mediated by Luther's *Commentary on Romans* also had a critical influence on John Wesley (1703–91), who was the founder of Methodism.

John's father was a Church of England clergyman. His mother Susanna also came from a clerical family. Both parents had links with nonconformists. John studied at Oxford and was ordained in 1725 and became a fellow of Lincoln College. Shortly afterwards, his brother Charles came to Oxford and he formed a small group with some friends to study religious books and to take Communion frequently. John joined the group and soon became its leader. The group was called the Holy Club, but was nicknamed Methodist, a name which stuck.

In 1735, John and Charles Wesley sailed as missionaries to Georgia in America. On board they got to know some Moravians, who were members of a Protestant group deriving from the Bohemian Brethren, who had come under the spiritual influence of Count Zinzendorf (1700–60). The Moravians stressed the need for a 'religion of the heart', based on intimate fellowship with the Saviour. When they reached North America, the Moravian leader Spangenberg asked John, 'Do you know Jesus Christ?' John replied, 'I know he is the Saviour of the world.' 'True, but do you know that he has saved *you*?', Spangenberg insisted.

The Wesleys hoped to work with native Americans, but ill health prevented this and they soon returned to England. Shortly afterwards, they met another Moravian, Peter Bohler, and very soon John and Charles Wesley both had profound spiritual experiences which were to be decisive for their life's work.

On 24 May 1738, John, after attending evensong at St Paul's Cathedral, went to an informal meeting where Luther's *Commentary on Romans* was being read. 'About a quarter before nine,' John wrote in his journal, 'while he [Luther] was describing the change which God works in the heart through faith in Christ, Christ alone, I felt in my heart an assurance was given *me* that God had taken away *my* sins, even *mine*, and saved *me* from the law and death.'

Charles had already experienced inner peace and assurance three days before, on Whit Sunday, 21 May 1738. On the following Tuesday, he wrote his 'conversion' hymn. It is worth quoting from it, as it illustrates both his recollection of his experience and also something of the Wesleys' theology and their evangelistic zeal.

> *'Where shall my wondering soul begin?*
> *How shall I all to heaven aspire?*
> *A slave redeemed from death and sin,*
> *A brand plucked from eternal fire,*

A Life-Changing Encounter

How shall I equal triumphs raise,
* Or sing my great deliverer's praise?*

Outcasts of men, to you I call,
* Harlots and publicans and thieves!*
He spreads his arm to embrace you all;
* Sinners alone his grace receives . . .*
Come, O my guilty brethren, come,
* Groaning beneath your load of sin! . . .*
He calls you now, invites you home;
* Come, O my guilty brethren, come!*[7]

More to modern taste is Wesley's still popular hymn 'O for a thousand tongues to sing' which also speaks of the experience of conversion and new life:

He breaks the power of cancelled sin,
* He sets the prisoner free;*
His blood can make the foulest clean,
* His blood availed for me.*[8]

Sadhu Sundar Singh

Another example of a life-changing encounter from a different century and a different continent is Sadhu Sundar Singh's (1889–*c.*1929) account of how Jesus Christ met with him. He was born of wealthy parents at Rampur in the Punjab in 1889 and brought up in a comfortable home. His parents were Sikhs, but were also interested in Hinduism. They read the scriptures and visited the places of worship of both religions. Of this period in his life, Sundar Singh, in a play on words, said, 'I was not a Sikh, but a seeker after Truth.' His mother encouraged an interest in religion and held up the ideal of a *sadhu* or holy man as the way of life he should adopt when he grew up. By the age of seven he knew most of the Hindu *Bhagavad Gita* by heart and by sixteen had read several other Indian scriptures. The Bible, however, to which he had been introduced at the Presbyterian mission school in the village, repelled him.

7

Indeed, as he says in his account of his conversion, 'I would tear up the Bible and burn it when I had the chance.' He was distressed that he could not find spiritual peace. Then, as he wrote:

> Three days after I had burnt the Bible, I woke up at about three o'clock in the morning, had my usual bath and prayed, 'O God, if there is a God, wilt thou show me the right way or I will kill myself.' My intention was that, if I got no satisfaction, I would place my head upon the railway line when the five o'clock train passed by and kill myself. I was praying and praying but got no answer... At 4.30 a.m. I saw something of which I had no idea at all previously. In the room where I was praying I saw a great light. I thought the place was on fire ... Then as I prayed and looked into the light, I saw the form of the Lord Jesus Christ. It had such an appearance of glory and love ... I head a voice saying in Hindustani, 'How long will you persecute me? I have come to save you; you were praying to know the right way. Why do you not take it?[9]

Sundar Singh went and told his father that he had become a Christian, but the family were far from pleased.

Later Sundar Singh, as a Christian, adopted the traditional way of life of a Hindu holy man or *sadhu*, living in great simplicity and wandering from village to village preaching and teaching. Much of his work at the time was in Tibet. In 1918, he travelled to south India and Sri Lanka (or Ceylon, as it then was) and then he went on preaching tours to America, Europe and Australia. On his return he continued his itinerant preaching in north India and Tibet and was last heard of in 1929.

Mother Teresa

Perhaps the best-known Christian of the twentieth century was Mother Teresa (1910–97), who will always be remembered for her work in India and especially in Calcutta. Agnes Gonhxa Boyaxhiu, to use her original name, was born in Albania/

Yugoslavia and brought up in a happy home. Her vocation came to her as a schoolgirl. She went to India as a member of a teaching order called the Sisters of Loreto. From her window in the convent she saw the slums of Motijhil and occasionally had to walk amongst the poor who lived on the streets of Calcutta.

Her second call – 'a call within a call', as she put it – was to devote herself to the poorest of the poor. In 1948, she left the relative security of the convent school, to devote herself for the rest of her life to serve Christ in the poor. After acquiring some medical knowledge, in 1949 she founded the Missionaries of Charity, whose members in their distinctive sari-like habit are now to be found all over the world.

Seeing Jesus in the Face of the Poor

In every generation there have been Christians who have seen Jesus most clearly in the face of those in need. In her commitment to serve the poor, Mother Teresa represents a dominant concern of Christian women today in Asia, Africa and Latin America.

Thérèse Souga from Cameroon says that 'Christ is the true human, the one who makes it possible for all persons to reach fulfilment and to overcome the historic alienations weighing them down . . . The realism of the cross every day tells me, as a woman of the Third World, that the laws of history can be overcome by means of crucified love.'[10]

The Korean theologian Chung Hyun Kyung likewise says that 'Asian women are discovering with much passion and compassion that Jesus takes sides with the silenced Asian women in his solidarity with all oppressed people. This Jesus is Asian women's new lover, comrade and suffering servant.'[11]

Lydia Lascano, a Filipino who worked for many years as a community organiser for slum-dwellers, sees Jesus both helplessly enduring suffering similar to that of Filipino women and as also actively present in the women's struggle for liberation.

A Personal Saviour

Many unknown Christians can recall the day and time that they discovered Jesus as 'their personal Saviour'. I can myself still vividly recall the moment at Holy Trinity Church, Cambridge, when, as an undergraduate, after a sermon by the well-known Bishop of Coventry, Cuthbert Bardsley, I knew the joy of the forgiveness of my sins. For many other Christians, the journey to faith is more gradual, although some of those who speak of a 'conversion experience' were already, like John Wesley, active church members. Whatever the initial experience of faith, it needs to be renewed each day.

The path to faith is not important, but what I wish to emphasise is that the experience of forgiveness, peace with God, union with Jesus Christ, is at the heart of a living Christian faith. Many Christians are reluctant to speak of such personal and intimate spiritual experiences. This may be why a number of young people, brought up in Christian homes, look to other faiths to help them discover God. They have perceived Christianity as a list either of teachings to be believed or of enjoyable ways of behaving to be avoided – not as a way to experience God. Yet revelation is not truth about God but encounter with the Living God.

Where Do You Start?

Friedrich Schleiermacher

To start a book on Christianity with religious experience is itself open to question. The great theologian and preacher Friedrich Schleiermacher (1768–1834), who has been called the father of modern Protestant theology, did so at the beginning of the nineteenth century, but was subject to strong criticism in the twentieth century by Karl Barth, whose emphasis on the objective revelation of God in Jesus Christ has dominated much theological thinking in the twentieth century.

Schleiermacher, the son of an army chaplain, was born at

Breslau in Lower Silesia. From an early age he thought about religious questions. At the age of fifteen, he became a pupil in a school at Niesky, which was run by Moravian brethren. Moravians, as we have seen with reference to the Wesleys, emphasised spiritual experience, especially warm emotional delight in the Saviour's love. In later years, Schleiermacher said that a revised Moravianism ranked for him as the ideal Christian life, although as a student at the Moravian seminary at Barby, he complained of its lifeless and dogmatic narrowness. Schleiermacher studied at the university at Halle and was ordained in 1794 into the ministry of the Reformed Church. In 1796, he became pastor of the Charité, a hospital and home for the aged just outside Berlin. Here, because for a time he shared an apartment with Friedrich von Schlegel, he found his way into the circle of German Romantic writers.

Schleiermacher became concerned that so many of the cultured people in Berlin in whose company he mixed had no use for religion. He shared their distaste for the arid philosophy of religion which had issued in Deism, which postulated a God who had created the world but who had little continuing interest in it. Deism had small room for personal experience of or relationship with God. On the other hand, the Moravians, amongst whom he had grown up, emphasised personal religious experience, but combined it with a narrow dogmatic belief. In 1798, his *On Religion: Speeches to its Cultured Despisers* appeared. He urged his readers not to concentrate on the doctrinal statements which they mocked, but on a 'sense and taste for the Infinite', or, in a phrase that he often used, on 'a feeling of absolute dependence'.

Schleiermacher argued that dogma and the petty and futile divisions of the church over belief and ritual were not what religion was really about. Religion, he said, is 'the immediate consciousness of the universal existence of all finite things in and through the infinite, and of all temporal things in and through the eternal'. Religion cannot be achieved by argument. It is the direct and unmediated sense of the totality of all there is bearing upon the individual. 'True religion is a sense and taste for the Infinite', which is experienced as an active movement towards the individual. This feeling Schleiermacher related to the common human experience of dependence. In the religious case, it is a feeling of absolute dependence. The fundamental intuition through which the Spirit of the World is apprehended is not a mere emotion, it is a response of the whole person to God. As we shall see in chapter 3, Schleiermacher claimed that Jesus was the person who had this sense of dependence on God in its fullest form.[12]

The Difficulties of Starting with Religious Consciousness

By grounding religious claims in human experience, Schleiermacher did not have to begin with metaphysical speculation nor by requiring intellectual assent to the dogmas of the church. Of course, other explanations of the experience are possible and Freud, for example, a century later, suggested that religion is a collective expression of neurosis and an attempt of individuals to find an escape from the realities of a hostile and indifferent universe. How too do you distinguish the religious experience of Christians from that of a Romantic poet such as Wordsworth or from the mystics of other religions? In the middle of the nineteenth century, a devout Hindu, Sri Ramakrishna (1836–86) claimed that he had followed not only several Hindu devotional paths, but the devotional practice of a Muslim and then of a Christian and that all led to the same spiritual experience. There has subsequently been much discussion about the nature of mystical or religious experience and many scholars would argue that there are varieties of spiritual experience. Even so, those who stress spiritual experience tend to see an affinity between the world's religions, whereas those who emphasise doctrinal belief stress the differences.

Further, if human beings are open to an experience of the Infinite and it is that relationship which is perfectly embodied in Jesus Christ, then, however great the gap, there is an affinity between Jesus and his followers. He is 'an elder brother'. Again as we shall see,[13] the twentieth-century Scottish theologian Donald Baillie compares the presence of God in Jesus Christ to the saint's closeness to the divine through grace. This is why Donald Baillie chose for the title of his book the Pauline phrase *God was in Christ* rather than saying 'Jesus is God'.

In the nineteenth century, the New Testament began to be studied in the same way as any other historical texts. Whilst this approach was disturbing for many Christians at the time, it again meant that defenders of Christianity, instead of calling for a leap of faith, could start from historical events and argue from them to the divinity of Jesus Christ. His divinity was seen as the perfection of his humanity and this fitted with the approach of Schleiermacher, who saw Jesus, whose consciousness was entirely taken up with awareness of God, as 'the ideal representative of religion'. This is a very different starting point from traditional Christian teaching which began with God, the Creator, who came to earth in Jesus Christ.

Karl Barth

The great twentieth-century proponent of the approach of traditional orthodoxy was Karl Barth (1886–1968), who developed the 'theology of the Word of God', also known as the 'theology of crisis' or 'kerygmatic theology', which is the theology of the preacher, so called because Barth said that the task of theology 'is one with the task of preaching; it consists in taking up and passing on the word of Christ'.[14]

Karl Barth was born in Basle, Switzerland. He was the son of a Reformed Church professor of church history and New Testament studies. Karl Barth studied at Berne, Berlin, Tübingen and Marburg. From 1911 to 1921 he was a minister of the farming and working-class congregation in Safenwil. There he began to reflect on and become increasingly critical of the optimism of nineteenth-century Protestant thought. He was shocked by the failure of his theological teachers in the face of current social questions and of the First World War. He joined the Religious Socialist movement, but soon saw that his real task was theological reflection and teaching.

In 1919, Barth's commentary on Paul's letter to the Romans, *Der Römerbrief*, shocked the theological world. It stressed the 'wholly otherness of God'. God, Barth argued, cannot be found by humans as the conclusion of an argument, or as the experience at the end of a religious or mystical quest. Rather, God speaks his Word through 'the strange new world of the Bible'. God takes the initiative in seeking that which was lost, finally coming to humanity in Jesus Christ, the Word made flesh. There is an infinite, qualitative difference between the Creator and his creatures and only God can re-establish a relationship that has been disrupted by human sin. Revelation is an 'event', on which the church should be utterly dependent.

From 1921 to 1935, Barth was professor of theology at various German universities, but he was then expelled by the Nazis and became professor at Basle in Switzerland. He published many works, but his *magnum opus* was *Church Dogmatics*, of which the first volume appeared in 1932. The work was unfinished at his death. His thought developed over the years and he came to see an increasing place for human co-operation with the initiatives of God.

It is his early writings which contrast most sharply with Schleiermacher and the dominant emphases of nineteenth-century Protestant theology. Barth held that there is no way from human beings to God, and his disciple Hendrik Kraemer (1888–1965) argued that religions, including Christianity, were vain human attempts to reach God. Human religious experience did not bring a person into contact with the Living God. That could only happen through repentance and faith in the gospel, wherein God came to man in Christ, to whom the Bible witnesses.

Different Starting Points for Discipleship

I hope this discussion of Schleiermacher and Barth makes clearer the issues involved in deciding where to start a book on Christianity. Do you start with God? It may seem the logical place to begin. The Bible starts with God creating the world, and many one-volume books on Christianity start with a chapter on God. For some Christians belief in God comes before commitment to Jesus Christ. Other people come to faith by reading about Jesus. Other Christians in their path to faith begin with an unexpected spiritual experience. For some that is clearly a meeting with Jesus Christ; for others it is a vaguer sense of 'a presence'. It is to the latter group that the Protestant theologian Paul Tillich spoke when in a famous sermon called 'You are Accepted', he said:

> Grace strikes us when we are in great pain and restlessness. It strikes us when we walk through the dark valley of a meaningless and empty life . . . Sometimes at that moment a wave of light breaks into our darkness, and it is as though a voice were saying: 'You are accepted. *You are accepted*, accepted by that which is greater than you, and the name of which you do not know' . . . If that happens to us, we experience grace.[15]

I have chosen to begin with a chapter on personal religious experience, then to think about the Jesus of the gospels and about what we may be able to know of the historical Jesus of Nazareth. After that I consider the claims Christians make for Jesus Christ and only then think about God the Creator. The second half of this book gives an outline history of Christianity and discusses the life and practice of a disciple.

An Autobiographical Excursus

This approach, not surprisingly, reflects something of my own spiritual journey. I was brought up in a Christian home. My mother was a devout Christian. My father, who was a very able sportsman, after a time as an army officer, followed his father's example and became ordained. About the time I was born, he gave up practising as a clergyman, although I do not think my arrival was the cause of his decision! My earliest memories of my father are as a soldier occasionally on leave during the Second World War. After the war, his main preoccupation was politics. His employment was spasmodic. He had an uneasy relationship with the Almighty. As a result religious questions were freely debated at home. The local church was very liberal in outlook and it came as a surprise to me at theological college to discover what other Anglicans believed. Almost every sermon I heard as a child – and there was some repetition! – was about either the Fatherhood of God or the brotherhood of man.

At the age of about twelve or thirteen, I nearly drowned. Reflecting on this led me to think that I had been rescued because God had some purpose for my life and, in the early 1950s, unaware of social work and many other options, the way to respond seemed to be to become a clergyman. I recall that I often felt closer to God and sensed the beauty of nature when I took the dog for a walk than I did at long-drawn-out church services. I went every Sunday to the early Communion and my prayer, in the words of the 'Prayer of Humble Access' from the *Book of Common Prayer*, was that 'Christ might evermore dwell in me and I in him'. Even then, my emphasis was on spiritual experience and I was uneasy with doctrine and ritual.

Already before my National Service, which took me to Libya and Cyprus, I had some interest in other religions, having heard talks by George Appleton, who had lived for some years amongst Buddhists in Burma, and Kenneth Cragg, a scholar on Islam. Also, thanks to the army, at the age of nineteen, I made the first of a number of visits to the Holy Land, where, especially in Galilee, I had a deep sense of the historical reality of Jesus.

The fact that for two years at Cambridge University, I studied history before studying theology, reinforced my historical approach to the faith. My thinking starts with the human historical Jesus in whom I see the presence of God. I do not start with God who comes down to earth.

My interest in other faiths led me, after university, to study for a year at Madras Christian College, where I tried to learn something about Hinduism and Indian philosophy. I also had the chance to stay in a number of Hindu homes. The poverty of so many people in India made a deep and lasting impression on me. I do not think I had in those days ever seen anyone in Britain sleeping on the street. My uncle, who in later years was a 'down and out', at least always slept in a Church Army or

Salvation Army hostel. Experience of the Church of South India and my marriage to Mary, who was a Methodist, inspired a deep commitment to the search for Christian unity. After my return to England and a time at Wells Theological College, I became a curate in London. Very quickly I also became involved in the World Congress of Faiths and started to do further studies on Hinduism. Through most of my ministry I have combined parochial responsibilities with engagement in interfaith work, both at local, national and international levels.

This book is not intended to be an autobiography nor a spiritual apologia! It attempts to give a picture of Christian faith, life and history. None the less, any book – indeed, as I shall be arguing, all knowledge – reflects the outlook and standpoint of the author. It is important for you, the reader, to be aware of my background and of my presuppositions, because these affect both what is included and also, as I have tried to show, my starting point.

Who Counts as a Christian?

It is also difficult to decide what to include because a religion is such a varied phenomenon. There are great varieties in practice and belief between different denominations and between different periods of history. Further, is a religion a matter of texts or rituals or behaviour?

Richard Gombrich, who is professor of Sanskrit at the University of Oxford and a social anthropologist has written:

> Whether we like it or not it would be blind not to admit that for most people in the modern world religion is first of all an identity, a label, a badge of allegiance of a group. What is your religion? it says on the form, and the terrorist asks the same question. Protestant and Catholic in Ulster, Hindu and Sikh in the Punjab . . . In this sense religion cannot be quite separated from politics or indeed from racism.

He continues by saying that in defining a religion, 'the first answer which occurs to someone from a Christian background is likely to be that religion is a matter of belief, particularly of belief in God. But half the world does not think in these terms. For them, religion is first and foremost what you do, not what you think. A Hindu or a Jew must avoid certain foods.'[16]

What do people mean when they say ninety per cent of the people in Britain are Christian, especially when perhaps no more than ten per cent attend church even once a month? Many of these so-called 'Christians' may not have been baptised, but they have been brought up in a country 'rooted in the Christian tradition'. They will have heard something about Christianity at school and will have holidays at the Christian festivals of Christmas and Easter.

The perspective of those of other faiths can help one see the pervasiveness, even today, of Christian influence in so-called 'Christian countries'. One British rabbi said that whenever he listens to *Thought for the Day*, a daily radio religious pep talk, Jesus repeatedly defeats the Pharisees 'six, love; six, love'. In Canada, where there is a separation of church and state, some Jews were upset when the mayor of a city switched on the Christmas tree lights. Yet, although associated now with Christmas, a Christmas tree is not a Christian symbol!

This question is relevant to civic occasions. If there is a religious service on Remembrance Sunday or Commonwealth Day is there any place in such services in a 'Christian country' for the participation of members of other faiths?

What again does it mean to say of someone, 'She never goes to church, but she's a good Christian'? It is a comment on her kindly way of life, not on her beliefs. In a similar way, when some people say of Britain, for example, that it is 'basically a Christian country', they mean that the accepted standards of behaviour and moral values derive from Christian teaching.

Dimensions of Religion

I thought it was hard enough to write a short book called *How to Understand Judaism*. It is difficult to define what it means to be

Jewish and hard to give a feel for a religion that is not one's own. It is almost equally difficult to define Christianity and to be fair to its enormous variety.

The twentieth century has seen considerable growth in the study of religions as an academic discipline and much discussion about what is involved in this study. Professor Ninian Smart, who has made important contributions to the study of religions, has suggested that a religion is a complex phenomenon with seven dimensions.

Ritual

The first is the practical or ritual dimension. This includes church services, with their patterns of worship, including the sacraments and preaching, festivals and rites of passage. Clearly this dimension is far more important in Orthodox and Catholic churches with their elaborate services than it is to austere Protestant churches or to members of the Society of Friends (Quakers), who sit together mostly in silence.

Experiential

The second area is the experiential or emotional. This has already been illustrated and I have indicated the importance that I attach to this.

Myth

The third dimension is the narrative or mythic. Each religion has its story or stories. The biblical story is that God created the world, including man and woman. Adam and Eve gave in to temptation, whereby sin entered the world. Only the saving death of God's Son Jesus offered a way of escape or salvation. At the end of time Jesus will come again to judge the world.

At one time, most Christians regarded this as factually true, but now most would regard it as a 'myth' or a story with a deep truth about the human condition. Although in popular usage the word 'myth' is taken as a falsehood or a fairy story, writers on religion use it to mean a traditional narrative involving supernatural or imaginary persons but which teaches significant moral or religious lessons. In this way the stories of Adam and Eve and Cain and Abel, even if such people never existed, illustrate the human experiences of failure, guilt, broken relationships and conflict.

Christianity centres on the story of Jesus Christ as told in the four gospels. There has been a great deal of dispute during the last two centuries on how much of that narrative is historical and how much is 'myth'. In part, the dispute reflects the attitudes and beliefs which a person brings to the story. For example, if a person thinks that miracles cannot happen, then they will not regard Jesus' miracles as historical.

The narratives are often reflected in the rituals, so these two dimensions are closely related. At Christmas, for example, countless nativity plays re-enact the story of Jesus' birth.

Doctrinal

The fourth dimension is the doctrinal or philosophical. This is the attempt to answer such questions as 'Does God exist?' or 'Did God make the world?' or 'Does God answer prayer?' Christianity traditionally has given considerable emphasis to correct belief. We shall see how important the creeds and other summaries of belief have been to many Christians, who have unchurched those with whom they disagreed and at times persecuted people whose opinions were regarded as unorthodox, whom they called heretics.

This dimension also includes the enormous amount of writing on theological and philosophical matters. Together with the emphasis on creeds or correct belief, there has also been the intellectual effort to grapple, for example, with questions of suffering and evil or to work out how Jesus could be both divine and human.

Ethical

Christians have also struggled to see what the central Christian story means for every aspect of life. Jesus' concern for the sinner, for example, has something to say about how criminals should be treated. His injunction to 'love your enemies' (Matt. 5:44) has led Christians to argue about whether or not they should take part in war. This fifth dimension is the ethical or legal.

Social

The sixth dimension is the social or institutional and is the one to which Richard Gombrich drew attention. It is about the community to which people claim to belong and their sense of identity. One difficulty, however, is that not all Christians recognise that others who claim to be Christian are really so. A decree of the Council of Florence (1438–45) said that 'The Holy Roman Church firmly believes, professes and proclaims that none of those who are outside the Catholic church – not only pagans, but Jews also, heretics and schismatics – can have part in eternal life, but will go into eternal fire.' Heretics and schismatics were those who thought of themselves as Christian but did not agree with the Holy Roman Church.

Such rigidity has changed, but even today Councils of Christian Churches argue about whether Unitarians, who reject the doctrine of the Trinity, may belong to such Councils. There are even sharper arguments about the Unification Church, which was founded by the Korean Sun Myung (b.1920), who is known as Reverend Moon. On Easter Day 1936, Moon claimed to have experienced a vision of Jesus Christ. The revelations which he received form the basis of Unification theology. In 1954 he established the Holy Spirit Association for the Unification of World Christianity. Yet although Reverend Moon regards himself as commissioned by Jesus Christ, the majority of Christians will have no fellowship with his followers who are often called 'Moonies'. This is partly because of disagreement about belief and partly because accusations have been made, firmly rejected by Unificationists, of brainwashing of converts. The point here, however, is that the question of how people define their religious identity may itself be a matter of dispute.

This question of identity can be important. According to the 1928 Church of England Prayer Book, the service of Burial was not to be used for the unbaptised. Baptism, the rite of entry into the church, defined who was or was not a Christian and, according to some Christian teaching, determined who would or would not go to heaven. This is why it was customary at one time to arrange an immediate baptism for a baby if it was thought that the child might not live. Religious identity may condition who can receive communion with whom, admission to a school or whether a person can be married in church. Where a church has a particular link with the state or is 'established', as is the case with the Church of England, this may be a cause of discrimination. This public face of religion, to which social anthropologists who study religion give particular attention, is important, although committed believers may wish to distinguish themselves, perhaps as 'born-again' Christians from so-called 'nominal' Christians.

Anyhow, it should be clear that the question of religious identity is complex!

Material

The seventh dimension identified by Ninian Smart is the material. This includes sacred buildings and sacred art. Christians have built churches of great beauty in many places, which are consecrated or set apart for the worship of God. Sometimes their upkeep is a drain on resources and some Christians may feel that the money would be better used helping the poor. It is also true that there are many people who are heirs to Christian culture and have a deep appreciation of cathedrals, Christian music and Christian art, who do not have a personal belief in Jesus Christ.

A Phenomenological Approach

The seven dimensions are inter-related and may help as a reminder of the various perspectives from which one may approach a religion. Other writers have suggested different models. One important approach is what is called the 'phenomenological'. This is the attempt to appreciate what a person's religious identity, belief and practice mean to that person. The student seeks, partly through the use of imaginative sympathy, to enter into the world of the believer.

My hope is that this book will be a doorway to the Christian world for those who do not consider themselves Christians, whilst helping those who do call themselves Christians to know more about the heritage into which they have entered. Because I have myself been met by the love of God in Jesus and seek to follow him, the book will be coloured by my own experience of and reflections upon the Christian faith, but I hope I shall be fair to those whose way of being Christian is very different to my own.

I hope, too, that whilst inevitably the book deals with externals it will point to the living experience at the heart of the faith. As the seventeenth-century poet George Herbert (1593–1633) wrote:

> *A man that looks on glass,*
> *On it may stay his eye;*
> *Or, if he pleaseth, through it pass,*
> *And then the heavens espy.*[17]

Any student of religions may look only on the glass. One may, as Jesus said, 'be ever seeing but never perceiving' (Mark 4:12). I hope I may be able to indicate how both Christian belief and practice flow from the living experience of God's forgiving love in Jesus Christ, but I hope also that the reader will pass beyond the words to appreciate the reality to which they point.

The classic books about religious experience are:
Rudolf Otto, *The Idea of the Holy* (1917).
William James, *The Varieties of Religious Experience* (1902).
Further information on this subject may be obtained from The Religious Experience Research Unit at Westminster College, Oxford OX2 9AT.
Ninian Smart discusses the Dimensions of Religion in the Introduction to *The World's Religions* (Cambridge University Press, 1989).

2

Who is Jesus?

Christian discipleship centres on faith in and the following of Jesus Christ. It is not, however, so easy to say who Jesus is. In speaking of Jesus, people may mean the historical person, Jesus of Nazareth, who lived in Palestine nearly two thousand years ago. They may mean the Jesus of faith, the living presence, whom believers claim 'walks and talks with them along life's narrow way'. They may mean both, and we shall need to try to explain the relationship between the Jesus of history and the Jesus of faith. In this chapter we try to discover what the historical Jesus of Nazareth was like.

What do we know about the Jesus of history? This also is not an easy question to answer. Many thousands of books have been written about Jesus; each with its particular emphasis. Perhaps that is not so surprising. I am writing this on the day of Princess Diana's funeral. For a week, every newspaper has been full of articles about her. Each author has his or her own memory of the Princess and even with all the words about her, the reader does not fully understand the complexity of her personality. A living person makes a particular impact on each other person he or she encounters. So with Jesus. We know him through the record left to us by those who were closest to him.

The Gospel Story

That record is in the four gospels. First I shall give an outline picture of Jesus as he has been known through the gospels to millions of Christians in many centuries and many countries. But then, we shall need to discuss the question of the accuracy of the gospels. Was Jesus really anything like the person presented in say Luke's or John's gospel?

Birth

The Christmas story celebrates the birth of Jesus to the Virgin Mary in a stable at Bethlehem. Luke tells us that Mary was living in Nazareth, a town in Galilee in the north of Palestine, when she had a vision of the Angel Gabriel. The angel told her that she was to give birth to a baby boy, who was to be called Jesus, which is the Greek for the Hebrew name Yeshua, which means 'God saves'. Although Mary was promised in marriage to Joseph, who was by trade a carpenter, she was still a virgin. Joseph was descended from King David. This meant that when the Romans, who occupied Palestine, ordered a census, he and Mary had to go to Bethlehem, the city of David. When they got there after four or five days' travelling, the town was so crowded that they could not find room at the inn, so they made do with the shelter of a cave, which was used as a stable for the animals. There Jesus was born.

Tradition has it that the first people to visit the Holy Family were local shepherds. Later, wise men, often pictured as kings, came perhaps from Persia. To escape King Herod's plot to kill the baby King Jesus, the Holy Family fled to Egypt. After Herod's death, they thought it was safe to return. They settled at Nazareth in Galilee. Little is known of Jesus' childhood and youth.

Baptism and Ministry

When Jesus was a young man, his cousin John started to call people to repent and be baptised in the river Jordan. Jesus too was baptised. As he came up from the water, 'he saw the heavens torn open and the Spirit, like a dove, descending upon him. A voice spoke from heaven, "Thou art my Son, my Beloved, on thee my favour rests" ' (Mark 1:10–11 NEB).

After a time in the wilderness, Jesus started a ministry, mostly around the lake of Galilee, preaching about God's kingdom and healing many who were ill. He collected quite a following and had twelve special companions, who became known as the disciples or apostles. Amongst the twelve were Simon Peter and his brother Andrew, and John and James, who were also brothers. Jesus' ministry aroused the opposition of some religious leaders, partly, it seems, because he was willing to mix with the outcasts of society and tell them of God's love and partly because he questioned some of the contemporary interpretations of the Torah or Jewish Law.

Death and Resurrection

Jesus met with more dangerous opposition in Jerusalem. It is not clear how often Jesus went there. In what was to be the last week of his life, he and his followers journeyed to Jerusalem. When he reached the Mount of Olives and drew near to the city, his supporters, in their enthusiasm, sat Jesus on a donkey and cut down branches of palm to wave, shouting: 'Hosanna! Blessings on him who comes as king in the name of the Lord' (Luke 19:38 NEB). Talk of Jesus as a king was enough to alarm the Jewish high priests and the Roman authorities.

Aware of the growing danger, Jesus at his last meal with his disciples, which was perhaps a Passover meal, warned them that he was likely to be arrested and put to death. After the meal, Jesus went with his disciples to an olive orchard at the foot of the Mount of Olives. Whilst he was praying there, a band of soldiers, who had been told where to find him by Judas Iscariot, who was one of the twelve apostles, came and arrested him. Jesus was taken before the Jewish authorities who handed him over to Pontius Pilate, who was procurator, or governor of Judaea from 26 to 36. Pilate condemned Jesus to death.

Jesus, after being flogged, was nailed to a cross – a cruel

method of execution, widely practised by the Romans – on what surprisingly has become known as Good Friday, because his death was for the 'salvation of the world'. His body was put in a new tomb, but when early on the Sunday morning, the day after the Sabbath, some of the women who had followed Jesus went there to prepare his body for burial, they found that the stone across the entrance to the tomb, which was a cave, had been rolled away and that the tomb was empty. The women and then other disciples claimed that Jesus was not dead, but risen from the grave and that he had appeared to them. The belief that Jesus died and was raised by God to new life – the Resurrection – is at the heart of the Christian message. It explains why Christians believe that Jesus is alive today and is their constant companion.

After forty days, during which the Risen Jesus appeared on occasion to his disciples, he ascended into heaven 'to the right hand of God' (Acts 2:33). The disciples expected his imminent return to act as God's judge and to bring in the kingdom of God.

Can we Trust the Gospels?

When Were the Gospels Written?

There are questions about almost every aspect of this story. Although we have some evidence from first-century Roman writers for the existence of a group of people who believed in Jesus Christ, we are dependent for our knowledge of Jesus on the four gospels. The first gospel to be written was probably Mark's in the early sixties in Rome. Luke's and Matthew's gospels were probably written between ten and twenty years later, although there is a persistent tradition that Matthew, one of the disciples, wrote a 'gospel' or collection of the sayings of Jesus in Hebrew. This is why until comparatively recently, Matthew's gospel was regarded as the earliest gospel. In fact, the present text of Matthew's gospel, in many passages, is almost word for word the same as Mark's gospel, which was written in Greek. Matthew, although his is the longer gospel, often abbreviates what Mark wrote. The view of the majority of scholars is that both Matthew and Luke used Mark's gospel, as well as some other material known to both of them, which scholars often call 'Q', from the German word 'quelle', which means 'source'. Matthew and Luke also both include some material found only in that gospel. Because of the common material in the first three gospels and because the writers look at Jesus from the same point of view, these gospels are known as the 'synoptic' gospels.

John's gospel is very different. It is debated whether John knew the other gospels. There are factual differences. John, for example, puts the incident of the cleansing of the Temple at the start of the ministry (John 2:12–22) whereas the other writers put it in the last week of Jesus' life. John makes clear that the Last Supper was not a Passover meal, whereas the other three gospels say it was (compare John 19:31 with Mark 14:12). There are also theological differences. In the synoptic gospels, Jesus did not wish his divine status to be openly proclaimed. When a man with an unclean spirit cried out, 'I know who you are – the Holy One of God', Jesus rebuked him and said, 'Be silent!' (Mark 1:25). In John's gospel, Jesus openly claimed, 'My Father and I are one' (10:30).

It is probably best to think of John's gospel as a meditation on the meaning of the life of Jesus rather than primarily a historical record, although at times he seems to preserve an early historical tradition. In the twentieth-century, there has been much debate about the identity of John. Was he the beloved disciple or was the book, as an ancient tradition suggested, written by an elder called John of Ephesus towards the end of the first century? It was felt that the gospel reflected Hellenistic ideas rather than a Jewish approach. In recent years, with the discovery of more Jewish literature which shows the great variety within Judaism at that time, a growing number of scholars have come to think that the fourth gospel derives from a 'heretical' Jewish-Christian community, maybe in Antioch, and dates to between 80 and 100.

It may be that none of the gospels is written by an

eyewitness. The material that the evangelists use had already been shaped by the preaching and teaching ministry of the church. Apart from the Passion narrative, the various incidents recorded in the synoptic gospels are only loosely connected and probably the links have been supplied by the evangelists. This would be consistent with the earliest stories about Jesus being passed on by word of mouth. If people tell a funny story, they remember the punch line, but often the context or characters are changed in different versions. In the same way, Jesus' followers would remember the key action or saying of Jesus but might be vague about where it happened.

In any case, Jesus' followers talked about him not from historical curiosity, but because they believed that he was the agent of God. They spoke of Jesus in the context of worship, preaching and teaching. In the same way, the evangelists were not like a modern biographer, trying to write a balanced history of a person's life. We have no reference to what Jesus looked like nor to whether he was tall or short. The evangelists wrote, as John put it in an appeal to the reader, that 'you may believe that Jesus is the Christ, the Son of God, and that believing you may have life in his name' (John 20:31).

Stories of Jesus Circulated in the Christian Community

The stories about Jesus which are recorded in the gospels, had first been told and retold in the teaching and preaching ministry of the church. This suggests that they had already been applied to the changing situation of the early Christian community. Take, for example, chapter 7 of Mark's gospel. A major issue in the early Christian community was whether gentiles should be welcomed into the church and if so, whether they had to observe Jewish rules about purity.[1] Mark's gospel is thought to have been written for the church in Rome, of which the majority of members were probably gentile. They would not have observed Jewish purity rules. In fact, Mark has to explain the Pharisaic practice of ceremonial washing of the hands before eating (Mark 7:3). Mark presumably included the story of the disciples eating without washing their hands as a justification for the behaviour of the Christians in Rome. Later, Mark quotes a saying of Jesus, 'Don't you see that nothing that enters a man from the outside can make him "unclean"? For it doesn't go into his heart but into his stomach, and then out of his body.' To this saying, Mark adds the comment, 'In saying this, Jesus declared all foods "clean" ' (Mark 7:18–19). Matthew omits this comment.

A more significant example of the way in which the early Christian community applied the teachings of Jesus to their own situation is in the interpretation given to some of the parables. Take, for instance, the parable of the Wise and Foolish Virgins (Matt. 25:1–13). Ten young women set out with oil lamps to meet a bridegroom to escort him to the bride's home for the wedding. The groom's arrival was delayed. The five 'foolish' women had not brought flasks of oil to replenish their lamps so had to go and buy some more. Whilst they were away, the groom arrived. By the time they got back, the wedding festivities had started and they were locked out. In Matthew's gospel, the parable follows a chapter about the signs of the End of the Age. 'No one knows about that day or hour, not even the angels in heaven,' Jesus said, 'Therefore keep watch, because you do not know on what day your Lord will come' (Matt. 24:36, 42). The parable, as we now have it, is a warning to be on the watch for Christ's Second Coming.

In the context of Jesus' ministry, it is more likely that the parable was a warning by Jesus to his immediate audience to recognise the moment – to be aware that the kingdom of heaven was at hand and to seize the opportunity of salvation and to welcome the bridegroom, whom Jesus elsewhere identified with himself (Mark 2:19). Central to Jesus' own preaching was the message that the 'kingdom of God is at hand' (Mark 1:15).

Why the Context Matters

That the early Christians reapplied the sayings of Jesus to their own situation is entirely proper. It is still the task of a good preacher. But it means that if we are to reconstruct the sayings of Jesus in their original context, we have, as it were, to reverse the process. The most significant difference, of course, is that the gospels are written in the light of the death and resurrection of Jesus. When Jesus spoke to the crowds in Galilee, they had no hint of these world-changing events. At times, the evangelists themselves recognise this. For example, John tells us that it was only after Jesus was raised from the dead that the disciples understood Jesus' saying, 'Destroy this temple and I will raise it again in three days' (John 2:19). Mark says that the three disciples who witnessed Jesus' transfiguration were only permitted to tell of this after his resurrection (Mark 9:9). Yet even if they tried, the evangelists could not put aside their knowledge of the crucifixion and resurrection and feel what the people of Galilee felt, any more than someone writing today about Jewish history in the 1930s can put aside their knowledge of the horror of the Holocaust or of the creation of the state of Israel.

Now, if the material in the gospels has been used and to some extent adapted to the changing needs of the early Christian community and it is written in the light of the belief that God had raised Jesus from the dead, there is room for much difference of opinion about what Jesus actually said and did. Traditional and conservative Christians will tend to regard the gospels as straightforward accounts of Jesus' life and death. That is probably how the majority of Christians hear readings from the gospels. Other writers put forward their own explanations, knowing that there is never enough evidence to disprove any theory, however unlikely it may seem to sober scholars. The more unlikely the theory, the more media coverage a book is likely to get. In fact, the uncertainty about Jesus is that which pertains to all our knowledge of the past. All accounts of the past are mediated to us through people who had their own interests and concerns.

In the same way, each of the evangelists was writing for a particular audience and had his special interests. Traditionally the author of the third gospel is said to be Luke, who was a gentile doctor. This gospel shows a particular interest in the gentiles and in healing miracles. It also emphasises the compassion of Jesus. It alone contains some of the best-loved parables, such as the story of the Prodigal Son or of the Good Samaritan, as well as Jesus' prayer on the cross, 'Father forgive them, they know not what they do' (Luke 23:34) and his words to the penitent thief, 'Today you will be with me in Paradise' (Luke 23:43).

Recognising the situation in which the evangelists wrote is important for several reasons. One is that at the time Matthew's and John's gospels were written, there was bitter argument between those Jews who believed in Jesus and those who rejected his claims. The hostility was intensified by the fact that when the Romans laid siege to the city of Jerusalem from 66 to 70, the Christian community fled (Matt 24:15–16 = Luke 21:20–21). The polemic of that period has soured Christian–Jewish relations through the centuries. John 8:44 implies that the Jews are 'children of the devil', whilst in Matthew 27:25, the Jewish people are said to have cried out for Jesus' crucifixion, saying 'His blood be on us and on our children.' Second, this polemic has also distorted our view of Jesus' relationship to the Judaism of his day. He has been seen as critical of it and in conflict with the Jewish religious leaders. There is much evidence, however, to show that the gospels are unfair to the Pharisees and that Jesus was himself a faithful Jew.

Another reason why the context is important is that in his own ministry Jesus' central message was that 'the kingdom of God is near' (Mark 1:15). After Jesus' death and resurrection, Jesus himself became the focus of the church's preaching. During his earthly life, did the people of Galilee, or even his disciples, recognise him as divine? Are the various titles given to Jesus in the gospels, such as 'Lord' or 'Son of God', ones that were used of him in his earthly ministry or were they first applied to the risen Christ by those who believed in him?

This bears significantly on how we picture Jesus and how we seek to reconstruct his earthly life and ministry. For many centuries, Christians have spoken of Jesus as God become man. Despite the attempts of the creeds, which we shall consider later, to balance his divinity and his humanity, the real subject of the gospels has seemed like a god in human disguise. Only gradually since the nineteenth century has it been accepted that

Jesus had the knowledge of a first-century human being. He did not, for example, two thousand years ahead of his time, understand computers, although keeping the knowledge to himself! Do Christians accept that Jesus had the emotions of an ordinary human being so that he could be angry or upset?[2] Did he have the sexuality of an ordinary man?

Perhaps because a historical way of thinking has become common, much liberal and critical scholarship during the last two hundred years has approached Jesus as a real and historical human being. The question then is where to locate his divinity. That is a matter to which we shall return in the next chapter.

The Life of Jesus Re-examined

Aware now of the complexity of the gospel records, we need to look again at the life of Jesus. How much of the traditional story survives the acid of historical scholarship? In my view, although details will remain uncertain, the impact of Jesus' magnetic personality shines out from the gospels.

The Virginal Conception

There has been much debate about the Virgin Birth or, as it is properly described, the virginal conception of Jesus. The two clear references in the New Testament (Matt. 1:18–25 and Luke 1:26–38) speak of the conception of Jesus in the womb of Mary 'from the Holy Spirit' and not by male agency. It is only a later second-century apocryphal gospel that speaks of Mary miraculously giving birth with her sexual organs intact.

It is uncertain whether other New Testament writers refer to the virginal conception. Perhaps John hints at this when he says that those to whom Jesus gave the right to become children of God were born 'not of natural descent, nor of human decision, nor of a husband's will, but were born of God' (John 1:14). Some see a reference to this tradition by Paul when he speaks of God's Son being 'born of a woman' (Gal. 4:4) and being 'as to his human nature a descendant of David'

(Rom. 1:3), but the evidence that Paul knew the tradition of the virginal conception is very uncertain. In Mark 6:3, Jesus is called 'son of Mary', rather than, as one would have expected, 'son of Joseph'. His opponents seem to have circulated rumours that Jesus was illegitimate. These are also mentioned and rejected in the account of Jesus' birth in the Qur'an, which says that in response to the angel's message, Mary replied, 'My Lord, how shall there be a son [born] to me, and man has not touched me?' to which the angel replied, 'Even so, God creates what he pleases' (Surah 3:46–47; cp. 19:20–21).

Some scholars who reject the tradition of a virginal conception say that the idea arose from a misreading of Isaiah 7:14, which in the New English Bible reads: 'Therefore the Lord himself shall give you a sign: A young woman is with child, and she will bear a son and will call him Immanuel.' Many other translations, following the translation of the Hebrew Scriptures into Greek known as the Septuagint, speak of a 'virgin' rather than a young woman, although the Hebrew word means a young woman and not necessarily a virgin.

Arguments based on biblical criticism are not decisive for or against belief in the virginal conception. The phrase in the creed, 'born of the Virgin Mary' emphasises the real humanity of Jesus against docetic views that, rather like a Greek god, Jesus had only the appearance of a man. Ambrose and Augustine believed that the transmission of original sin was related to the carnal desires aroused by procreation. That Jesus was asexually conceived explained for them how Jesus was free from original sin. Some Christians today, however, reject the doctrine of the virginal conception just because it seems to undervalue human sexuality.

For some traditional Christians the doctrine of the virgin birth is integral to belief in Jesus' divinity. More liberal Christians would however find other grounds for their belief in Jesus and may be either agnostic about or reject the tradition. The Roman Catholic church speaks of Mary as 'ever virgin' and holds that the brothers of Jesus (Mark 3:31) were in fact half-brothers, children of Joseph by a previous marriage. In both Catholic and Orthodox churches high veneration is paid to the Virgin Mary, who is sometimes called 'Mother of God' or *Theotokos*, the 'God-bearer'.

The Birth of Jesus

According to a tradition not mentioned in the Bible, Mary's parents were Joachim and Anne. They are said to have lived in Jerusalem. Before Mary conceived, her cousin Elizabeth, who was thought too old to have children, also became pregnant. Luke begins his gospel by telling of the angel's message to Elizabeth's husband, Zechariah, and of the meeting of the two pregnant women, probably at the village of Ein Kerem, which is now on the outskirts of Jerusalem. On meeting Elizabeth, Mary praised God in a hymn known as the Magnificat. At the church built on the site, the words of the Magnificat are reproduced in many languages. Zechariah and Elizabeth's son, who, in obedience to an angel's instruction was called John, became as John the Baptist the precursor or herald of Jesus' own ministry.

The exact date of Jesus' birth is impossible to determine. The first mention of 25 December as his birthday is not until 336. The day was probably chosen in opposition to the pagan feast of the Birth of the Unconquerable Sun. Even the year of Jesus' birth is not known for sure, although it is usually now thought to be about 6 BCE. The most definite date is for the beginning of John the Baptist's ministry. This can be fixed with considerable certainty to 28/29 CE, the fifteenth year of the Emperor Tiberius (Luke 3:1). Matthew says that Jesus was born perhaps a couple of years before the death of Herod the Great, who died in 4 BCE. (Matt. 2, especially verse 15). Luke, who also says that Jesus was born when Herod was king (Luke 1:5), relates Jesus' birth to a census conducted when Qurinius was the governor of Syria (Luke 2:2). This census is also mentioned by the Jewish historian Josephus as the cause of a rising against the Romans by the Zealots. The date, however, is 6 or 7 CE. There is no evidence of an earlier census and it is very unlikely that a Roman census would have been held whilst Herod the Great, who was an allied king, was in power. The general view is that Luke's chronology is mistaken. Some attempts have been made by astronomers to date 'the star in the east' which led the wise men to Bethlehem. It was suggested by the seventeenth-century astronomer Johannes Kepler that in 7 BCE there was a conjunction of Jupiter, the planet of kings, with Saturn, the protector of the Jews, in the Zodiac sign of Pisces, which designates Palestine.

Jesus' birth at Bethlehem has been questioned, because it seems unlikely that in a census people would be required to travel to the home of their ancestors. In Matthew's gospel, the assumption seems to be that the Holy Family already lived in Bethlehem. Because of the threat to their baby's life from Herod the Great, they fled to Egypt. When Herod died, they thought it was safe to return, but not to Bethlehem, so they settled in Nazareth in Galilee. Historical accuracy may, however, not have been the evangelists' main concern. They wanted to show that Jesus the Saviour had been born in the city of David, who was the greatest king of Israel (Luke 2:11). In their genealogies both Matthew and Luke, in different ways, show that Jesus was descended from King David. The tradition of the flight into and return from Egypt may also have been developed to match the experience of the people of Israel, whom God rescued from slavery under Pharaoh. Some scholars sometimes feel that the traditions have been tailored to fit the prophecies!

Even if the date and place of Jesus' birth may be uncertain, the claim that God entered human history is central to traditional Christian belief, as the British poet Sir John Betjeman (1906–84) indicated in his poem 'Christmas':

> *And is it true? And is it true,*
> *This most tremendous tale of all,*
> *Seen in a stained-glass window's hue,*
> *A Baby in an ox's stall?*
> *The Maker of the stars and sea*
> *Become a child on earth for me?*
>
> *No love that in a family dwells,*
> *No carolling in frosty air,*

> *Nor all the steeple-shaking bells*
> *Can with this single Truth compare –*
> *That God was Man in Palestine*
> *And lives to-day in Bread and Wine.*[3]

The Jewish World in which Jesus Grew Up

We have no direct information about Jesus' childhood, apart from stories in Luke 2. We have to fill in the picture from what we know of life in Galilee at that time. Mary's well in the centre of Nazareth was until recently the only source of water and must have been the place to which Jesus went with his mother to collect water. Many pilgrim sites are uncertain, but there are places where one can feel, despite the passing of two thousand years, the link with the historical Jesus.

Joseph is said to have been a carpenter, although since much wood was used in building, he was probably a builder as well. Presumably, when there was work, Joseph made an adequate living, although the family would have lived very simply by modern Western standards. Mary would have made the clothes for the family. They would have lived on home-made bread, fish from the Sea of Galilee, fruit, eggs and milk. Sparrows were used for meat. The lamb, killed for the Passover, was a luxury. A peasant's home would probably have been one room. At night the family slept on a platform and the animals were brought inside as well.

Education was provided for Jewish boys at the synagogue school, where Jesus would have learned Hebrew, the language in which the Jewish scriptures were written. At the start of his ministry Luke tells us that he read from the scroll of the prophet Isaiah (Luke 4:16–21). The language of the people was Aramaic.

As a Jew, Jesus would have been brought up to pray and praise God and to obey God's teaching or Torah. He would have learned of Jewish faith and history not only at school, but also in the home, especially from observance of the Sabbath and from participating in the various festivals. Luke says that every year Jesus' parents went up to Jerusalem for Passover and that when Jesus was twelve he went with them. He became separated from his parents who eventually found him in the Temple (Luke 2:41–50).

At the heart of Jewish faith is the belief that God, the creator of the world and the Lord of History, rescued the people of Israel from slavery in Egypt and entered into a covenant with them at Sinai. In gratitude to God, the Jews responded by seeking to obey the Torah which God had given them. Torah is often translated 'Law', but it has a richer meaning. Torah is God's teaching by which he shows the holy people how to live. Although Christians have sometimes spoken of the Law as a burden,[4] most Jews regarded it as a privilege. The Psalmist spoke of the Law as 'the joy of my heart' (Ps. 119:111).

The Jewish cultic ritual centred on the Temple in Jerusalem, which had been rebuilt by Herod the Great. A model of how Jerusalem would have looked at that time, which can be seen in Jerusalem today, shows how magnificent the Temple was and how it dominated the city. Animal and cereal sacrifices were offered regularly by the priests. Pious Jews would go to Jerusalem for personal ceremonies and some of the major festivals (Luke 2:22, 41).

Sadducees and Pharisees

The high priests in Jerusalem belonged to the party of the Sadducees. Much of the creative religious leadership at the time, however, came from the Pharisees. The main dispute between the Pharisees and the Sadducees was over what was called the 'oral Law' or 'oral Torah'. Both groups accepted the authority of the 'written Torah' – the books of the Hebrew Bible. Particular authority attached to the first five books of the Bible – the books of Moses. The Pharisees believed there was another source of authority called the oral Torah, the traditional interpretation of the scriptures that had been handed down from generation to generation, right from the time of Moses. The Jewish historian Josephus (*c.*37–*c.*100), who wrote in about 90 CE, described the difference in this way:

> The Pharisees have delivered to the people a great many observances by succession from their fathers, which are not

39

written in the laws of Moses: and for that reason it is that the Sadducees reject them, and say that we are to esteem those observances to be obligatory which are in the written word, but are not to observe what are derived from the tradition of our forefathers.[5]

A major point of dispute was about belief in the resurrection, which the Pharisees accepted and the Sadducees rejected (Acts 23:6–8).

The Pharisees, although they have had a bad press from Christians, made a creative contribution to the understanding of God. The origins of the movement are obscure, but the general view is that by the first century BCE, they were bringing about profound and lasting changes in Judaism. They had a new perception of God as concerned for the individual. God was not just the God of Abraham, Isaac and Jacob – the God of the nation. God watched over and cared for each member of the people of God. Everyone, therefore, and not just the priests, was expected to observe the Torah, which the Pharisees applied to contemporary life by giving oral interpretations of it. The Pharisees gave new names to God, such as 'the Holy One' or 'Our Father who art in heaven'. They developed the synagogue as a centre of teaching.

Most of our knowledge of the Pharisees comes from the second-century literature of the rabbis, who were the heirs of the Pharisees. It is not clear exactly what the Pharisees taught nor how influential they were at the time of Jesus. Certainly the gospels often refer to the Pharisees and on many occasions show Jesus in dispute with them. A growing number of scholars, however, think Jesus was close to the Pharisees. The pattern of his ministry with its emphasis on teaching and the reinterpretation of the oral Torah and on healing the sick is that of an authentic rabbi. Like the Pharisees, Jesus emphasised the *Shema* ('Hear O Israel') and the primacy of love. Jesus taught the resurrection of the dead. He stressed his intimate link with the Father, and his meals with his disciples are similar to the meals which the Pharisees shared with each other.

According to Matthew, Jesus said, 'Do not think that I have

come to abolish the Law and the Prophets; I have not come to abolish them but to fulfil them' (Matt. 5:17). His disputes with the Pharisees were internal arguments. We know of various sub-groups of Pharisees, such as the Hasidim, or 'saints', who went beyond the letter of the law. Rabbis often argued strenuously with each other. Indeed, those who belong to the same religious group can be fierce in their disagreements, even though they have a great deal in common, as has been shown by the recent arguments in the churches about whether women should be ordained. One leading New Testament scholar, E. P. Sanders, has said, 'We know of no substantial disputes about the Law, nor of any substantial conflict with the Pharisees.'[6] For example, arguments about Sabbath observance are recorded in the gospels. Yet there was no disagreement that the need to save life had precedence over Sabbath rules. There was however regular dispute about whether an illness was life-threatening or whether the healing could wait until tomorrow.

In their attempt to grow in holiness by carefully observing rules about food and purity, the Pharisees may have kept them-selves apart from ordinary people, rather as some vegetarians are reluctant to eat with those who have chosen meat, or as the early Methodists, with their stress on temperance, kept them-selves apart from those who drank alcohol. Jesus, however, saw his mission as to the lost children of the house of Israel and was prepared to mix with those who were regarded as sinners.

Scribes
The Sadducees and the Pharisees are the two Jewish religious groups most frequently mentioned in the gospels. The term 'scribe' is often linked with the Pharisees. Some have suggested that they were the leading Pharisees. Others see it as a term for those who could read – 'clerks' – who offered their services to the people and who may have belonged to various religious groups, although probably most of them were Pharisees.

Essenes
In the twentieth century the Essenes have attracted much interest because of the discovery of the Dead Sea Scrolls. Early

in 1947, a Bedouin shepherd accidentally found fragments of ancient scrolls inside some earthenware jars in caves high up on the rock face near the Dead Sea. The very dry climate had helped to preserve them. The shepherd had no idea of their significance and value. In the following decade, more scrolls were discovered in other nearby caves.

Altogether, eleven more or less complete scrolls were found, and thousands of fragments. There are extracts from all the books of the Hebrew Bible, except the book of Esther, as well as other religious compositions and works belonging to a particular Jewish sect. Gradually, the scrolls have been pieced together and translated. Subsequent excavation nearby at Qumran unearthed the buildings of a monastic community. The inhabitants are usually thought to have been Essenes, who are mentioned by Josephus as an important group, numbering about four thousand. The Essenes separated themselves from ordinary society and lived apart in communities. They did not marry. Like the early Jerusalem church (Acts 2:44), they held all goods in common. They disapproved of the temple priesthood and cult. The scrolls were presumably from the Essenes' library and had been hidden to protect them from the Roman army.

Because John baptised not far away in the river Jordan, and because Jesus, at the start of his ministry, spent forty days in the Judean wilderness nearby, it has been suggested that John, who had an ascetic way of life, and perhaps Jesus, were influenced by the Essenes, but this remains speculation.

The Essenes expected a final cataclysmic conflict between good and evil. A rather similar picture is found in some of the Pauline and Johannine writings. Earlier in the twentieth century, scholars attributed this to the influence of Hellenistic dualism, but now scholars accept a Jewish background to the concept of a cosmic struggle of good and evil. A similar outlook is to be found in some of the apocalyptic Jewish literature of the period, such as 1 Enoch. It is important to stress that in both Christian and Jewish apocalyptic the power of God is in the end always stronger than the forces of evil.

Samaritans

If the Essenes avoided other people, most Jews avoided the Samaritans. When Jesus asked a Samaritan woman for a drink of water, she expressed surprise. 'You are a Jew and I am a Samaritan woman. How can you ask me for a drink?' John adds an explanatory note that 'Jews do not associate with Samaritans' (John 4:9). The origins of this dislike dated back to 722 BCE, when the Assyrians destroyed the capital of the northern kingdom of Israel and deported many of the inhabitants. Those who were left eventually mingled and intermarried with the pagan people who were settled in the land. When the Jews of the southern kingdom, who after the fall of Jerusalem in 597 BCE were taken into exile in Babylon, eventually returned to Judea, they would have nothing to do with the 'impure' northerners. Jesus on more than one occasion spoke kindly of the Samaritans. Of the ten people whom he healed of leprosy, it was a Samaritan who came back to thank Jesus (Luke 17:11–19). It was also a Samaritan in one of Jesus' stories, who unlike the priest and Levite, stopped to help the man who had been attacked by thieves (Luke 10:25–37).

Zealots

If the Essenes shunned society and expected heavenly intervention to overthrow Satanic powers, the Zealots were prepared actively to hasten the process, identifying the occupying Roman army with those forces of evil. During the period of the Maccabees, who in 168 BCE led a revolt against the Seleucid ruler Antiochus Epiphanes, the Jews had for a time reasserted their independence. Throughout the period of Roman rule, there were a series of armed uprisings against them, which the Romans cruelly suppressed. One of Jesus' disciples was known as 'Simon the Zealot' (Luke 6:15), but it seems clear that Jesus rejected a military struggle against the Romans, although some of the people wanted to make him king (John 6:15). On Palm Sunday, he chose to ride into Jerusalem on a donkey, echoing the prophecy of Zechariah: 'See, your king comes to you, righteous and having salvation, gentle and riding on a donkey' (Matt. 21:5 and Zech. 9:9).

Jews of the Diaspora

To complete this picture of Judaism at the time of Jesus, it is important to remember that many Jews lived in the Diaspora, outside the land of Palestine. The two greatest centres were in Babylon and Alexandria, which was said to have contained about a quarter of a million Jews. Both were great centres of Jewish scholarship. The famous Rabbi Hillel was of Babylonian origin, whilst Philo, one of the greatest Jewish philosophers, lived in Alexandria.[7] Many Jews lived at Antioch in Syria. The Acts of the Apostles shows there were Jewish communities in many cities of Asia Minor. Paul himself came from the 'well-known city of Tarsus in Cilicia' (Acts 21:39 JB). There were many Jews in Rome. Throughout the Roman Empire, Jews were permitted to practise their religion, which with its ethical monotheism was respected by many gentiles, even if Jews also suffered from some popular prejudice.

The Political Situation

Palestine itself was under the control of the Romans, although some areas were under puppet kings, such as Herod Antipas (Matt. 14:1). There is some mention of Jesus having contact with Roman officers. For example, he healed a centurion's servant and marvelled at the centurion's faith (Matt. 8:5–13). In his last week in Jerusalem, he painfully experienced the power and cruelty of empire, although, as he died, it was a centurion who said, 'Surely this man was the Son of God' (Mark 15:39).

Palestine had been exposed to Hellenistic influence for at least two hundred years. Sepphoris, which was Herod Antipas' capital until he built the city of Tiberias, was less than five miles from Nazareth, but is not mentioned in the gospels. Devout Jews would have avoided what they regarded as the corrupting influence of Hellenistic culture.

Jesus' Baptism and Ministry

The centre of Jesus' ministry was Capernaum, a town at the north end of the Sea of Galilee. The present site is dominated by the remains of a third-century synagogue, probably on the site of an earlier one. Nearby is a church over a site identified as the house of Peter. Mark tells us that at the beginning of his ministry, Jesus was walking beside the Sea of Galilee and called Simon and Andrew and John and James, the sons of Zebedee, all of whom were fishermen, to be his followers. They went to Capernaum, where Jesus taught in the synagogue and drove out an evil spirit, and afterwards went to the home of Simon and Andrew and healed Peter's mother-in-law who was ill in bed (Mark 1:14–31).

Jesus' ministry, following his baptism and period in the wilderness, began, according to Mark, with the announcement, 'The time has come, the kingdom of God is near. Repent and believe the good news!' (Mark 1:15). Jesus made present the kingdom of God by word and deed. For the gospel writers, the miracles were signs of the kingdom. John says of the miracle at the wedding in Cana of Galilee, at which Jesus changed water into wine, that this first miracle 'revealed his glory and his disciples put their faith in him' (John 2:11). The driving out of demons was seen as evidence of the overthrow of Satan's kingdom (Mark 3:20–30).

The miracles of Jesus are a problem for many people today. They ask, 'What really happened?' but that was not a question which interested the evangelists. Instead, they ask the reader, 'What do you think about the person who performed the miracles?' At the time of Jesus most people believed that holy men could perform miracles. Jesus' opponents did not question the fact of the miracles, but said that Jesus performed them in the power of the devil (Mark 3:32).

What today might be regarded as psychiatric illness was at that time considered to be possession by evil spirits. Some people have tried to give 'natural' explanations to the miracles. For example, it has been suggested that most of the crowd whom Jesus is said miraculously to have fed with five loaves and two small fish, had brought packed meals with them, but were reluctant to share these until he set the example (John 6:5–15). Perhaps, when Jesus walked on the water, he knew of some stepping stones, hidden just beneath the surface (John 6:16–21). It has even been suggested that the guests at the wedding in Cana (John 2:1–11) were so drunk that they did not notice that they were being served water instead of wine! Such an approach assumes that in theory everything can be given a natural explanation and that miracle stories belong to a pre-scientific superstitious age. Today, however, with greater awareness of the psychosomatic nature of much illness, there is renewed interest in spiritual healing.

The nature miracles create more difficulty. Atheistic materialists, who do not believe in God, understandably reject the idea of divine intervention. Even Christians are divided. Those who believe that miracles are refuted by modern science may view them symbolically rather than literally, saying, for example, that the stilling of the storm (Mark 4:35–41) shows that God is with the believer in the storms of life. Other Christians are concerned about the idea of an interventionist God. Why, if God 'miraculously' cures some people, does he allow others to suffer excruciating pain? Are not the laws of nature an expression of God's guiding providence? Other Christians so stress the full humanity of Jesus, that they question whether he exercised supernatural powers.

I do not myself doubt that a person of great spiritual authority can give someone who is ill release from guilt and new hope which may make recovery possible. I find the raising of Lazarus from the dead (John 12) more difficult to accept as historical, although its symbolic meaning as brought out by John is powerful. Unless the resurrection of Jesus is interpreted only as a change of attitude in the disciples from deep gloom to new hope, it seems to me difficult for Christians altogether to discount the possibility of divine intervention. God, I believe, wills the wholeness of all people, but never forces divine grace upon them. The longing of the sick for recovery and other people's prayers for them may unstop the channels of grace.

Today probably most people primarily see the miracles as

evidence of Jesus' compassion. Indeed, Mark in introducing the account of the feeding of the crowd said that 'Jesus had compassion on them' (Mark 6:34). In the story of the healing of the blind beggar Bartimaeus (Mark 10:46–52) or of the healing of the woman who had a haemorrhage and who touched Jesus in the crowd (Luke 8:42–48), there can again be seen his concern for the individual.

The Kingdom of God

For the gospel writers, however, both Jesus' miracles, especially the exorcisms, and his teaching were evidence of his authority and were signs of the kingdom. A great deal in recent times has been written about 'the kingdom of God'. It may be better to translate the term as 'the rule of God', which suggests a relationship to God rather than a state. Even the term 'rule of God' sounds male, authoritarian and undemocratic. One modern version of the Lord's Prayer begins: 'Holy One, our only Home, Hallowed be your name. May your day dawn.' In speaking of the kingdom, Jesus seems to have been talking about those who live consciously in awareness of the love of our Heavenly Parent. They have no need to worry. Themselves forgiven, they forgive others and bear no enmity. This new way of life is described in the Sermon on the Mount (Matt. 5–7). Such people reflect the love of God. It is possible to live now in this way, and where people do so, God's gracious presence is already a reality, although the confidence is that more and more people will come to live in this way.

Some of the New Testament writers seem to have pictured the kingdom in more objective and less personal terms. They would have been influenced by the role model of contemporary rulers. For example, in Luke's version of the Parable of the Talents, the king on his return gave orders that his enemies who did not want him to be king should be brought to him and be killed in his sight (Luke 19:27). Pictures of the terror by which rulers in the ancient world sought to maintain their authority ought not to be applied to God's exercise of his rule and should not, in my opinion, be used to suggest that Jesus taught that the wicked would burn for ever in hell. The evangelists' ideas of the kingdom were also coloured by apocalyptic literature which pictured a sort of 'star wars' conclusion to world history in which God's armies of the righteous would destroy the wicked.

Some New Testament passages suggest that there was a strong expectation that the kingdom was about to come. According to Mark, Jesus said, 'I tell you the truth, some who are standing here will not taste death before they see the kingdom of God come with power' (Mark 9:1). The second letter to the Thessalonians speaks of 'the Lord Jesus . . . revealed from heaven in blazing fire with his powerful angels. He will punish those who do not know God and do not obey the gospel of our Lord Jesus' (2 Thess. 1:8). John, however, suggests that it is not the Son's task to punish people. Jesus, he said, came to show God's love, and people bring suffering upon themselves by rejecting that offer of light and love. Judgment is self-inflicted. 'For God so loved the world that he gave his one and only Son, that whoever believes in him shall not perish but have eternal life. For God did not send his Son into the world to condemn the world but to save the world . . . Whoever does not believe stands condemned already . . . Everyone who does evil hates the light' (John 3:16–20).

Clearly some early Christians expected the return of Jesus in their lifetime. There are, however, cautionary remarks. When, in Acts 1, the disciples just before his ascension ask Jesus if he is about to restore the kingdom to Israel, they are told, 'It is not for you to know the times or dates the Father has set by his own authority' (Acts 1:7). The end of John's gospel contradicts a rumour that John was to live until the Lord's return. Luke's writings, like John's gospel, play down ideas of an imminent return.

Some Christians today, as they have through the centuries, continue to try to predict the date of Christ's second coming. Most churches retain the belief in the Second Coming – the Church of England Communion service includes the words, 'Christ will come again', which everyone is expected to say – yet there is no great expectation that the second coming is about to take place. The belief is a way of affirming that the future belongs to God. Few Christians probably have a clear picture of what they expect will happen at the end of time. Some hope for the kingdom of God to come on earth – as Jesus taught his disciples to pray – but others expect the denouement of history in another world. Others are more interested in a future life in the next world rather than in the destiny of human society. The law of thermodynamics suggests that eventually the world is running down – but not for millions of years. Many Christians do not speculate about the future, but are sufficiently occupied struggling for peace and justice, for which the kingdom of God is a symbol, amidst the conflicts of the day.

The kingdom, understood as a believer's relationship of trust in God, is the subject of many of Jesus' parables. Just as a merchant will sell all his possessions to buy a priceless pearl, or the man who discovers buried treasure will sell his belongings to buy the land where the treasure is buried, so God's kingdom is worth any sacrifice. Like a mustard seed or yeast, the kingdom grows through the power of God. Disciples are not to be down-hearted if there are weeds amid the crops. Although some seed is wasted, the good seed will bear a harvest (Matt. 13). The faithful are not to be discouraged by persecution and setbacks; God's kingdom will be established.

Several parables insist that the kingdom of God's love is offered freely to all who repent and turn to God. One of the best-known parables is the story of the Prodigal Son in Luke chapter 15. A father had two sons. The younger asked his father for his share of the inheritance and then set out for a far-off land. There he wasted the money on riotous living. When his funds were exhausted, he tried to get work, but the only job he – a Jew – could get was to look after pigs. He decided to return to his home country and ask his father for work as a servant. Whilst he was still some way from home, the father saw him, ran out to greet him, kissed him, ordered that he be given a robe, a ring and sandals and arranged a celebration. The elder son, however, refused to go to the party and complained that although he had worked hard all his life for his father, he had never been given a party, so the father went out to plead with him as well. Some of Jesus' opponents, instead of rejoicing that Jesus was mixing with and preaching to the rejects of society, criticised him for his actions. Jesus told other parables to defend his mission to sinners, such as the parables of the Lost Sheep and the Lost Coin (Luke 15) as well as the story of the Labourers in the Vineyard.

An owner of a vineyard went out early to employ some workers. He promised to pay them a denarius each for a day's work. He went back three times and each time found some men who still had not found work, so he engaged them as well. At the end of the day, he first paid those who had only started work in the afternoon and gave them a denarius. Those who had toiled all day expected to get more, but the master said, 'Didn't you agree to work for a denarius? I want to give the man who was hired last the same as I gave you. Don't I have the right to do what I want with my own money? Or are you envious because I am generous?' (Matt. 20:15).

There is a tendency of those who wish to live holy and upright lives to cut themselves off from those whose morals are more questionable. The Essene community, as we have seen, went to great lengths to keep themselves unspotted by the world. Jesus, however, insisted that God's generous love is for all – just because he had created them and they were his children. Jesus pointed out that if a man has an ox or an ass that falls into a pit, he goes to great trouble to rescue the animal. Why then, Jesus asked, is it surprising that God wants to recover his erring children?

There is however a human tendency of the righteous to want to see others punished for their wrongdoing. Jesus insisted that no one is righteous, but that all people depend on the generous mercy of God. Paul said the same: 'All have sinned and fall short of the glory of God, and are justified freely by his grace through the redemption that came by Christ Jesus'(Rom. 3:23–4). It is still a matter of dispute whether people need first to repent before they can receive God's forgiveness or whether the initiative is with God and that it is only as a person experiences the accepting love of God that they recognise their failures and wrongdoing and ask for help. Jesus in his ministry came to seek and to save, and in his teaching gave a picture of God, whose outflowing and forgiving love seeks to draw all people to himself. Too often the church has not been so welcoming – although it has been said that the church exists for sinners and not for saints.

This mission to the outcasts may well have been related to Jesus' sense that his ministry was a decisive moment in God's purposes. Some Jews expected that in the new age, God would welcome back the sinners of the children of Israel. Indeed, in Isaiah 44:22, God had promised, 'I have swept away your offences like a cloud . . . Return to me, for I have redeemed you.' When Jesus went to the home of Zacchaeus, who was despised because of his work as a tax-collector for the Romans, Jesus said, 'Today salvation has come to this house, because this man, too, is a son of Abraham. For the Son of Man came to seek and to save what was lost' (Luke 19:9–10). Jesus defended his actions against his critics by stressing that God's forgiving love was available to all and that the angels of heaven rejoiced whenever a sinner repented.

There was also some expectation that at the end time the twelve tribes of Israel would be restored. This may explain Jesus' choice of twelve disciples. There is some disagreement in the gospel records about their names, but not about the highly significant number twelve. Another hope for the new age was that the Temple would be renewed. It may be that when Jesus drove out the moneychangers and those who sold animals for sacrifice, he was not just objecting to the commercialisation of a holy place, but symbolically warning of the Temple's forthcoming destruction and the replacement of the sacrificial cult by worship in spirit and in truth (John 4:21–4).

There was also some expectation that at the end time there would be a gathering in of the gentiles. Zechariah, for example, had promised that 'many nations will be joined with the Lord in that day and will become my people' (Zech. 2:11 and 8:20–22; see also Isaiah 56:6–8). The early Christian community claimed that in opening its doors to the gentiles, this prophecy was being fulfilled (Rom. 9:25).

This brings us back to the kingdom. The sense that the

kingdom was at hand and that a new age was dawning gives coherence to Jesus' ministry, but such a belief would have been controversial, just as a generation ago many white South Africans could not see how the apartheid regime could ever be changed. Those who speak of change are always threatening to those who have a vested interest in the status quo. It is not necessary, however, to vilify Jesus' opponents, as Christians have often done with regard to the Pharisees. It is more accurate to recognize that good people can sincerely disagree.

The Death of Jesus

The gospels are probably mistaken when they on occasion suggest that the Pharisees were involved in the plot to kill Jesus. Over the centuries, Christians have blamed the Jews for the death of Jesus, even though he was crucified, which was a Roman form of execution. It may be that the high priests and some of the Sadducees wanted Jesus out of the way, lest the Romans used a 'rebellion' as an excuse to take away the Jews' few remaining liberties. John pictured a meeting of the Sanhedrin, the supreme Jewish council and court of justice at that time, at which it was said, 'If we let him go on like this, everyone will believe in him, and then the Romans will come and take away both our temple and our nation.' To which Caiaphas, the high priest commented, 'You know nothing at all! You do not realise that it is better for you that one man die for the people than that the whole nation perish' (John 11:48–50).

It seems likely that the gospel accounts try to shift the blame for the crucifixion of Jesus from the Romans to the Jews. It is interesting that in popular Christian devotion, it is often assumed that the Palm Sunday crowd which greeted Jesus with cries of 'Hosanna' was the same crowd that on the following Friday shouted out, 'Crucify him'. But the latter may have been a 'rent-a-mob'. We are told that Jesus could not be arrested in public for fear of the people and that Judas told the authorities where they could arrest Jesus when no crowd was present

(Mark 12:12; Luke 22:6). As he was led to crucifixion, the women of Jerusalem wept for him (Luke 23:27, 48).

There is much uncertainty about the historicity of the gospel accounts of the various trials. According to Mark, after Jesus had celebrated his last supper with the disciples, he went with them to a place called Gethsemane, where he prayed, '*Abba*, Father, everything is possible for you. Take this cup from me. Yet not what I will, but what you will' (Mark 14:36). Whilst he was at prayer, a crowd, armed with swords and clubs, led by Judas Iscariot came to the garden and arrested him. They took him to the high priest, where accusations were made against Jesus. Then the high priest asked Jesus directly, 'Are you the Christ, the Son of the Blessed One?' 'I am,' Jesus replied, 'And you will see the Son of Man sitting at the right hand of the Mighty One and coming on the clouds of heaven' (Mark 14:61–2).[8] At this, the high priest cried out, 'Blasphemy!', and concluded that Jesus deserved to die.

It was, as far as we know, against Jewish law to hold a meeting of the Sanhedrin at night. This may, however, have been a preliminary hearing as Mark refers later to another meeting very early in the morning (Mark 15:1). It was also unacceptable to condemn a person out of his own mouth. It is questionable whether what Jesus is reported as saying was actually blasphemous. In any case, it is quite possible that in his account of the trial, following the practice of some ancient historians, Mark wrote what he thought would have been said, rather than attempting to give a verbatim record of the trial's proceedings. That is to say, by the time Mark wrote his gospel the key issue in dispute between the early Christians and the Jewish community was whether or not Jesus was the Christ. Mark brilliantly highlights the central issue, but it is more likely, historically, that Jesus was put to death by the Romans because he was a trouble maker. According to Mark, Jesus after the second hearing was taken before Pilate. Pilate wanted to set him free, but gave in to Jewish demands. We know, however, from other evidence that Pilate was eventually recalled to Rome for cruelty. He was not a squeamish man and had little concern for Jewish sensitivities.

By the time Mark's gospel was written, however, some Christians, including perhaps Peter and Paul, had been put to death by the Emperor Nero. Christians were the object of Roman hostility. It would only increase Roman hostility were they to think that the founder of Christianity had himself been put to death for sedition. There seems to have been an attempt to whitewash Pilate – with even his wife dramatically pleading for Jesus' innocence (Matt. 27:19).

Many Christians continue to accept the historical accuracy of the gospel accounts, which have formed the basis for dramatic re-enactment of Jesus' passion over the centuries. They need, however, to be challenged because the way in which Christians have heard the story of Jesus' passion has inflamed prejudice and hatred of Jews and has been a cause of persecution in every century – most of all in the horrors of the Holocaust.

Since that ghastly event, most churches have repudiated the false charge of deicide, which implied that the Jews were accursed by God because they put the Son of God to death. Some Jewish leaders may have colluded with the Romans, but Jesus suffered a Roman penalty because he was regarded by the Romans as a rebel. In any case, it is morally wrong to blame future generations for the actions of their parents. In Christian theology, responsibility for the death of Jesus rests with God (Acts 3:17–8), or with all people, because it is believed that Jesus died for the sins of all people. As a hymn writer puts it,

> Twas I, Lord Jesus, I it was denied thee:
> I crucified thee.[9]

Muslims, out of respect for Jesus, deny that he really died. God, they say, would have raised a *faithful* servant to heaven and not allowed him to be killed. According to the Qur'an, the Jews said, ' "We killed the Messiah, Jesus, son of Mary, the messenger of God", though they did not kill him and did not crucify him, but he was counterfeited for them . . . Nay, God raised him to himself' (Surah 4:155–59). The Christian creed, however, insists that Jesus died and was buried.

The Resurrection

If there is uncertainty because we lack historical evidence about who was responsible for the death of Jesus, there are questions about his resurrection because it is a supra-historical occurrence. The Christian claim that Jesus, after he had died and been placed in a tomb, was raised to new life by God, is a belief in a unique event. Historians rely on parallels, and the activity of God does not count as a historical explanation. There is some historical evidence for the resurrection, but the central issue is a matter of faith.

The biblical arguments for the resurrection of Jesus are threefold. First, his tomb was found empty. Second, several members of the early Christian community claimed that the Risen Jesus had appeared to them. Third, Jesus' resurrection was said to fulfil Scripture.

According to John, very early on the first day of the week, Mary Magdalene went to the tomb and saw that the stone had been removed from its entrance. She ran and told Peter and 'the other disciple whom Jesus loved', who also came to the tomb and saw that it was empty. Matthew's gospel mentions a rumour that the disciples, despite an armed guard at the tomb, had stolen the body. Yet the opponents of the early Christians never produced a body. Some modern scholars cast doubt on the tradition that Jesus was buried in the tomb belonging to Joseph of Arimathea. They think it more likely that a criminal's body, when removed from the cross, would have been flung into a common grave.

There are several accounts of the Risen Lord appearing to disciples. John says that he spoke to Mary Magdalene while she was still in the garden near the tomb, as well as later in the day to all the disciples, except Thomas, who was not there. Thomas, often called 'Doubting Thomas', insisted that he would only believe if he himself saw the nail marks in Jesus' hands. A week later, the Risen Jesus appeared again to the disciples and this time Thomas was with them. Thomas, now the true believer, hailed the Risen Jesus as 'My Lord and my God' (John 20:28).

Paul, in his first letter to the Corinthians, summed up the message that he had received in these words:

> that Christ died for our sins according to the Scriptures, that he was buried, that he was raised on the third day according to the Scriptures, and that he appeared to Peter, and then to the Twelve. After that, he appeared to more than five hundred of the brothers at the same time, most of whom are still living, though some have fallen asleep. Then he appeared to James, then to all the apostles, and last of all he appeared to me, as to one abnormally born. (1 Cor. 15:3–8)

It is interesting that Paul counts his vision on the Damascus road as an appearance of the Risen Lord, as this seems to conflict with the Acts of the Apostles which implies that the resurrection appearances came to an end after forty days (Acts 1:3).

Paul mentions the argument from the Hebrew Scriptures. In Luke's gospel, there is a story of two disciples travelling to Emmaus on the first Easter day, who were joined by a stranger, who explained to them that Moses and all the prophets had said that the Christ had to suffer before entering into his glory (Luke 24:26–7; cf. Acts 3:17ff.). It is not always evident, however, that the passages quoted by the early Christians as evidence that the resurrection of Jesus Christ was foretold by the prophets, originally had the meaning that they put upon them.

Although the various scriptural arguments for the resurrection of Jesus are open to question, modern writers insist that some explanation is needed of what empowered the early disciples to spread the message of Jesus across the world. Millions of Christians today, as in every generation, witness that in their experience 'Jesus is alive'.

This conviction is central to Christian faith, but it remains a matter of belief. Christians vary from those who picture the resurrection as the reanimation of a corpse to those who understand it in more spiritual terms and might look for a parallel in group hallucinations. Although Thomas was invited to touch the wounds made by the nails, the Risen Christ is not portrayed in the gospels as a reanimated corpse. He could pass through doors. Paul in 1 Corinthians 15 speaks of a 'spiritual body' (1 Cor. 15:44). The Risen Jesus was seen only by believers, not by the general public. It has been said of the empty tomb that however early the women had been, they would not have seen the stone being rolled away. The evangelists are not describing an ordinary physical happening. It seems quite likely that Mark's gospel originally ended at chapter 16, verse 8, with the words, 'Trembling and bewildered, the women went out and fled from the tomb. They said nothing to anyone, because they were afraid.' The resurrection could not be described; it could only be known to those who believed. It is later writers who tend to treat the resurrection as an ordinary, objective event.

Often in Christian hymns, the resurrection is sung of in triumphalistic terms as the defeat of evil and death. Both, however, remain very evident in the world and this is one reason why many Jews do not believe that Jesus was 'the Messiah'. He has not delivered the redemption that the Messiah was expected to bring. Sadly, some Christians have even used the resurrection as an argument against the Jews, suggesting that by it God showed that Jesus was right and the Jews wrong. At the same time, some Christians have so spiritualised redemption as the promised reward of the individual in the next world, that they have ignored the suffering and evil of human life in this world.

The resurrection is perhaps best understood as a hope. It is both an affirmation of faith that the way of self-giving love embodied by Jesus can never be defeated and a commitment to live in that love. John, in his gospel, was careful not to separate the death and resurrection of Jesus. Easter is not a happy ending after the horror of Good Friday. Good Friday and Easter Day belong together. John wanted his reader to see that it was the cross itself which revealed the glory of God (John 12:16, 23). John used for the crucifixion the deliberately ambiguous word 'lifted-up', which suggested both the physical lifting up on the cross and the exaltation to glory (12:32). Easter, for John, was the recognition that the self-giving love shown on the cross revealed the heart of God.

Further, John suggested that through Jesus' glorification on the cross, the Spirit became present to the believer (John 7:39). Some commentators think that the words with which John records Jesus' death, 'He bowed his head and gave up his spirit', were also intended to mean that as he died he handed over the Spirit to the few representative believers who stood at the foot of the cross (John 19:30.[10] Luke, in the Acts of the Apostles, separates chronologically what John holds together theologically. Luke pictures Good Friday and Easter being followed by a period of forty days in which the Risen Jesus appeared to the disciples before leaving them and ascending into heaven. Ten days later, at Pentecost, the Holy Spirit came upon the disciples 'like the blowing of a violent wind' (Acts 2:2).

Pentecost, or Whitsun, is sometimes spoken of as 'the birthday of the church'. But this is to move from the historical Jesus to the Jesus of Christian faith, although it is only through the sometimes distorting medium of that faith that we have a glimpse of the man from Nazareth.

Two quite short lives of Jesus are C. H. Dodd, *The Founder of Christianity*, (Collins, 1971) and Donald Coggan, *The Servant-Son* (SPCK, 1995). Rather longer are E. P. Sanders, *Jesus* (Penguin, 1993), and Günther Bornkamm, *Jesus of Nazareth* (Hodder and Stoughton, 1960).

An imaginative book which creates the atmosphere of the time is Gerd Theissen, *The Shadow of the Galilean* (SCM Press, 1987).

Books by E. P. Sanders and J. Jeremias are useful for the relationship of Jesus to the Judaism of his day, as is Hyam Maccoby, *Judaism in the First Century*, (Sheldon Press, 1989) and John Riches, *The World of Jesus* (Cambridge University Press, 1990).

3

Is He the Christ, the Son of God?

Christians through the centuries have in many different ways tried to communicate their experience of being met by God in Jesus Christ.

John in the Prologue to his gospel says, 'No one has ever seen God; but God's only Son, he who is nearest to the Father's heart, he has made him known' (John 1:18 NEB). The claim is that in their relationship to Jesus, men and women are in relationship to God. We all know the irritating experience of trying to speak to the manager of a company or to a consultant and finding that we cannot get past a receptionist or assistant. Christians believe that Jesus is not just an angel or messenger of God, but, as the Nicene creed puts it 'very God'. Jesus, in John's gospel, tells Philip, 'Anyone who has seen me has seen the Father' (14:9).

Paul speaks of 'the revelation of the glory of God in the face of Jesus Christ' (2 Cor. 4:6 NEB). John says, 'We saw his glory, such glory as befits the Father's only Son' (John 1:14 NEB). Modern readers may miss the full significance of the word 'glory'. The glory of God is a way of speaking of God himself. Moses on Mount Sinai asked God, 'Show me your glory.' God replied, 'You cannot see my face, for no one may see me and live,' but God placed Moses in a cleft of the rock and covered him with his hand and allowed Moses to see only his back (Exod. 33:12–23). In this passage, the term glory means the same as the Presence of God or the *Shekinah* of Jewish theology. The term glory is often used by the prophets. The rabbis also used it, occasionally of God himself, but more often of the presence of God in the world. Frequently the *Shekinah* is associated with light. It rests predominantly on Israel. The *Shekinah* supports the sick, rests on the worthy married couple and takes proselytes under its wing. The Jewish scholar Alan F. Segal says that 'there was in the Bible a human theophany, a human appearance of God, often called the angel of the Lord but also called the *Kavod*, God's glory'. Paul claimed that he had himself seen the *Kavod*, God's glory just as Ezekiel did. 'And this *Kavod* had the features and face of Jesus.'[1]

This is an astonishing claim and made at most within a generation of Jesus's death. In Matthew and Luke also there is the verse, 'All things have been delivered to me by my Father. No one knows the Son except the Father, and no one knows the Father except the Son and any one to whom the Son chooses to reveal him' (Matt. 11:27 = Luke 10:22).

To speak of Jesus just as a good man, a great ethical teacher and a healer of the sick is to fail to do justice to the evidence of the New Testament. It is, of course, possible to say that the early Christians were wrong, but not, to my mind, to deny that they claimed to have encountered God in the person of Jesus Christ.

New Testament Claims for the Divinity of Jesus

It is difficult to know to what extent the disciples were aware of God's presence in Jesus prior to his being raised from the dead. Indeed, to what extent was the human Jesus himself aware of his divine status?

The gospels tell of an occasion when Jesus took three disciples, Peter, James and John, up a high mountain and was transfigured before them, so that his clothes became dazzling white. They had a vision of the true glory and divine nature of Jesus. Just before, in response to Jesus' question, 'Who do you say that I am?', Peter had answered 'You are the Christ' (Mark 8:29; Matt. 16:16 gives Peter's reply as, 'You are the Christ, the Son of the living God'). Many modern scholars think that the gospel accounts of both Peter's confession and the transfiguration were written in the light of the resurrection. Some indeed suggest that the transfiguration was originally a resurrection appearance.

In India today, there are those such as Sai Baba (*b.*1926), who are regarded as divine by their followers. At many ashrams in India, devotees will just sit in the presence of the holy person – *darshan.* Indian concepts of divinity are different from those of Judaism, Christianity and Islam, which are often called the Semitic religions. Even so, Indian experience suggests that some people are, even during a person's lifetime, willing to regard their teacher as 'divine'. Some critical scholarship seems to me too saturated in the presuppositions of the rational Enlightenment. Some Indian holy figures are also aware of their own special relationship to the divine. Of course, there are examples of arrogance and deceit, but other holy figures radiate goodness and love. Some contact with the pattern of Indian devotion to a holy person has helped me to see how even in his lifetime Jesus may have been felt to make God present in a special way. The immediate reaction to his ministry, according to Mark, was that everyone was amazed and praised God: 'We have never seen anything like this' (Mark 2:12). It was noted that Jesus spoke with authority and not like the teachers of the Law (Matt. 7:29).

Having been trained in a very critical approach to the New Testament that saw the material as largely shaped by the early church in the light of the resurrection, I have come to think that Jesus was indeed aware of a unique vocation, even if he did not consciously think of himself as the unique Son of God. The calling of twelve disciples, the cleansing of the Temple, the entry into Jerusalem on a donkey, were highly symbolic actions, which appear to have been deliberately planned by Jesus and of which the significance would have been clear to his contemporaries. Further, Paul himself had a premonition of the danger that awaited him in Jerusalem (Acts 20:22–3), and other great leaders, such as Martin Luther King, have sensed the danger of their mission. In the same way, it is likely that Jesus was aware of the risks that he ran in going to Jerusalem and consciously chose a non-violent confrontation with the authorities (Luke 18:31).

Critical New Testament studies, in contrast to the traditional Christian assumption that Jesus was God on earth, have started from the historical Jesus of Nazareth. They have perhaps, however, taken too limited a view of historical possibility.

If that is the case, arguments about when titles were first used of Jesus may be of only limited significance. Does it matter if Jesus did or did not speak of himself as Son of God? Those who believed that they had been met by God in Jesus Christ used many different ways to try and communicate their conviction. The first Christians used language and imagery familiar to them from the Hebrew Bible. The Fathers of the church, who shaped the classical creeds, thought in the categories of Greek or Hellenistic philosophy. Today new ways are needed to communicate the significance of Jesus. There has, however, often been a tendency in the church to sanctify a particular phrase or title and to use that as a touchstone of orthodoxy.

Son of Man

'Son of Man' is the term that the gospels suggest Jesus most often used of himself. There have been heated debates among modern scholars about the meaning of the term and attempts to find parallels in Hellenistic and Jewish literature. The term is used in three ways.

The first is as a roundabout way for a speaker to refer to himself. When Jesus went to the home of Zacchaeus, Luke tells us that Jesus justified his action by saying that 'The Son of Man [meaning 'I'] came to seek and to save what was lost' (Luke 19:10). Some scholars, however, think 'son of man' is only an overliteral Greek translation of an Aramaic expression for 'a man' or 'someone'. In that case, in the saying 'The Son of man is lord of the Sabbath,' the term just means 'man', so this is just a general statement that the Sabbath exists for human refreshment and renewal and that Sabbath rules are not sacrosanct. Most translations, however, take the verse as referring to Jesus as Son of Man, who, because of his divine status can dispense with Sabbath laws.

The second context in which the title is used is with reference to Jesus' death. In Mark's gospel, immediately after Peter had confessed that Jesus was the Christ, Jesus 'began to teach them [the disciples] that the Son of Man must suffer many things and be rejected by the elders, chief priests and teachers of the law and that he must be killed and after three days rise again' (Mark 8:31). It may be, especially as the Greek word *pais* can mean both 'son' and 'servant', that the title was a way of interpreting Jesus' ministry in the light of passages in Isaiah which speak of a Suffering Servant, who was called to be a 'covenant for the people and a light for the gentiles' (Isa. 42:6). The Servant was destined to be 'despised and rejected by men' (53:3), but would 'bear the iniquities of many' (53:11).

The third use of the title was in predictions about the end time. Matthew says that 'at that time the sign of the Son of Man will appear in the sky, and all the nations of the earth will mourn. They will see the Son of Man coming on the clouds of the sky with power and great glory. And he will send his angels with a loud trumpet call, and they will gather his elect from the four winds, from one end of the heavens to the other' (Matt. 24:30).

Some scholars think that Jesus used the title of himself in all three senses, whereas others think that he never used the title at all and that it was given to him by the first Christians. Some think that Jesus used it in only one or perhaps two of the three meanings. My own view is that he used the title of himself and, by reference to the Suffering Servant passages in Isaiah, he also used the title to prepare his followers for his death. Jesus seems to have been convinced that his death was required of him by his Father and that his Father would vindicate him. I doubt, however, whether the detailed predictions of the second coming are from the lips of Jesus.

Messiah

Christians have often spoken of Jesus as 'Messiah'. This Hebrew term means 'Anointed' and the Greek version *Christos* (Christ) quickly became a title for Jesus. Although at the time there was only limited Jewish speculation about the Messiah, Jewish expectations of the Messiah were very varied.[2] The predominant view was that the Messiah would be a human and earthly deliverer and not a divine figure. It was expected that the Messiah would usher in God's rule of peace and justice.

It is questionable whether Jesus used the title of himself. If he did so, he needed radically to reinterpret it so as to reject any idea of leading an armed uprising.

Son of God

The title 'Son of God' in Mark's gospel, rather than deriving from Jesus himself, seems to be used by the evangelist to emphasise the true nature of Jesus. It is used in the opening verse of the gospel to announce what the book is about. It is used at Jesus' baptism, so that the reader knows the true nature of Jesus. It is used by those possessed with demons, who were thought to have supernatural insight. The title also occurs at the transfiguration. At Jesus' trial, the high priest, on behalf of the Jewish people, rejected the application of the title to Jesus, whereas at his crucifixion, a Roman centurion, on behalf of the gentile world, declared, 'Surely, this man was the Son of God.'[3]

To the first believers, who were Jewish, Jesus' sonship would have been understood as indicating God's special favour and Jesus' moral obedience. In Psalm 2:7, God says to the King of Israel, 'You are my Son; today I have become your Father.' Coronation implied adoption by God, because in the ancient world a king was regarded as a quasi-divine figure. At his baptism, the words of the Psalm were applied to Jesus. John particularly emphasised Jesus' obedience to the Father. 'I have come down from heaven not to do my will but to do the will of him who sent me' (John 6:38). Jesus told the Jewish leaders,

'Do not believe me unless I do what my Father does' (John 10:37). In his final prayer to the Father, Jesus said, 'I have brought you glory on earth by completing the work you gave me to do' (John 17:4). The Synoptic gospels also emphasised Jesus' obedience in their account of his agony in the Garden of Gethsemane, when Jesus prayed '*Abba*, Father, everything is possible for you. Take this cup from me. Yet not what I will, but what you will' (Mark 14:36).[4]

Lord

The term 'Lord' or *Kyrios* in Greek was quickly adopted by gentile Christians as a title for Jesus. It may have been used during his ministry as a respectful form of address, but in both Jewish and Hellenistic religions it was a title applied to God.

There can, I think, be little doubt that the writers of the New Testament regarded Jesus as divine. The hymn quoted by Paul in Philippians speaks of Christ Jesus 'being in very nature God' (Phil. 2:5). The emphasis on his divinity, the Canadian scholar Larry Hurtado suggests, was brought about by praying and singing hymns to Jesus, by celebration of the Lord's Supper, by confession of faith in Jesus and prophetic pronouncements of the risen Christ.[5] Even so there seems to have been some hesitation to speak of Jesus simply as 'God' and those verses which appear to do so in English versions of the New Testament may have been mistranslated. For example, the translation of Romans 9:5 is disputed. Compare the New International Version which says that from the Israelites comes the human ancestry of 'Christ, who is God over all, for ever praised', with the New English Bible which says that from the Israelites, 'in natural descent, sprang the Messiah. May God, supreme above all, be blessed for ever.' In the latter translation, the doxology does not refer to Christ. Jewish opponents of Paul rejected his belief that Jesus was the Messiah; they did not accuse him of departing from the monotheism which was central to Jewish belief.

The fourth gospel went furthest in its claims for Jesus. Jesus said to Philip, 'Anyone who has seen me has seen the Father . . .

I am in the Father and the Father is in me' (John 14:9–10, see also 8:48–58). The Johannine community seems to have felt that their beliefs were still within the bounds of Jewish monotheism, but rabbinic Judaism, which was emerging after the fall of Jerusalem, was less sympathetic to the speculative forms of Judaism found in apocalyptic literature, and felt that the Christians had gone too far. By that time those who believed in Jesus were being expelled from some synagogues (John 16:2).[6]

Councils and Creeds

The Doctrine of the Trinity

Unlike the New Testament writers, the early Fathers of the church had little hesitation in speaking of Jesus as God. Ignatius (*c.*35–*c.*107), the prophet-bishop of Antioch and a martyr, wrote, 'Our God, Jesus the Christ, was conceived by Mary.' Clement (*fl. c.*96), Bishop of Rome, spoke of the 'living God that suffered and is worshipped'. It was not until the fourth century that the deity of the Holy Spirit was so clearly articulated.

How did the teachers of the early church affirm the divinity of Jesus and the Holy Spirit whilst also claiming to believe in Only One God? The answer was the doctrine of the Trinity, that there is One God in three persons. The answer, however, was not convincing to Jews and Muslims and has continued to be a puzzle to many people, including some Christians. The biblical justification for the doctrine is sometimes found in Matthew 28:19; 1 Peter 1:2 and Isaiah 6:3, but none of these passages speak of a God who is eternally three in one.

It is easy to get bewildered by what may seem the philosophical hair-splitting of the doctrinal debates of the early church. Essentially the orthodox Church wanted to defend its conviction that in the person of Jesus Christ and in the experience of God present in Christian life and worship, the believer was met by very God. Neither Jesus nor the Holy Spirit were intermediaries. Christians thought of God as Creator or Father, as Redeemer or Son, and as Sanctifier, the one who makes us holy, namely the Spirit. The usual questions to a person seeking baptism or confirmation are still:

Do you believe and trust in God the Father who made the world?
Do you believe and trust in his Son Jesus Christ, who redeemed humankind?
Do you believe and trust in his Holy Spirit, who gives life to the people of God?

By the doctrine of the Trinity Christians have, however, wanted to say more than that God's activity is known in three ways. The doctrine is intended to give an insight into the very nature of God. God is not a solitary monad. Just as no human being can live fully in isolation from other people, since in this world it is only possible to be a self in a field of selves, so the interior nature of God is relational.

It is important to recognise that traditional beliefs about the Trinity and about the status of Jesus Christ, which are often called Christology, were shaped by opposition to views which the majority of Christians felt were untrue to scripture and to their experience of faith. It has to be admitted that the doctrinal controversies were coloured by political concerns, especially after the emperor had become a Christian and wanted to use the religion to unify his subjects. The language of the argument, in which opponents were denounced as heretics and 'anathema' or 'accursed', may seem unchristian, but shows how passionately Christians of that time felt about these issues. None the less, the resulting divisions of the church were to weaken it in the eastern Mediterranean world and make it vulnerable to the spread of the new religion of Islam in the seventh century.

Arius

One of the most important controversies about both the oneness of God and the divinity of Jesus was sparked by Arius (c.250–c.336), who was a priest in Alexandria. He sought to protect the absolute sovereignty and transcendence of God and held that God could not be present in a human life. Jesus was only divine in the sense that he had been 'divinised'. He was subordinate to God and a creature, however unique and perfect. 'There was', Arius said, 'a time when he [Jesus] was not.' Arius was strongly opposed by St Athanasius (c.296–373), who was Bishop of Alexandria. For a time the party who supported Arius was in the ascendant and Athansius more than once was ousted from his diocese. Nevertheless his view triumphed at the Council of Nicaea (modern Iznik in north-west Turkey), which was an assembly of bishops convened by the Emperor Constantine, held in 325. A creed was agreed that said that Jesus was 'of one substance' (*homoousios*) with the Father. The creed known as the Nicene Creed, however, which includes the affirmation that Jesus Christ is 'of one Being with the Father' and which is still used by many churches, probably dates to a later council held at Constantinople in 381.

Three Persons in One God

The tendency of Eastern Christian thought has been to start with the evident distinction of persons in the Trinity and then to try to understand the mysterious unity of God. Gregory of Nyssa, (c.330–c.395), who was bishop of Nyssa, but exiled for a time by the Arian party, used this analogy: 'We may be confronted by many who individually share in human nature, such as Peter, James and John, yet the "man" in them is one.'[7] The Eastern approach can sound as if Christians believe in three gods. Western thought started from the unity of God. Augustine used this famous analogy: the Father is the lover, the Son the loved one and the Holy Spirit the love between them. Modern theologians, who work with traditional terminology, try to hold together the two approaches. It is also pointed out that the term translated 'person' meant in the Greek world a mask and not, as in modern usage, a centre of self-consciousness.

Jewish and Muslim Objections

To Jews and Muslims, the Christian position did not satisfy their insistence on monotheism. Although the Qur'an always refers to Jesus in respectful terms, it denies the doctrine of the Trinity and that God had a Son. Surah 112 says clearly: 'He is God, One, the ever self-sufficing, the Eternal. He does not beget and he was not begotten, and there is not any like him.' The suggestion that God had a Son is dismissed in several places. One verse will serve as an example. 'Wonderful originator of the heavens and the earth! How could he have a son when he has no consort and He (Himself) created everything, and He is the knower of all things' (Surah 6:102).

One or two modern Muslim writers, rather than just repeating the condemnation of Christian doctrine have tried to understand it, but they are the exception. Sayyid Ahmad Khan wrote, 'In the western world "father" is a term applied to the originator of something . . . the son is he whom God has formed with his hands . . . If we would express it in Arabic idiom, then father means *rabb* (Lord) and "son" *al-'abd al-maqbul* (the chosen servant) and these meanings agree exactly with the application of these terms in the Old and New Testaments.' A Persian writer, Shin Parto, in his Life of Jesus wrote, 'The Christians say he is Son of God, but it is better to call him Son of Love, one who was born in love, taught men love, and was crucified for love and liberty.'[8]

Jews, also, insist upon a pure monotheism. In the Middle Ages, Jewish thinkers argued about whether Christianity should be regarded as polytheistic.

The great teacher Moses Maimonides (1135–1204) thought Christianity was both idolatrous, because of the use of icons, as well as polytheistic, because of the doctrine of the Trinity. Maimonides wrote, 'Know that this Christian nation, who advocate the messianic claim, in all their various sects, all of them are idolaters . . . All Torah restrictions pertaining to idolaters pertain to them.'[9]

'If someone believes that he [God] is one, but possesses a certain number of essential attributes, he says in his words that he is one, but believes him in his thought to be many. This resembles what the Christians say: namely, that he is one but also three, and that three are one.'[10]

The twelfth-century French scholar, Rabbenu Jacob Tam, also known as Jacob ben Meir (1100–71), however, held that Christians were not idolaters because Christianity was monotheistic.

The eleventh-century Spanish theologian, Judah Halevi (1075–1141), whilst arguing the absolute superiority of Judaism over Christianity and Islam, regarded both the other religions as having a role in preparing for the Messiah, because they helped to spread monotheism.[11]

In the twentieth century, and especially since the establishment of the state of Israel, there has been renewed Jewish interest in Jesus and a number of books have been written about him by Jews. Many of them concentrate on the historical Jesus. One Israeli writer, Pinchas Lapide, claimed that 'Jesus is closer to me than to many a Christian theologian in Europe today.'[12] He gave various reasons for this assertion. He and Jesus lived in the same place, namely the Holy Land, with its geography, weather and fauna and flora. The mother tongue of both was Hebrew and Aramaic. Both regarded the Hebrew Bible as sacred Scripture. Both he and Jesus had an Oriental imagination, shown in the stories which Jesus told, and both shared a concern for the history and people of Israel.

Various attempts have been made to relate Jesus to the Jewish life of his day. Some Jewish scholars picture Jesus as a charismatic holy man or *hasid*. Others think he was a patriotic rebel. Rather than speaking of him as a false Messiah, it has been suggested that Jesus should be seen as a 'failed Messiah'. Others have seen him as a preacher who was close to the Pharisees.

Jews, however sympathetic to Jesus, cannot accept that a human being was divine. A few Jewish scholars are prepared to see that in Jesus there is a disclosure of God similar to that at Sinai, which is the bedrock of the Jewish experience of God. Rabbi Irving Greenberg has said that God who chose once can choose and choose again. Rabbi Tony Bayfield, the Director of the Reform Synagogues of Great Britain, has written:

> The God of Abraham, Isaac and Jacob, indeed of Sarah, Rebekah, Rachel and Leah, is my Jewish God . . . Christ comes to the dialogue room and I experience him perhaps in something of the same way in which Christians experience the God of Abraham, Isaac and Jacob. Fascinating, perplexing, enlightening, puzzling, distinctive – not my God. And yet, as it were – and paradoxically – an outpouring and an outreaching of the Ein Sof, the 'Without End', whom I believe, both Jews and Christians address.[13]

Although Jews and Muslims reject the Christian claim that Jesus was divine and the Trinitarian understanding of God, both religions, like Christianity, struggle with the way in which the transcendent God relates to the transient world. Christians often argue that, as in human life the most adequate form of communication is by personal meeting rather than the written word, so God's fullest revelation also needed to be a human life. Jewish and Muslim critiques of Christian doctrine, however, should remind Christians that they too believe in Only One God and need to beware of ways of stating the divinity of Jesus which appears to compromise this.

Raimundo Panikkar, a Catholic priest and brilliant scholar who is of mixed Indian and Spanish descent, who has been a pioneer of interfaith dialogue, has developed the doctrine of the Trinity as a framework for Christians to relate to other religions. He describes three aspects of the divinity and three corresponding forms of spirituality. The first is the silent apophatic dimension, which transcends any human concepts, which he relates to the Father who expresses himself only through the Son. The second is the personalistic dimension, which Panikkar relates to the Son, who is the personal mediator between God and man. The third is the immanent dimension, which relates to the Spirit. Panikkar suggests that the apophatic spirituality of the Father is similar to the Buddhist experience of Nirvana, whilst the personalistic approach relates to the Jewish and Muslim stress on the Word of God. The immanent spirituality of the Spirit resonates with the Hindu sense of the non-duality of the self and the Absolute.[14]

The discussion about the relationship of Christianity to other religions has given new relevance to a long-standing dispute between the Roman Catholic and the Orthodox Churches about the relation of the Holy Spirit to the other two persons of the Trinity – the so-called '*filioque*' ('and the Son') dispute. The Western Church has insisted that the Holy Spirit proceeds from the Father and the Son and witnesses to the Son. The Orthodox Church, seeing the Father as the source of unity, holds that the Holy Spirit proceeded only from the Father. This has allowed teachers of the Eastern Orthodox churches to affirm the activity of the Holy Spirit in all cultures. His Beatitude Archbishop Anastasios of Tirana has written that the Holy Spirit, who the Orthodox liturgy repeatedly says is ' "present everywhere filling all things" . . . is the Spirit of Truth working and inspiring human beings in their longing and search for truth in any religious setting'.[15]

Christology

The Chalcedonian Definition

Besides questions about the unity of God there were also long debates about how Jesus could be both God and Man.

Arius, who, as we have seen, said that Jesus was created by God and was not himself God, claimed that God had adopted Jesus, perhaps at his baptism. To Arius' opponents, this meant that to be met by Jesus Christ was not to be met by God himself and that to worship Jesus, if he was only a creature, was idolatry. At Chalcedon, a city near to Constantinople, a council was held in 451, which drew up what is known as the Chalcedonian Definition, that Christ is to be acknowledged in 'two natures . . . concurring into one person and *hypostasis*'. The word *hypostasis* literally means 'one subsistence or substance', although, to add to the complication, it was used in rather different senses by different theologians. The intention of the Chalcedonian Definition was to affirm the unity of Christ's person, but it had the effect of destroying the unity of the church.

Is He the Christ, the Son of God?

Those who held that there was only one nature in Christ, the Monophysites, were never reconciled to the Chalcedonian position, and the Oriental churches, such as the Syrian, Coptic, Ethiopian and Armenian Orthodox still reject the formula.

A third position was taken by the Nestorians, who not only held that there were two natures in Christ, but that there were also two distinct persons, the one divine and the other human. They, therefore, rejected the Chalcedonian view that there was only one *hypostasis* in Jesus.

In the spring of 1997, I visited the ancient capital of China, X'iang. Besides visiting the Terracotta Army, we went as well to the Provincial Museum, known as the 'Forest of Stelae'. Amongst these inscribed pillars is one from 781 CE which records the presence of Nestorian Christians who presented to the emperor a copy of the Bible, which had been translated by a Syrian called Raban. The stone says that the emperor was impressed by the scriptures and ordered that a monastery dedicated to the new religion should be established in the city. Centuries later, Marco Polo made contact with some Nestorian Christians when he travelled to China in the fourteenth century.

This visit reminded me of how little many Western Christians know of the ancient churches of the East. By calling them 'heretical', Mediterranean Christians forgot about their existence. The so-called 'Nestorian Church' is properly called the 'Church of the East' and is the ancient church of Persia. Nestorius was an interesting character and a very holy man. He was Patriarch of Constantinople from 428 and died in about 451. There is some doubt whether he actually taught 'Nestorian' doctrines or merely opposed theological innovations. For example, he resisted those who called Mary the 'Mother of God' (*Theotokos*, literally 'bearer of God') and his condemnation may have been because of ecclesiastical rivalries.

Modern Christological Debate

The Chalcedonian Definition failed to unite the church, partly because it does not so much provide a solution as define the problem.

None the less, because of other theological disputes, it was not until the nineteenth century that Christology again became a major subject of discussion. It is probably true that until the nineteenth century most Christians thought of Jesus as God who lived a human life. Now a considerable number of Christians see his divinity in some special feature of his humanity, such as his intense awareness of God, or his total self-giving and sacrificial love.

Liddon and Strauss

One of the last well-known statements of the classical position was made by the Anglican scholar Canon Henry Liddon (1829–90) in his 1866 Bampton Lectures on *The Divinity of Our Lord and Saviour Jesus Christ*. The lectures were in part a response to David Strauss's *The Life of Jesus*, of which the novelist George Eliot (1819–90) was a translator. It has been said that 'it is impossible to be more radically sceptical than Strauss'.[16]

Strauss (1808–74) regarded the gospels as almost entirely the mythical creation of the early church. The miraculous was banished from the plane of history. In reply, Liddon argued that the claims that Jesus made for himself in the gospels could only be explained in two ways. Either Jesus was an impostor or he was, as catholic theology claimed, God incarnate. The agnostic intelligentsia of Europe, Liddon argued, could not admire the moral virtues of Jesus whilst dismissing his claims to be divine. If he was not God, he was a fraud and therefore no example of morality – a popular summary of the argument was that Jesus was 'either mad, bad or God'. For Liddon, Jesus was without qualification God. The divine attributes of omnipotence and omniscience were to be ascribed to the incarnate Lord. Liddon was slightly uneasy about the verse in which Jesus said that only the Father knew the date of the End, but claimed that 'the knowledge infused into the human soul of Jesus was ordinarily and practically equivalent to omniscience'.[17]

A nineteenth-century hymn illustrated by the use of paradox the belief that the incarnate one was also possessed of the full powers of God.

> *O wonder of wonders that none can unfold,*
> *The Ancient of days is an hour or two old,*
> *The Maker of all things is made of the earth,*
> *Man is worshipped by Angels, and God comes to birth.*[18]

Such an attitude is alien for many Christians today. Schooled in a historical approach to the world, they see Jesus as a historical figure, with, as we have already suggested,[19] the knowledge of a first-century Jew and with human emotions and feelings.

Schleiermacher

Further, in their attempt to explain the divinity of Jesus many liberal and critical scholars start with the human Jesus. This was the approach of Friedrich Schleiermacher.

For Schleiermacher, as we have seen,[20] the essence of religion lay in the individual's feeling of dependence upon the Infinite. Jesus embodied an absolute dependence on God and it was the 'glorious clearness' of the God-consciousness which Jesus exhibited that was the reason to call him divine. Schleiermacher accepted that there are other mediators of this sense of absolute dependence. He gave little importance to the resurrection of Jesus and believed that the disciples had attained a full measure of faith in him during his lifetime. Human redemption for Schleiermacher was achieved by the incorporation of believers into Jesus' God-consciousness.

Ritschl

Looking for Jesus' divinity in some outstanding quality which he displayed is an approach that has been adopted by a number of Christian thinkers. The important German Protestant theologian Albrecht Ritschl (1822–89) saw Jesus as the symbol and representative of the moral law. Ritschl's starting point was in the Christian church, the fellowship of believers, historically derived from and actually dependent upon Jesus Christ, whose will was identical with God's purpose for humankind. The deity of Jesus could only be recognised from within the church and was not derived from history but from experience. 'By what he has done and suffered for my salvation Christ is my Lord, and by trusting for my salvation to the power of what he has done for me, I honour him as my God.' This emphasis was especially important as scholars became more aware of the complexity of historical research into the life of Jesus.

The Quest for the Historical Jesus

During the nineteenth century, a number of writers tried to write historical biographies of Jesus, which, as we have seen, was not the purpose of the evangelists. A famous example was the *Life of Jesus* written by Joseph-Ernest Renan (1823–92). His aim was to rescue Jesus from the embellishments of later over-enthusiastic disciples. Miracles were dismissed as legends. 'No miracle has ever taken place', he wrote, 'under conditions which science can accept. Experience shows, without exception, that miracles occur only in times and countries in which miracles are believed in, and in the presence of persons who are disposed to believe in them.' His aim was to highlight the high moral teaching of Jesus and he gives an attractive picture of Jesus.

The problem with Renan's book and other lives of Jesus was that they were very selective in the material that they used and were liable to create a Jesus who was in their own image. This was pointed out by Albert Schweitzer (1875–1965), a brilliant theologian and musician, who later settled in equatorial Africa as a missionary doctor, in his famous book *The Quest of the Historical Jesus* (Eng. trans. 1910). Schweitzer's criticism of the approach of the great philosopher Friedrich Hegel (1770–1831) to the historical also applied to other biographers of Jesus. 'He is like a spider at work. The spider lets itself down from the roof and after making fast some supporting threads to points below, it runs back to the centre and there keeps spinning away. You look on fascinated, and before you know it you are entangled in the web.'[21] Schweitzer particularly drew attention to the apocalyptic passages in the gospels which were ignored by modern writers. He claimed that Jesus saw himself as the one who was to inaugurate the Final Kingdom. He expected the imminent end of the world and this conditioned his 'unrealistic' ethical teaching. Yet even though Jesus was wrong in his expectation, Jesus still makes the demand of absolute love upon us by his own example. Jesus cannot be reconstructed by historical research but known only by those who obey his call.

Schweitzer ended his *Quest of the Historical Jesus* with a memorable passage:

> He comes to us as One unknown, without a name, as of old by the lakeside, he came to those men who knew him not. He speaks to us the same words: 'Follow thou me!' and sets us to tasks which he has to fulfil for our time. He commands. And to those who obey him, whether they be wise or simple, he will reveal himself in the toils, the conflicts, the sufferings, which they shall pass through in his fellowship and, as an ineffable mystery, they shall learn in their own experience who he is.[22]

Bultmann

One significant attempt to avoid the ambiguities of history, similar in some ways to that of Albrecht Ritschl, was made by Rudolf Bultmann (1884–1976), a German theologian who was much influenced by the writings of the philosopher Martin Heidegger (1889–1976). A brilliant and radical New Testament critic, Bultmann despaired of any certainty about the life of the historical Jesus. His long two-volume *Theology of the New Testament* devotes only thirty pages to 'The Message of Jesus'. He was concerned that Christian faith should not be at risk by some new historical discovery. He was also keen to 'demytho-logise' the biblical message so that it would be accessible to his contemporaries. He found in Heidegger's analysis of human existence in terms of authentic being, a way of communicating the gospel. The response of faith to the preaching of the cross of Christ, he claimed, could liberate us from anxiety and inauthentic living, which is characterised by bondage to the past, fear of the future and a search for this-worldly securities, to experience the joy of authentic living which is based on the reality of love which frees men and women from the burden of the past. Bultmann insisted that this new authentic life was only possible through faith in Christ, although some critics questioned this.

'God Was in Christ'

For myself, as I have suggested, I do not think the ambiguity of the historical evidence prevents us from having an outline picture of Jesus. I see in his life and death the embodiment of the boundless love of God. I am, therefore, sympathetic to the attempt to see his divinity in his humanity and find most helpful an influential book written in 1947 by the Scottish theologian, Donald Baillie (1887–1954) called *God Was in Christ.* Baillie tried to explain the incarnation in terms of the paradox of grace. The essence of this, he wrote, 'lies in the conviction which a Christian man possesses that every good thing in him, every good thing he does, is somehow not wrought by himself but by God'.[23] Paul, for example, said, 'By the grace of God I am what I am' (1 Cor. 15:10). There is also a verse in the familiar hymn 'Our blest redeemer' by Henriette Auber (1773–1862) which says:

> *And every virtue we possess,*
> *And every victory won,*
> *And every thought of holiness*
> *Are his alone.*[24]

This sense of God acting in them is familiar to the devout Christian. Baillie then suggested that 'this paradox of grace points the way more clearly and makes a better approach than anything else in our experience to the mystery of the Incarnation itself; that this paradox in its fragmentary form in our own Christian lives is a reflection of that perfect union of God and man in the incarnation on which our whole Christian life depends, and may therefore be our best clue to the under-

78

standing of it'.[25] Baillie made clear that what is only fragmentary and fleeting in the experience of the Christian is complete and continuous in the person of Jesus Christ.

In the 1960s, Bishop John Robinson, whose book *Honest to God* provoked a theological furore, developed this position. He spoke of Jesus as 'the man for others':

> It is in Jesus, and Jesus alone, that there is nothing to be seen, but solely the ultimate, unconditional love of God . . . It is as he empties himself not of his Godhead but of himself . . . that he reveals God. For it is in making himself nothing, in his utter self-surrender to others in love, that he discloses and lays bare the Ground of man's being as Love.[26]

Partly because of Baillie's book, a number of more liberal Christians today prefer, as I do myself, to say 'God was in Christ', echoing Paul (2 Cor. 5:19 KJV), than to say baldly, 'Jesus is God', although this assertion is part of the basis of the World Council of Churches. To say without qualification 'Jesus is God' seems to overshadow his humanity and to obscure the Trinitarian nature of Christian belief. Christian worship, properly understood, is of God the Father through His Son Jesus Christ and in the power of the Spirit; it is not worship of Jesus by himself, although this might be the impression given by a number of modern hymns.

Jesus as the Christ

Some theologians have sought to distinguish between Jesus and the Christ. One example is the influential thinker Paul Tillich (1886–1965), who was born in Prussia and moved to the USA in 1933, after he had become the first non-Jewish academician to be banned by the Nazis. By Jesus, Tillich meant the man of Nazareth, who was a historical person, even if our knowledge of him is uncertain. By Christ he meant the principle of New Being, which is the eternal principle of God's self-revelation, which his contemporaries recognised in Jesus.[27]

Other writers, such as Raimundo Panikkar who has been mentioned already, have made a distinction between the Logos

– the eternal principle of God's self-revelation – and Jesus of Nazareth in whom that principle is expressed. They suggest that the same eternal principle may be recognised in other great spiritual teachers such as the Buddha and Lord Krishna, and that too exclusive a focus on Jesus is liable to ignore the evidence of God's presence in the other great faith traditions of the world.

Such a view is also the usual Hindu reaction to Christian claims that Jesus was the unique Son of God. For example, Gandhi, who despite being influenced by Christian teaching remained a Hindu, said, 'I cannot ascribe exclusive divinity to Jesus. He is as divine as Krishna, or Rama or Mohammed or Zoroaster.'[28]

'The Myth of God Incarnate'

Recently, some Christian thinkers have questioned whether the language of the doctrines of the Trinity and of the Incarnation continue to have any meaning. At least, they say, they should be seen as significant 'myths' rather than as having factual content. The alarm that such views cause to more traditional Christians is increased by the confusion caused by the word 'myth'. 'Myth' has the popular meaning of 'a widely held but false notion'. Scholars, on the other hand, as we have seen earlier, mean by it 'a traditional narrative involving super-natural persons', of which the truth is not literal but to be understood as illuminating the meaning of human life. Radical thinkers, such as those who in the 1970s contributed to the book *The Myth of God Incarnate*,[29] should not be seen as rejecting the Christian faith, but as trying to hold on to its essential meaning in terms of a way of life, in the face of the uncertainty of historical knowledge and the view of some philosophers that all knowledge is a human construct.

We come back to the question, to which Schleiermacher and Barth gave very different answers, about the extent to which the Christian message can be fitted in to contemporary ways of thinking. This is also seen in the difference between those who see Jesus as in some way embodying a universal principle, as is the case of theologians in the tradition of Schleiermacher, and those, like the great Swiss theologian Karl Barth, who stressed that humans can in no way sit in judgment on God's revelation. Together with Pastor Martin Niemöller, Barth drafted the Barmen declaration (May 1934), which was the basis on which the Confessing Church opposed National Socialism and those Christians who colluded with it. The first article of the Declaration summed up Barth's theological standpoint: 'Jesus Christ, as He is attested for us in Holy Scripture, is the one Word of God which we have to hear and which we have to trust and obey in life and in death.' Barth in his later years somewhat modified his position, but he stressed that the basis of Christian understanding is faith in God's revelation in Jesus Christ and this cannot be subject to human judgment.

The Atonement

Although we have focused on Jesus' divine status, for many people their experience of him as Saviour is more significant. The World Council of Churches in its basis, which has already been mentioned, says it is a 'fellowship of Churches which accept our Lord Jesus Christ as God and Saviour'. Often, as Ritschl suggested, it is in the experience of being forgiven through the cross of Christ that people come to recognise Jesus as their Lord. The peace and joy of that pardon is so complete that it could only come from God.

There have been many attempts to explain how the cross is effective in making people one with God. The technical term is the doctrine of the Atonement, although this has never been officially defined in the same way as the doctrines of the Trinity and the Incarnation.

The Penal Theory

Some Conservative and Evangelical Christians have tried to make the so-called 'substitutionary' or 'penal' theory of the atonement a touchstone of true belief. This theory, also known as the 'juridicial' theory, regards sin as an infinite offence to

God. God is so holy that he cannot look upon sin and because God is just, a punishment must be exacted for sin. That punishment was met by Jesus Christ, who was punished instead of sinners. As Paul says, 'God made him [Jesus] who had no sin to be sin for us, so that in him we might become the righteousness of God' (2 Cor. 5:21). Literally interpreted, this leads to the claim that Christ is a substitute for each individual who, because of sin, deserves the penalty of death. Christ is punished instead of the sinner. As Paul Gerhardt (1607–76) wrote in a hymn:

> *Mine, mine was the transgression,*
> *But thine the deadly pain.*[30]

Expiation for Sin

Another theory, especially associated with Archbishop Anselm (*c.*1033–1109) is that Christ, who is spoken of as 'the Lamb of God who takes away the sin of the world', is the sinless offering who makes a universal expiation (or compensation) for the sins of all people. As a seventeenth-century hymn put it:

> *For if thy Lord had never died*
> *Nought else could sinful man betide*
> *But utter reprobation.*[31]

It is questionable whether either theory has the biblical support that is claimed for it. The real difficulty, to my mind, is that they separate Jesus from God, giving a picture of an unforgiving God whose pardon could only be bought by a bloody sacrifice.

The Victory of the Cross

Another theory, known as '*Christus Victor*' (Christ the Conqueror) pictures Christ on the cross overcoming the power of evil. This speaks powerfully to many African Christians. 'The devil is a reality in Africa,' write Elizabeth Amoah and Mercy Amba Oduyoye from Ghana,

* * *

Witches actually operate to release life-denying forces into the world. Individual people may be possessed and used by negative forces to prevent life-affirming and life-giving environments and activities. Evil is real, and evil is embodied in persons as well as unleashed on people by spiritual forces. Further, the spirit world is a powerful reality in Africa ... Such a cosmology calls for a Christology that consciously deals with the relation of Christ to God, the relation of Christ to the spirit world and how the Christ, in the context of the belief in spirits stands in relation to Africans in their dependence on God.[32]

I recall too as a student in India walking with a Church of South India pastor to a very remote village in Andhra Pradesh. On the way, we saw a deadly snake. I sensed the fear of those who lived in a world which they believed was controlled by evil forces, from whom Christ could deliver them.

Many traditional Christians believe in the devil and that some people are possessed by evil spirits. As the fourth-century Latin hymn writer Prudentius (b.348) put it:

> *Begone, thou crooked serpent,*
> *Who, twisting and pursuing,*
> *By fraud and lie preparest*
> *the simple soul's undoing:*

> *Tremble, for Christ is near us,*
> *Depart, for here he dwelleth,*
> *And this, the Sign thou knowest,*
> *Thy strong battalions quelleth.*[33]

The dangers of belief in the devil can be that one is tempted to demonise opponents, as, for example, when Christians have spoken of Jews as children of the devil. The belief can also seem to question God's ultimate responsibility for all that God created. My own picture is of God's redemptive love eventually reconciling all beings to the divine, which is suggested by Paul's vision of the time when God will 'be all in all' (1 Cor. 15:28). Victory is not the defeat of evil but its redemption. Although such a view would be shared by many liberal Christians it is not the view of the majority of Christians.

'Love to the Loveless Shown'

The theories of the Atonement so far mentioned are all sometimes called 'objective', which is to say that Jesus' death on the cross made an objective factual difference to sin and to human beings' relationship to God. So-called 'subjective' theories see the cross as a revelation of God's love which brings about an inner change in the believer. The willingness of God's Son to accept a brutal and unjust death should move us to repentance and the acceptance of God's mercy. The human analogy of the father and the prodigal son is taken as the key to understanding the atonement. As a Swiss theologian, Paul Wernle, wrote: 'How miserably all those finely constructed theories of sacrifice and vicarious atonement crumble to pieces before this faith in the love of God our Father, who so gladly pardons. The one parable of the Prodigal Son wipes them all off the slate.'[34]

This theory of the atonement is particularly associated with Peter Abelard, a brilliant thinker and one of the most colourful of medieval church figures. He described much of his life in his *History of My Troubles*. He was born in 1079, a son of a knight. He sacrificed his rights of inheritance by going to France to study philosophy. His views often brought him into dispute with his contemporaries and he was twice condemned for heresy. Whilst teaching in Paris, he was also given a private pupil called Héloïse, with whom he fell in love and by whom he had a son called Astralabe. The couple married secretly, but her father was furious. Abelard was castrated and embraced the monastic life, whilst Héloïse was forced to become a nun. Abelard argued that the love of Christ, shown in his life and passion, called forth a human response of love. 'The purpose and cause of the incarnation', he wrote, 'was that God might illuminate the world by his wisdom and stir it to the love of himself.' For Abelard, Jesus is the great teacher and example who arouses a responsive love in human beings. Such love is the basis of reconciliation and forgiveness, and he liked to quote Luke 7:47, 'Much is forgiven to them that love much.'

The New Testament

The variety of pictures used to illustrate the significance of Jesus' death reflects the New Testament, where many different images are used. The letters of Peter for example draw attention to Jesus' patience under suffering, which are seen as a fulfilment of the 'Suffering Servant' passage in Isaiah 53:2–10. Peter also compared Jesus' death to that of the scapegoat and the Passover Lamb. The letter to the Hebrews argues that Jesus' perfect self-offering brought to an end the sacrificial system of the Temple. It is not surprising that a similar variety of interpretations and illustrations are to be found in subsequent Christian devotion.

Believers in every generation have found peace in fellowship with the Crucified and Risen Saviour. At times, it has been external enemies or a threatening environment which has been most troubling. For others, inner guilt and self-reproach have been a heavy burden. Today, perhaps fewer Christians in Europe and America have such a keen sense of sin as seems to have been felt by Christians at the time of the Reformation. A comparison of Reformation and contemporary liturgies shows a change of emphasis. There is perhaps also more emphasis on what Christians might through the grace of Christ become, rather than on the legacy of past sin, whether inherited or original or actual sin. Asian and African Christians, on the other hand, are very aware of the suffering and evil that dominates so many lives.

For me it is the example of Jesus' self-giving love which is the moment of truth in which, in the light of Christ, I both know my sin and that despite it I am loved and accepted as I am. In the famous words of Isaac Watts,

> *When I survey the wondrous cross*
> *On which the Prince of glory died*
> *My richest gain I count but loss*
> *And pour contempt on all my pride*
>
> *Were the whole realm of nature mine*
> *That were a present far too small*
> *Love so amazing, so divine*
> *Demands my soul, my life, my all.*[35]

The Man for Others

Some Christian devotional literature dwells so much on the punishment that Christ suffered for our sake that it seems to have an unhealthy preoccupation with his blood and the torture that he suffered. After the horrors of mass genocide in this century, it is hard to speak of Jesus' agony as uniquely awful, horrible as it was. Instead, Jesus may be seen as representative of all who suffer, voicing their agony in an uncaring world. This is the sentiment of the modern hymn writer Timothy Rees (1874–1939):

> *Today we see your passion*
> *Spread open to our gaze*
> *The crowded street, the country road*
> *Its Calvary displays . . .*
>
> *The groaning of creation*
> *Wrung out by pain and care*
> *The anguish of a million hearts*
> *That break in dumb despair;*
> *O crucified Redeemer*
> *These are your cries of pain;*
> *O may they break our selfish hearts*
> *And love come in to reign.*[36]

For quite a number of people today, it is a concern for those who suffer that may lead them to discipleship. Jesus is the victim, whom those who suffer can feel is one with them. He also identified himself with the struggle for human dignity and freedom and so attracts those Christians who are committed to agencies for the relief of poverty and campaigns for world-wide social and economic justice. This Christology is perhaps to be found most clearly in some of the Christian songs of protest. For example, in Sydney Carter's 'Judas and Mary', Jesus says:

> *'The poor of the world are my body,' He said,*
> *'To the end of the world they shall be;*
> *The bread and the blankets you give to the poor*
> *You'll find you have given to me,' He said,*
> *'You'll find you have given to me.'*[37]

Jesus identified with the poor and needy. In *Honest to God*, John Robinson wrote: 'Christ was utterly and completely "the man for others", because he *was* love, he was "one with the Father", because God is love.'[38]

Jesus the Liberator

But Jesus was also one who struggled against injustice. For female theologians from Africa, Asia and Latin America, Jesus, besides identifying with the poor, is a model of true humanity who can inspire others to struggle for liberation. They note the place that women occupy in the gospel story. Women ministered to him during his ministry and it was to women that he first appeared after he had been raised from the dead. 'The gospel', writes Thérèse Souga, a Catholic from Cameroun, 'leads me to discover that Jesus bears a message of liberation for every human being and especially for those social categories that are most disadvantaged.'[39] Louise Tappa, a Protestant from Cameroun, says in the same way, 'The Christ of history is the one who defined his mission as a mission of liberation.'[40]

A statement entitled 'Asian Church Women Speak', from a conference held in Manila in 1985, said,

We rediscovered Christ's liberating and salvific mission

which encompasses all; we encountered the Christ of the poor... Most of all we felt confirmed by Christ's radical breakthroughs and supportive stance for women during his time. We saw Mary, the mother of Jesus, no longer as a passive ethereal being, detached from the suffering millions of Asia. We now see her in a new light, as a strong woman who can identify and be with today's grieving mothers, wives and daughters in the bitter fight for freedom.[41]

Women from Latin America say the same: 'The Bible is a book about life and liberation . . . The Gospels restore to women our human dignity as persons loved and cherished by God.'[42] Indeed, women from all three continents, Africa, Asia and Latin America, say that 'In the person and praxis of Jesus Christ, women of the three continents find the grounds of our liberation from all discrimination: sexual, racial, social, economic, political and religious . . . Christology is integrally linked with action on behalf of social justice and the defence of each person's right to life and to a more humane life.'[43] This means that Christology is about apartheid, sexual exploitation, poverty and oppression.

Such a view of the saving work of Christ leads to political action, but this is very controversial. The Christology being developed today in Africa, Latin America and Asia is likely to promote as heated arguments as any that shook the Church in the ancient world.

For a fuller discussion of the some of the issues in the first part of the chapter see James D. G. Dunn, *The Parting of the Ways* (SCM Press, 1991), which has a full bibliography, and his *Christology in the Making* (SCM Press, 1989); and R. Brown, *An Introduction to New Testament Christology* (Chapman, 1994). The writings of G. L. Prestige and J. N. D. Kelly are valuable for the doctrinal debates of the Patristic age. For more recent theological debate, H. R. Mackintosh's *Types of Modern Theology* (Nisbet, 1937), and J. M. Creed, *The Divinity of Jesus Christ* (Cambridge University Press, 1938), both reprinted by Collins/ Fontana, are useful, and also John Macquarrie's *Twentieth*

Century Religious Thought (SCM Press, 1963). D. M. Baillie's *God was in Christ* (Faber and Faber, 1961) is important for Christology, as are G. Aulén, *Christus Victor* (1931, SPCK, 1961), and F. R. Barry, *The Atonement* (Hodder and Stoughton, 1968), for the doctrine of the Atonement.

4

God

William Temple (1861–1944), a great Archbishop of Canterbury, said once that he was never aware of not having believed in God. Looking back, I feel the same is true in my case. This, however, is perhaps the experience of only a minority in secular Western society, although opinion surveys suggest that even there the majority of people believe in the existence of God. Rather fewer perhaps consciously try to shape the way they live in the light of that belief.

Questions about whether or not there is a God are commonplace today. There was a strong case for beginning this book with a discussion about this before thinking about Jesus Christ. Yet for many Christians it is an experience of Jesus Christ that makes belief in God real.

In large parts of the pre-modern world perhaps most people, like Archbishop Temple, never seriously questioned the existence of God. Admittedly the Psalmist talks about 'the fool [who] says in his heart, "there is no God" ' (Ps. 14:1), and the Buddha dismissed speculation about a creator god as unimportant. Even so, the world of the Bible was one of many gods, in which the people of Israel were called to witness to the Oneness of God.

God in the Hebrew Scriptures

The ancient Middle Eastern world believed in God, and indeed in gods. Arguments were about who was the true god and about the nature or character of God. Christianity, like Islam, has been shaped by its inheritance from Judaism. The belief in One God, the creator of the world, the Lord of history and the upholder of moral values is the witness of the Hebrew Bible and the gift of the Jewish people to the church (Rom. 9:4).

The first book of the Bible, Genesis, begins with the creation of the world by God.[1] Stories from pre-history follow: about the fall of Adam and Eve and their expulsion from the Garden of Eden; Cain's murder of his brother Abel; the flood and Noah's ark; and the building of the tower of Babel. Biblical history begins with God saying to Abram, as Abraham was then called, 'Leave your country, your people and your father's household and go to the land I will show you. I will make you into a great nation and I will bless you' (Gen. 12:1–2).

Abraham

Abraham's father, Terah, originally lived in Ur of the Chaldeans. Ur in Mesopotamia is near the mouth of the river Euphrates at the top of the Persian Gulf. It was at the centre of Mesopotamian civilisation, which was established by the end of the fourth millennium BCE and which saw the development of agriculture, of city states and the discovery of the wheel, of pottery and of writing. About 1950 BCE, the Third Dynasty of Ur came to an end and the city was sacked and destroyed. About this time, Abraham's father set out from Ur and travelled along the Euphrates to Haran. The religion in Mesopotamia was a developed polytheism, with gods ranged in a complex pantheon. The Bible admits that the Israelites' ancestors worshipped 'other gods' in Mesopotamia (Josh. 24: 2).

Abraham was told by God to leave Haran and to go to Canaan. His obedience to God was tested by the demand that he should offer his only son, Isaac, as a sacrifice – although at the last moment a voice from heaven called out, 'Do not lay a hand on the boy . . . Now I know that you fear God, because you have not withheld from me your son, your only son' (Gen. 22:12). It is not clear whether Abraham should be described as a monotheist, that is to say, someone who believes there is only one God. Sometimes he is described as 'henotheist', who is a person who does not reject polytheism but who himself only worships one god – the god of his tribe.

Moses

The decisive moment of revelation was to Moses at Mount Sinai. The God who revealed himself to Moses affirmed his identity with the God of Moses' forefathers. 'I am the God of your father, the God of Abraham, the God of Isaac, and the God of Jacob' (Exod. 3:6). God went on to say that he had seen the suffering of the Israelites, Abraham's descendants, who at the time of Joseph had come to Egypt to escape a widespread famine and had become slaves to the Egyptians and their rulers, known as Pharaohs. Now, God said he was going to rescue the Israelites from slavery and Moses was to be their leader.

Moses was reluctant to accept the call and asked God what he should say when people asked him the name of God. God replied, 'I am who I am. This is what you are to say to the Israelites: "I am has sent me to you" ' (Exod. 3:14). An alternative translation is 'I will be what I will be'. Most commentators agree that there is a future reference, meaning that God said, 'I will be what tomorrow demands.' God is known in relationship and is capable of responding to human need. God is not an object to be known. The French thinker, mathematician and theologian, Blaise Pascal (1623–62) wrote on a paper, dated 23 November 1654, which was stitched into the lining of his coat and found after his death, 'God of Abraham, God of Isaac, God of Jacob, not of the philosophers and scholars. Certainty. Certainty. Feeling. Joy. Peace.' The great reformer, Martin Luther (1483–1546) paraphrased God's answer as 'I am God on whom you must fully rely and not trust in other creatures.' The God who revealed himself to Moses was a God who invited humans into a personal relationship of trust and obedience. It was to be an exclusive relationship, like that of lovers. There was to be no worship of other gods and no idolatry. Much of the early history of Israel is the struggle to maintain the pure worship of God and to resist the polytheism and idolatry of neighbouring peoples.

After a prolonged struggle with Pharaoh, God indeed rescued the Israelites from Egypt. Then, at Mount Sinai, God made a covenant with the people. They were to be a holy people, a model community and for their guidance God gave them the Law or Torah. The Torah includes many detailed rules and it was elaborated over the centuries in what is known as the oral Torah. The underlying principles of the Law are proclaimed in the Ten Commandments, which make clear men and women's duty to God and to other people.

Jesus affirmed the importance of the Law (Matt. 5:17) and at the Reformation, several churches included a reading of the Ten Commandments at the Communion service.

Under Moses, who led the Israelites to the edge of the Promised Land of Canaan, the people had been taught to recognise God as the one who had saved them from the Egyptians and who had protected them through the wilderness and who required holiness and moral behaviour. God was the protector, Lord of history and guardian of morality.

In Canaan

In Canaan, the Israelites were surrounded by the nature and fertility worship of Baal and other gods. It was a long struggle to maintain the pure worship of One God. At the same time, God was now seen to be the Creator and the one who provided food and harvest. As the Psalmist wrote:

> You care for the land and water it,
> You enrich it abundantly.
> The streams of God are filled with water
> to provide the people with corn . . .
> The meadows are covered with flocks
> and the valleys are mantled with corn.
> they shout for joy and sing. (Ps. 65:9, 13)

It was probably at this time that the cult of animal sacrifice, which centred on the Temple in Jerusalem, was fully developed.

The sacrificial offerings came to an end with the destruction of the Temple in Jerusalem in 70 CE. Even, so sacrificial language has remained part of Jewish and Christian devotion, and often Jesus' death has been explained by images of sacrifice.

Exile

Despite the efforts of the prophets, the people were often unfaithful to God. According to the biblical writers, they were punished for this by the destruction of the northern state of Israel in 722 BCE and by the destruction of Jerusalem in 593 BCE, which was followed by the exile in Babylon of the leading citizens of Judah. There, the Jews may have come in contact with Zoroastrianism. Zoroaster,[2] who proclaimed an ethical monotheism, taught that there are two opposing forces in creation: the Bounteous Spirit of Mazda and the destructive power of Angra Mainyu. Each person's eternal fate would be determined by the choice he or she made between them. 'There are two primal Spirits, twins renowned to be in conflict . . . the better and the bad. And those who act well have chosen rightly between these two, not so the evil doers' (Ys. 30:3). It may be from Zoroastrian influence that some Jews developed the picture of a cosmic struggle, which is to be found in apocalyptic literature. The world is seen as a battleground between the angels of God and Satan and his army. For the virtuous there is reward in the next life and for the wicked eternal punishment.

After the return from the exile in Babylon, when the state of Judah was re-established, Jews came increasingly under the political and cultural influence of the Hellenistic world. This offered both a threat and a challenge. Jewish thought, particularly in the writings of the philosopher Philo, was influenced by Plato and other Greek philosophers. Jews also had the opportunity to make their beliefs known to a wider world. On the other hand, various Hellenistic practices, such as gymnastic sports which involved nudity were a danger to traditional behaviour. Some Hellenistic rulers, such as Antiochus Epiphanes, also tried to subvert Jewish religious life and this caused revolts, such as those led by the Maccabees.

God in Ancient Greek Thought

Greek thinking about God, as Pascal indicated, was different from that of the Bible. Yet it has been influential in the development of Christian thought, because it was in the terms of Greek philosophy that the creeds of the Church were formulated.

Plato

The Greek consciousness of God was dominated by the philosophical impulse. The emphasis was upon reason, often in isolation from other human faculties. Plato (c.428–348BCE), for example, regarded the 'inspired utterances of poets and prophets as, at best, symbolical adumbrations or shadows of truth and, at worse, the source of degrading superstitions'.[3] Fundamental to Plato's thought is the conviction that truth cannot be found in everyday life and sensible reality, but in a more real or ideal realm of unchangeable or eternal forms, which are the blueprint and pattern of the world. The everyday world is transitory and perishable and most people take this as the real world. In fact, they are trapped in a cave and see only the shadows of reality. The soul, which is immortal, struggles to rejoin the eternal realm. Plato makes a sharp contrast between the physical everyday world and the eternal world. This is reflected in a world-weariness to be found in some expressions of Christianity.

Aristotle

Aristotle (384–322BCE), Plato's most brilliant pupil, thought there was a great chain of being from pure matter, which is unknowable, at the bottom, to pure form, which is God, at the top. God is engaged in unending self-contemplation. He is not involved with the world. He moves it as the beloved moves the lover, without needing to stir; he is the Unmoved Mover. As John Ferguson (b.1921) a great classical scholar, wrote, 'one of the paradoxes of history is that the profound and subtle medieval scholastics succeeded in identifying this Unmoved Mover with the ever-working Father of Jesus'.[4] Certainly Greek influence encouraged them to seek for rational proofs of God's existence. It also lay behind the traditional doctrine that God is impassible and immutable. This is the claim that God is not subject to action from without, changing emotions from within or feelings of pain or pleasure caused by another being. God does not change. These doctrines, however, seem to some Christians to be in tension with the belief that God is love and a number of modern theologians, as we shall see, speak about the 'Suffering God'.

Plotinus

Despite modern objections, the classical Christian doctrine of God has been shaped by Greek thought and particularly by the Hellenistic philosopher, Plotinus (c.205–270CE). His thought centred on the One, beyond personality, beyond reality, beyond thought, beyond definition, beyond comprehension. All things aspire to It, from It the whole universe is derived by a process of flux or emanation. Beneath the undifferentiated One or the Good, which is at the summit or chain of beings, is the intelligible world of ideas, and beneath it is the world soul, which is the creator or orderer of the material world. The highest life is the ascent of the soul to mystical and ecstatic union with the One – the flight of the alone to the Alone. This is achieved by ascetic practices, whereby the soul turns progressively from the sensuous and intellectual realm. Plotinus spoke of God as Love, but he used the Greek word *eros* in contrast to *agape*, which was another Greek word for love used by Christians. Plotinus decisively influenced the development of Jewish, Christian and Islamic mysticism and his influence can also be seen in the development of Christian monasticism.

W. R. Matthews, who was Dean of St Paul's Cathedral, London, once suggested that somebody should write an imaginary conversation between Plato and Jeremiah, whom he regarded as the greatest person of the Hebrew Bible.[5] They represent the two strands of thought about and experience of God, which Christianity tries to hold together in its thinking about the character of God.

Is God Real?

To those who today think about God, the first question may not be about the character of God, but about whether God exists and whether God made the world.

A child who is told that God made the world and everything that is in it often asks, 'But who made God?' This question, which is natural enough, is in fact a misunderstanding of what is meant by God. God, to the believer, is not an object amongst objects or a cause in a series of causes. God is, whether or not this or any other universe exists. God, the absolute and real, is the unproduced Producer of all that is. God is Being.

To the unbeliever, on the other hand, language about God is a surrogate language about humanity or human persons. Theology is in fact anthropology. Thus, to Sigmund Freud (1856–1939), a founder of psychoanalysis, God is the projection into supposed reality of human fears, neuroses and abject needs. To Ludwig Feuerbach (1804–72), a German philosopher, God is the projection of human ideals which can never be realised. To Karl Marx (1818–83), a political theorist, God is a projection caused by the requirement to perpetuate conditions of alienation in the interest of one class or party.

The division between the theist who believes in the reality of God and the atheist who denies this reality and regards talk about God as in reality talk about humanity, is not entirely clear cut. In addition to those people who call themselves 'agnostic', because they say that they do not know, there are some Christians, such as Don Cupitt (b.1934) who adopt a 'non-realist' position. They claim that all our knowledge is a human creation. Talk about God, which may be beneficial for human life and society is mythological. It is a way of making sense of our experience, but does not have an objective referent.

Believers will admit that God cannot be known in the fullness of the Divine being, because God is transcendent, beyond human experience. What is called apophatic theology says that we can only say what God is not – 'Neti, Neti', 'not this, not that', as the famous Hindu text puts it. God, as mystical theology insists, cannot be spoken of, but must be experienced. Classical

Christian theology, however, has accepted that it is possible to speak of God by the use of analogy. For example, Christians speak of God as 'our Father'. God is not exactly like a human father. He does not engage in biological reproduction. Yet in being the origin of life and providing for the possibility of life, God behaves in a way which is not dissimilar to that of a human father. God, Jesus suggested, in being willing to forgive those who do wrong, acted as we would expect a human father to behave. When, in speaking of God, we use language which derives from human experience, it is not univocal. It never applies exactly to God, but to the believer it is not without meaning. Yet, the critic might ask, 'If God is like a father, why did he allow millions of people to die in the Holocaust?' The believer then probably says God is not exactly like a human father. Some critics have gone on to suggest that the believer makes so many qualifications that his or her use of words loses all meaning. Indeed, the philosopher A. N. Flew (b.1923) spoke of the death of God by a thousand cuts. Any word used of God, he said, was so qualified by the believer, that it had lost all meaning.

A major preoccupation of some Western theologians in the twentieth century has been the question of what language can be used of God. Indeed, when as a student I went from Cambridge to Madras, I found it refreshing to escape from debate about whether it was possible to speak of God, if there is a God, to discussions which presupposed mystical knowledge of God as a valid source of our knowledge of reality. To the mystic, it is the experience of Divine Reality, which is convincing. This is why I began this book with Venkayya's prayer, 'O great God, who art thou? Where are thou? Show thyself to me.'[6]

My study of Hindu philosophy also raised the question of whether the Eternal should be spoken of in personal or impersonal terms. Sankara (c.788–820) who was the most influential proponent of Advaita Vedanta, held that Brahman or the Absolute is the underlying reality of all appearance. Reality is non-dual. Theism, in his view, was a lesser stage of knowledge, but this position was rejected by Ramanuja (11th or 12th century), who developed a school known as Visistadvaita. Is God in very essence best thought of in personal terms or is that a human projection on to the Eternal? I doubt whether that is a question that can be answered, despite the discussions of Idealist philosophers such as Josiah Royce (1855–1916) and Bernard Bosanquet (1848–1923). Yet most Christians because of their experience of a personal relationship with God will think of God in personal terms.

Arguments for God's Existence

Even if the chief Christian evidence for the reality of God is an invitation to 'taste and see that the Lord is good', some Christians have offered intellectual arguments for the existence of God. Some people still find these persuasive, whereas others find this approach arid.

There are three main arguments for the existence of God, known as the Cosmological, the Ontological and the Teleological. These Proofs, including additional variants, are sometimes known as the *Quinque Viae*, which is Latin for 'five ways', because this is how Thomas Aquinas (*c.*1227–74), the Angelic Doctor whose writing has exercised a profound and lasting influence on Catholic philosophy and theology, summarised them at the opening of his *Summa Theologiae*.

There are various forms of the **Cosmological** argument. It may start from the existence of the world which requires an explanation, or it may start from the fact that everything in the world has a cause, therefore the world itself must have a cause. So God is the First Cause. Critics suggest it is improper to leap from what happens in the world to the origins of the universe itself. Others suggest that certain kinds of infinite regress are possible, so that because everything has a cause it does not follow that there is a first cause. Such a view has echoes of the Buddhist rejection of belief in a creator god. Modern defenders of the cosmological argument see it as an expression of the human mind's search for intelligibility in the world.

The **Ontological** argument was first formulated by Anselm (1033–1109), who was Archbishop of Canterbury. Anselm claimed that since anyone can think of 'a being than which no greater can be conceived', such a being must exist at least in the understanding. But we could not think of such a being if that being were not a reality, which is to say we would not have the idea of God if there were no God. Such a concept is not a creation of the human mind. This argument was criticised by Thomas Aquinas but put forward in different forms by the great philosophers René Descartes (1596–1650), Baruch Spinoza (1632–77), Gottfried Wilhelm Leibniz (1646–1716) and Georg Wilhelm Friedrich Hegel (1770–1831), although it was criticised by Immanuel Kant (1724–1804). The argument still has both critics and defenders.

The **Teleological** argument, sometimes called the argument from Design, starts from the signs of order and purpose in the world. Thomas Aquinas noted that natural bodies act to obtain the best result. An animal, for example, avoids danger and does not hurt itself on purpose. Knowledge, he said, cannot move towards an end or purpose unless directed by some being with knowledge and intelligence. For example, an arrow has to be directed by an archer.

The argument was severely criticised by David Hume (1711–76) in his *Dialogues on Natural Religion* (1779). It was, however, restated by William Paley (1743–1805), who in a famous comparison suggested that if the existence of a watch requires a watchmaker, so the existence of the world requires the existence of God. His *Natural Theology* (1802) was required reading for British students of theology into the twentieth century and the book had a considerable influence on Charles Darwin. In the twentieth century the argument has been restated by F. R. Tennant in his *Philosophical Theology* (1928), and by R. Swinburne in *The Existence of God* (1979).

Many Christians, who would not be able to name any of these arguments, probably use them in unsophisticated forms. Some would stress the sense of purpose in life and their conviction that there is a moral order. Belief in God, they might say, gives meaning to life. Others might, as the Psalmist did (e.g. Ps. 104), point to the beauty of the world and the intricate interdependence of all life as evidence of a Creator. Others, however, like the poet Alfred Tennyson (1809–92), who was influenced by the writings of the naturalist Charles Darwin (1809–82), see the apparent cruelty of the natural world as alien to the idea of a God of Love. Tennyson wrote:

> *[Man] . . . trusted God was love indeed*
> *And love Creation's final law -*
> *Though Nature, red in tooth and claw*
> *With ravine, shrieked against his creed.*[7]

Darwin's Theory of Natural Selection

Many people today have a considerable awareness of the natural world thanks to the films of David Attenborough and others. These show one species hunting and feeding on another. None the less, the contemporary Oxford theologian, Keith Ward (b.1938), points out that although Charles Darwin spoke mostly of life on earth as a 'war of nature', he occasionally struck a different note, as when he wrote, 'I can see no limit to the amount of change, to the beauty and infinite complexity of the co-adaptations between all organic beings.'[8] 'The metaphor of a war of nature', Keith Ward writes, 'here gives way to a different metaphor: that of a developing emergent whole, with increasingly complex and beautiful co-adaptedness among organic life-forms, and which pictures nature as expressing a continuous growth in harmonious complexity.' Keith Ward, referring to the Gaia hypothesis of the inter-relatedness of all life, continues:

> On the newer, more holistic, picture, suffering and death are inevitable parts of a development through conflict and generation of the new . . .What God wills, and consequently what the process will eventually produce, is not the triumph of the strong, but the triumph of virtue, of beneficence, compassion and love. The ultimate evolutionary victory, on the theistic hypothesis, does not go to the most ruthless exterminators and most fecund replicators. It will go to beings who learn to co-operate in creating and contemplating

values of many different sorts, to care for their environment and shape it to greater perfection. It will go to creatures who can found cultures in which scientific understanding, artistic achievement and religious celebration of being can flourish.[9]

The Creation

Charles Darwin's theory of natural selection questioned the benevolence of God, but more immediately it questioned the biblical account of creation and the authority of the Bible itself.

The Bible starts with an account of the creation of the world, which God accomplished in six days (Gen. 2:2). In 1830, Sir Charles Lyell (1797–1875), the leading geologist of Victorian England, published his *Principles of Geology*, which showed from the study of rocks that 'creation' was a much slower process than would appear from the Bible. He suggested that it took not six days but many millions of years. Nearly thirty years later, Charles Darwin argued for abandoning the biblical view that God created separate species 'each according to its kind' (Gen. 1:24). Instead, he argued from a mass of evidence collected in different parts of the world, that 'species' had originated by natural selection, by adaptation to the environment and by gradual evolution.

Then in 1871, in his *The Descent of Man*, Darwin argued that human beings, far from being made 'in the image of God' (Gen. 1:27), were only a highly developed species of anthropoid apes. Not only could the Bible account not be taken literally, the process of evolution left little room for the miraculous. As Cardinal John Henry Newman (1801–90) observed, new scientific thought 'increased vastly the territory of the natural at the expense of the supernatural'.[10] The world did not seem under the control of God. Others felt humanity had been degraded. The Tory politician Disraeli (1804–81) said, 'The question is this – Is man an ape or an angel? I am on the side of the angels.' Others suggested that the biblical 'days' were in fact aeons.

Although there are some Christians, such as the Creationists in the USA, who insist on the literal accuracy of the biblical account of creation, the majority of Christians would now see the stories as mythological. They assert that the universe is dependent on God and that men and women have a relationship with God or are made in God's image. The myths go on to illuminate the human experience of sin and evil.

The Bible suggests that the world had a beginning. Admittedly, the early church father, Origen (c.185–254) held that creation is an eternal process, but this view was rejected by the early church, although some theologians in the twentieth-century have subscribed to it. Many Christians have held that the world had a beginning in time, although Augustine took over from Plato's *Timaeus* the suggestion that the world and time originated together in a single creative act.

The idea of a beginning may fit the 'Big Bang' theory of the origin of the universe, but the primary purpose of the Christian doctrine of creation is to affirm that the world is not self-existent but dependent on a purposive being. It is more about meaning than about the process whereby life came into existence. As Oliver Quick, who was Regius Professor of Divinity at Oxford from 1939 to 1943, wrote, 'It is because the Christian believes himself to have been made for God, that he believes also that God made him. And the belief so grounded cannot be upset by anything that natural science may discover about the temporal origin of mankind.'[11]

Is the World Made by a Loving Creator?

To many people it is not perhaps the question of how the world was made which is the difficulty, but whether it gives evidence of a loving Creator. We have already seen that people draw different conclusions from their observation of the natural world. Some see beauty and the amazing intricacy and inter-connectedness of life, others see the cruelty of one animal preying on another. Perhaps an even greater difficulty is the experience of sin and evil, reinforced in our own times by cruel wars and horrible genocide.

The Holocaust, in which some eleven million people, more

than half of them Jews, were killed by the Nazis, destroyed many people's faith in God and has led other believers to question traditional pictures of God. The Nobel Prize Winner, Elie Wiesel, wrote:

> *Never shall I forget the little faces of the children, whose bodies I saw turned into wreaths of smoke beneath a silent blue sky.*
> *Never shall I forget those flames which consumed my faith forever.*
> *Never shall I forget that nocturnal silence which deprived me, for all eternity of the desire to live,*
> *Never shall I forget those moments which murdered my God and my soul and turned my dreams to dust.*
> *Never shall I forget these things, even if I am condemned to live as long as God Himself. Never.*[12]

Whilst the tragedy of the Holocaust is especially poignant for Jewish people, who believe themselves to be the chosen people of God, it is an agonising concern for all believers in God. Indeed, some Christian theologians have said that all theology now has to start after the Holocaust, because 'there is no God to whom I could pray with my back turned toward Auschwitz'.[13]

The Problem of Evil

The problem of suffering and evil is that if God is all-powerful and all-loving, why does God allow evil? Part of the answer is in terms of human freedom. If love is of supreme value, love cannot be compelled, it can only be given. If God who is Love seeks a relationship of love with human beings, they have to be free to respond or to reject divine love. Human freedom is not only moral, but is part of human creativity, which in part is what Christians understand by saying that men and women are made in the image of God. Indeed, in giving birth to children, they share in God's work of creation. Human freedom implies the freedom to disobey God's will and to hurt others.

Much of the evil in the world can be attributed to human wrongdoing. This does not seem to explain the unfairness of life, and much traditional teaching has suggested that in the next world those who are virtuous and those who suffer will be rewarded in heaven and wrongdoers will be punished in hell. Some Christians feel that such teaching has been used by the unscrupulous to exploit others and that it has made some Christians reluctant to battle for social justice in this world. It is not sufficient to regard this world as a 'vale of soul-making' nor to assume that a heavenly reward can compensate for the appalling suffering some people have endured. How can there ever be compensation for those children who were murdered in the Holocaust?

This is a complex issue and the theological arguments may seem unhelpful and detached to a person in the midst of acute suffering. Even so, they are important to the Christian understanding of the nature of God.

God is said to be all-powerful or omnipotent. If, then, God is able to do anything, can God do the logically impossible, such as making a square circle? The answer of most theologians is no, although Thomas Aquinas notes that scripture says that God has 'made foolish the wisdom of the world' (1 Cor. 1:20). Equally, it is said that God cannot create a free being who is unable to do wrong. This issue was most sharply focused in Islam, which especially stresses the power of God. Nothing happens unless God wills it. How then, it was asked could human beings be held accountable on the Day of Judgment? At one extreme, the Jabriya taught absolute predestination, which really makes a mockery of human freedom. This view was eventually rejected by orthodox Islam. Other Muslims, known as the Qadriya, held that as God's agents on earth, humans have delegated power. The mediating position of the Maturidites was that all possibilities are created by God, but that human beings have the responsibility to 'acquire' actions out of the possibilities and thus become accountable.

Christians have had similar debates, with views ranging between those who advocated 'Double Predestination', which is the view that God determines those who will be saved and those who will be damned, and Pelagians who hold that human beings have freedom to choose or deny God. Probably a general view would be that God may allow what God does not actively will. A parent will give a growing child considerable freedom and will allow him or her to ride a bicycle. The parent does not want or will the child to fall off and be hurt.

Like the Qur'an, the Bible, and especially the Hebrew Bible, assumes that all that happens is the direct will of God. Many Christians, besides recognising a measure of human freedom, also acknowledge that the world operates according to certain God-given laws of nature. Thus fire can be used to provide warmth and heat for cooking, but it can be misused to destroy buildings and human life. Yet without the constancy of natural laws, no scientific advance or medical discoveries would be possible.

I recall hearing a sermon in which the preacher told how 'miraculously' he missed his aeroplane and thus God saved his life – because otherwise he would have been the victim of an air disaster. Yet does this imply that just as God willed to save the one man, God also willed to destroy the other two hundred passengers?

There are those who argue not only that God cannot do the logically impossible, but that God chooses to withdraw to encourage human freedom. Does this mean that the future is genuinely open? Traditionally God has been spoken of as omniscient, knowing all things, including the future. Some contemporary writers suggest that the future is not predetermined but dependent on human beings who are free to respond to God's will or to bring upon themselves self-destruction. As the Jewish philosopher Hans Jonas has written, 'We literally hold in our faltering hands the future of the divine adventure and must not fail Him, even if we would fail ourselves.'[14] Another Jewish thinker, Arthur A. Cohen, has used what has become a well-known analogy. 'It is man', he writes, 'not God who renders the filament of the divine incandescent or burns it out.'[15]

The Suffering God

To say the future is in human hands is not to imply that God is indifferent. Rather the reverse. Whilst God does not control, God appeals to the conscience of the world through the victims of its agony. God identifies with their suffering, which, it is hoped, will change the way people behave. As the Asian Christian Choan-Seng Song wrote of the victims of Indochina, 'In the refugees' faces distorted with agony, someone must have perceived the face of God distorted with pain. In the disfigured bodies of the children fallen victim to hunger and bullets, someone must have seen God disfigured with horror.'[16] 'On the cross', writes Phillip Berryman in his summary of Latin American Liberation Theology, 'God takes on human suffering, becomes himself "a crucified God." '[17]

Christ on the cross is the representative of all who suffer, and in Christ, God identifies with them. Like the parent who comforts the child who falls off a bicycle, God cannot undo the injury, but God can share the pain. The German theologian Dorothee Sölle has written, 'God consoles us as a mother does. She cannot magic away the pain (although that occasionally happens!), but she holds us on her lap, renewed, sometimes in darkness without light.'[18] Another female theologian from Korea, Dr Chung Hyun Kyung, told the World Council of Churches Canberra Assembly, 'I rely on the compassionate God who weeps with us for life in the midst of the cruel destruction of life.'[19]

In her book *Struggle to be the Sun Again*, Chung Hyun Kyung vividly describes the suffering of many Asian women, 'whose bodies are beaten, torn, choked, burnt and dismembered'. In their brokenness, they long for a full humanity and see this vision in the biblical teaching that men and women are created equally in God's image.[20]

Although it is quite common for Christians today to speak of God as 'The Suffering God', for many Christians it is not enough to see God as only the voice of the victim and as the one who identifies with those who suffer. They would wish to emphasise the power of love and that it is in the end stronger than force. Oliver Quick wrote that even by the light of reason, love can be seen to have an inherent omnipotence. A love that is not destroyed by hatred is invincible. The power of love 'converts even suffering itself into something active and creative and makes the very forces of evil, even through the apparent completeness of their triumph over it, nevertheless subserve its own purpose of good'.[21] The Anglican theologian W. H. Vanstone (b.1923) puts this poetically in a now well-known hymn:

> *Love that gives, gives ever more,*
> *gives with zeal, with eager hands,*
> *spares not, keeps not, all outpours,*
> *ventures all, its all expends.*
>
> *Drained is love in making full,*
> *bound in setting others free,*
> *poor in making many rich,*
> *weak in giving power to be*
>
> *Therefore he who shows us God*
> *helpless hangs upon the tree;*
> *and the nails and crown of thorns*
> *tell of what God's love must be.*
>
> *Here is God: no monarch he,*
> *throned in easy state to reign;*
> *here is God, whose arms of love*
> *aching, spent, the world sustain.*[22]

The Cross as Victory

If some modern writers, and especially feminist and Asian theologians stress the power of suffering love, much of classical Christianity, as we have seen, speaks of the death and resurrection of Jesus in terms of victory over or deliverance from evil.

This image has a long history in Christian art. Richard Harries (b.1936), the Bishop of Oxford, has written:

* * *

The first scene of Christ on the cross does not appear until the fifth century. Before that time the main images were ones of deliverance. Sometimes the motifs were those of late antiquity, but they were predominantly drawn from the Hebrew scriptures and include such scenes as Daniel in the lion's den; Shadrach, Meshach and Abednego being delivered from the burning fiery furnace; and the story of Jonah, which ends in triumph and which the early church took as a foreshadowing of the death and resurrection of Christ. From the gospel it was above all the scenes of the raising of Lazarus and the healing of the paralytic that appeared. When Christ is first depicted on the cross, as in a series of four ivory panels dating from about 420 CE in the British Museum, he is strong and triumphant. Christ as a suffering, battered figure did not emerge for a further 400 years. What spoke to the condition of Christians in the first 900 years was the strong Christ who saves us from fate, evil, all forms of malevolent power and death.[23]

Yet the language of victory may suggest that the believer has to conquer his or her shadow nature rather than integrate it. This has led at times to an unhealthy repression of the Christian's full humanity. It has equally encouraged Christians to conquer and destroy those perceived to be the enemies of faith. My hope is not so much for the ultimate destruction of evil as its redemption. Other contemporary Christian voices warn that by over-much emphasising the triumph of Christ, Christians diverted their attention from the need to tackle the evil and exploitation in the world. An emphasis on deliverance, especially if it is focused on the next world, may lessen concern for those who suffer in this life.

Hope of Another Life

None the less, many Christians through the centuries have set their hearts and their hopes on the heavenly Jerusalem. Because the subject is inherently speculative, there is some imprecision in Christian teaching. All souls will be judged, but there is talk both of a Last Judgment at the end of time and of souls being judged after they die. They are judged both in terms of their faith in Christ or lack of it and by their behaviour. The righteous are rewarded by the beatific vision – the joy of seeing God. The wicked are condemned to the punishment of hell. According to catholic teaching, those who have not committed unforgivable sin go to the state of purgatory, from which after due punishment they ascend to the beatific vision. Limbo is an intermediate state for those, such as unbaptised infants or the righteous who lived before Christ, who deserve neither the reward of heaven nor the punishment of hell.

In company with a number of contemporary Christians I am uneasy with this scheme. First, the picture of God who judges and punishes is incompatible with the character of God as revealed by Jesus Christ. God wills all people to be saved. The miseries of hell are the suffering people bring upon themselves by their wrongdoing, rather than penalties inflicted by an offended Deity. Further, such punishment or suffering should be remedial – a way by which souls come to a true knowledge of themselves and are opened to divine love. Universalists, of which I am one, hope that in the end all souls will recognise and accept the gracious love of God and that God's love by its nature is never withdrawn. Others think that a soul may be so shut in on itself that it may cease to be. Freedom, it is said, must include the freedom for ever to reject divine love.

Another difficulty with the traditional scheme is that if virtue is rewarded and vice punished, virtue is hardly disinterested. Yet the essence of love is that it is freely given without expectation of reward. This is expressed in the words of a famous hymn, which is said to have been written in Spanish by St Francis Xavier (1506–52), who was the 'Apostle of the Indies and of Japan' and which was translated by the English Catholic E. Caswall (1814–78):

My God, I love thee; not because
I hope for heaven thereby

Nor yet because who love thee not
Are lost eternally . . .

Then why, O blessed Jesu Christ,
Should I not love thee well,
Not for the sake of winning heaven,
Or of escaping hell;

Not with the hope of gaining aught,
Not seeking a reward;
But as thyself hast loved me,
O ever-loving Lord.[24]

The sentiment is similar to that of the Muslim mystic Rabi'a al-Adawiyya (*c.*713–801) of Basra, who had a lasting influence on Sufism. She said: 'O my Lord, if I worship you from fear of hell, burn me in it; if I worship you in hope of paradise, exclude me from it. But if I worship you for your own sake, then do not hold me back from your eternal beauty.'[25]

For some Christians, their pictures of heaven and hell have helped them cope with the sufferings and injustices of life. But does the final end, however perfect, make sense of life's horrors and tragedy? Even if the evil will in the end get their deserts and the innocent their reward, does this compensate for the agony of the victims? Can any reward compensate for the horrors of Auschwitz or the genocide in Rwanda?

In a famous scene in *The Brothers Karamazov* by the Russian novelist Fyodor Dostoevsky (1821–81), the story is told of a general who deliberately sets a pack of hounds on a boy who had accidentally injured one of them. Ivan draws two conclusions from this story. First, it would be wrong under any circumstances for the mother to forgive the general for what he did. Second, Ivan says that no heaven, however blissful, could make up for what had happened. 'Too high a price is asked for harmony; it's beyond our means to pay so much to enter. And so I hasten to give back my entrance ticket . . . It's not God that I don't accept, Alyosha, only I most respectfully return Him the ticket.'[26]

Those who reject Ivan's arguments say that only at the end

of the creative process, when it can be seen as a whole, will we be in a position to judge God. On the other hand, if the future is not predetermined and the creative process is not a play-back of a pre-recorded programme with a happy ending, we may need to accept that there are real tragedies, such as the Holocaust, for which there is no compensation.

In my view, Christians rightly affirm their belief that death is not the end and that the God who gives life gives also new life. The quality of human love and divine love have an inherently deathless quality. Yet I am not persuaded that the hope of another life answers the problem of life's unfairness and suffering, and if it diverts us from addressing those injustices, it offers us comfort at the expense of the agony of other people. The way of self-giving love, the way of the cross, is right whether or not it ushers in a utopian reign of God. I doubt whether the human Jesus on his way to the cross knew that resurrection awaited him. It was enough for him to be obedient to the Father and the disciple should pray for a similar obedience, hopeful that no act of goodness nor any expression of love is ever wasted.

The Holy Spirit

Although the Holy Spirit has already been mentioned several times, the Third Person of the Holy Trinity, who has often been neglected in Western theology, deserves at least a paragraph to himself.

In his last discourse to his disciples, according to St John's gospel, Jesus promised that after his death, he would send them the Paraclete, a word variously translated a 'counsellor', or in older English a 'comforter' or 'strengthener' or 'advocate' to be with them. The Holy Spirit, whose coming is celebrated at Pentecost or Whitsun, would stand by the disciples, Jesus said, especially when they were persecuted, like a defence counsel; he would make the world aware of its sin, and would bring the disciples together in a loving community. The distinction between the presence of the Risen Christ and the Holy Spirit is not always clear, either in John or Paul (see 2 Cor. 3:17). Jesus said that the Spirit 'will bring glory to me by taking from what is mine and making it known to you' (John 16:15). One could perhaps say that the Holy Spirit transforms knowledge about Jesus into awareness of a living presence.

The Spirit is known in the Christian community, but those who recognise the Spirit see his activity in the whole of life, present everywhere, filling all things. The Pentecostal churches and the charismatic movement emphasise both baptism in the Spirit and the Spirit's continuing post-conversion work, which may be seen in external signs such as speaking with tongues, healing and exorcism, which is the casting out of evil spirits. Pentecostalists have shown a mixed reaction to the Toronto Blessing, a recent phenomenon in which a concentrated outpouring of the Holy Spirit is shown by falling or resting in the Spirit, laughter, shaking and crying. Paul insisted that the greatest spiritual gift is love (1 Cor. 13:13).

Jostein Gaarder, *Sophie's World* (Phoenix, 1995), is a readable introduction to the history of Western philosophy.

W. R. Matthews, *God in Christian Thought and Experience* (Nisbet, 1930), covers many of the issues, as does the recent book by B. Studer, *Trinity and Incarnation* (T. & T. Clark, 1993).

Jürgen Moltmann, *The Trinity and the Kingdom of God* (SCM Press, 1981), is an important book.

Keith Ward, *God, Change and Necessity* (Oneworld, 1996), is a careful refutation of scientific atheism.

W. H. Vanstone, *Love's Endeavour, Love's Expense* (Darton, Longman and Todd, 1977), and Austin Farrer, *Love Almighty and Ills Unlimited* (Fontana, 1966), give rather different responses to questions about God and suffering.

On the Holy Spirit, see John V. Taylor's *The Go Between God* (SCM Press, 1972), and G. W. H. Lampe's *The Seal of the Spirit* (Longman Green and Co., 1951).

5

Many Mansions

For a time we lived as a family in the Old Deanery at Wells in Somerset. This is a historic house, dating back before the time of the Tudors. King Henry VII slept there in the early years of the sixteenth century and Sir Walter Raleigh's nephew, who was Dean of Wells at the start of the Civil War, may have been murdered in the house.

It was fascinating to try to trace how the building had been altered and adapted over the centuries by every generation. The same is true of the church. It is like a body. It is a continuously developing organism, so the history of the church – indeed of any religion – is a story of continuity and change and the church today has been shaped by the past. But Christianity is not one 'house'. There are many different churches and denominations and 'houses' in almost all the countries of the world. In a few pages, it is only possible to pick out the highlights.

In looking at the central beliefs of Christians we have already seen wide differences. In part, these are reflected in denominational divisions, but many of the differences are cultural or to do with church order or caused by political influence, or they reflect different temperaments and patterns of worship. Yet in the bewildering variety, there is continuity. Although, for example, Christians may come to scripture with very different presuppositions, it is the same scripture that they approach. Again, one may attend the Eucharist in another country without any knowledge of the language or local ceremonies, and yet recognise the Eucharistic action of blessing and breaking bread and blessing the cup.

There was a time when it was presumed that there was a single truth of a religion that could be identified and that those who had different beliefs were wrong and perhaps heretics who should be shunned. Some people still have this approach. A growing number of people recognize that 'truth' is related to the person who thinks and speaks. Thus today people acknowledge a variety of theologies – such as Liberation theology, Black theology, Feminist theology. I recall that when I was a student a number of books were being written on New Testament theology which made the attempt to argue that there was one consistent theology in the New Testament. Now it is recognised that Peter and Paul and James and the author of the Letter to the Hebrews had very different ways of expressing their belief. Christian faith, as we have suggested, is not, in the first instance, acceptance of certain intellectual dogmas, but trust in the Living God. Theological reflection may be compared to several critics viewing a statue from different positions. The standpoint of the beholder colours what is seen.

With such an approach it is possible to rejoice in the enormous variety of Christian churches. Visitors from the West to Jerusalem are sometimes bewildered by the many different denominations represented there – such as Ethiopian or Abyssinian or Coptic, as well as Catholic and Orthodox and Lutheran and Anglican. They may also be surprised to meet Christian pilgrims from Korea and the Philippines, as well as from Cyprus, Italy and Texas. Yet the visitor might also marvel that the Christian faith has taken root in an amazing variety of cultures, although it has to be said that such an ecumenical spirit has seldom been characteristic of the churches. Christian history has been marked by fierce argument, persecution of opponents, division and even religious wars.

The Early Church

Jews and Gentiles

There seem to have been some heated disagreements in the early church, although they have been glossed over in New Testament writings. The main one, about the attitude of Jews, Jewish believers and gentile believers to each other, has had a lasting effect on Jewish–Christian relationships. The main question, discussed in the Acts of the Apostles and in Paul's letters, was whether gentiles could become members of the church and on what terms. The so-called 'Judaisers' insisted that any gentile believer in Jesus had to be circumcised and become a Jew. Paul strenuously resisted this position (Gal. 2:14–16). His attacks on the Jewish Law in his epistles do not seem to have been on the Torah as such, although this is how they have often been understood, but upon those who insisted that gentile believers were required to observe all the commandments of the Law. According to Acts 15, Paul, at the Council of Jerusalem, won the support of Peter and James and the other members of the Jerusalem church for his position that gentile believers did not need to be circumcised. It was agreed, however, that they should 'abstain from food sacrificed to idols, from blood, from the meat of strangled animals and from sexual immorality' (Acts 15:29).

The Jerusalem church, which was headed by James the brother of Jesus, remained within the Jewish fold, although James is said to have been killed by the Jews in 62 CE. The leadership of the Jerusalem church passed to another blood-relation of Jesus. When, in the late sixties, the Romans laid siege to Jerusalem, the Christians fled to Pella, a gentile town east of the river Jordan, where they survived for a time.

Early Christian writers speak of two groups of Jewish Christians, the Nazarenes and the Ebionites. The Nazarenes held that Jesus was the Messiah, the Son of God, and that his teachings were superior to those of Moses and the prophets. They held that Christians of Jewish descent should observe the Jewish Law. The Ebionites, however, held that Jesus was only a prophet. Some of the Ebionites accepted the virgin birth, but others held that Jesus was the son of Joseph and that the Christ descended upon him at his baptism. The Ebionites repudiated Paul because they held that he had rejected the Law. It seems, in fact, that Paul did not argue against Jewish believers in Jesus continuing to keep the Law, but he rejected any attempt to impose the Law on gentile believers.

Increasingly the church did try to stop Jewish believers in Jesus from keeping the Jewish Law. In the middle of the second century, Justin Martyr said that he would accept those who continued to observe the Torah into Christian fellowship, provided they did not seek to persuade gentile Christians that they too had to follow the Mosaic Law. Justin admitted that other gentile Christians did not show the same leniency.[1] By the fourth century, the church had ruled that it was heretical even for believers of Jewish birth to observe the Law. Augustine wrote that 'the ceremonies of the Jews are both baneful and deadly to Christians and whoever keeps them whether Jew or gentile, is doomed to the abyss of the devil'.[2] In recent years, to the anger of many in the Jewish community, some Christians of Jewish descent, such as the Messianic Jews, have tried to observe much of the Torah while affirming that Jesus is the Messiah. More widely the church has attempted to recover its Jewish roots, recognising that the developments of the early centuries impoverished the church and were a cause of lasting bitterness between members of the two religions.

The Spread of the Faith

By the end of the first century, the membership of the church was predominantly gentile. Indeed, by the time that Paul wrote his letter to the Romans, only a generation after the resurrection of Jesus, the church in Rome was already mostly gentile. The Acts of the Apostles tells of Paul's missionary journeys. There are also stories about the missionary travels of other apostles. There is a tradition that Thomas went to southern India and that Bartholomew was martyred in Armenia.

The first churches were mostly in urban areas, founded by

Christians who followed the trade routes from city to city. By the middle of the second century, in parts of Asia Minor, Christianity had spread widely to the smaller towns and even into the countryside. We know little about the expansion of Christianity in the second century, but by the end of that century Christians were to be found in every province of the Empire, as well as in Mesopotamia. Even in Britain there were Christians in areas not under Roman control, according to Tertullian, who wrote in about 208. St Alban, the first English martyr, may have died under Emperor Septimius Severus (*c.*209), although some scholars date his death to the persecutions under the Emperor Diocletian (*c.*305).

The growth of the church was even more marked in the third century, especially in the eastern part of the Empire. We know a little about how this happened from the writings of Gregory, later known as Thaumaturgos or 'Worker of Wonders' (*c.*213–*c.*270), who was one of the leading third-century Christians in Asia Minor. He was a native of Pontus and reared as a pagan. He was from a wealthy family and for part of his education he travelled to Palestine, where he came under the influence of Origen. Gregory became a Christian and on his return to Pontus, he was persuaded to become bishop. He set about trying to convert the rest of the people in the diocese. He was so successful that it was said that when he became bishop he found only seventeen other Christians there and that when he died, about thirty years later, there were only seventeen pagans. He made conversion easier by substituting festivals in honour of Christian martyrs in place of the old pagan festivals.

Another area where the church grew steadily was north Africa, at the time the granary of the Roman Empire. There the church was Latin-speaking and produced great writers and leaders such as Tertullian (*c.*160–*c.*225), who was brought up in Carthage, and Cyprian (d.258), who was a pagan orator who was converted to Christianity in about 246 and who, two years later, was elected Bishop of Carthage.

Persecution

Until the fourth century Christians were at constant risk of persecution from the Roman authorities. Ten major persecutions are enumerated, beginning with Nero in the first century and ending with one launched by Diocletian early in the fourth century. The account of Nero's persecution comes from the Roman historian Tacitus (*c*.56–*c*.120), writing about fifty years after the event. He says that Nero, to escape the ugly rumour that he had given orders to start the great fire of Rome, tried to pin the blame on the Christians. They were accused of hatred of the human race. They were wrapped in the hides of wild beasts and then torn in pieces by dogs. Others were fastened to crosses which were set on fire to illuminate a circus that Nero was staging in his gardens. According to tradition, both Peter and Paul died in these persecutions.

An interesting correspondence on the punishment of Christians survives between Pliny the Elder (*c*.61–113), who had been sent to reorganise the province of Bithynia, and the Emperor Trajan (*c*.53–117; ruled 98–117). Pliny said that he had not previously had to deal with Christians. He did not know whether any allowance was made for the age of the accused nor 'whether pardon is given to those who repent' nor 'whether punishment attaches to the mere name apart from secret crimes, or to the secret crimes connected with the name'.[3] In reply, Trajan wrote that Christians 'are not to be sought out, but if they are accused and convicted, they must be punished – yet on this condition, that whoso denies himself to be a Christian, and makes the fact plain by his action, that is by worshipping our gods, shall obtain pardon on his repentance, however suspicious his past conduct may be'.[4] The Emperor Hadrian (76–138; ruled 117–38) made clear that slanderous accusations against Christians were unacceptable and that it had to be proved that they had acted contrary to the laws.

Jews were exempt from emperor-worship, but that exemption did not extend to Christians. Refusing to join in the worship of the emperor may have been an offence. Certainly Christians avoided pagan festivals. Vicious rumours circulated about their immorality and that they ate human flesh and drank human blood. At a more intellectual level, Porphyry (*c.*232–*c.*303), an early leader of the Neoplatonists, pointed to some of the discrepancies in the Christian scriptures.

The most severe general persecution took place in the middle of the third century under Emperor Decius (249–251). We do not know his motives, but he seems to have wanted to reinstate the old gods of Rome. In 251 Decius was killed in battle and for the time being Christians were spared, but under Valerian (253–260) persecution was redoubled. The last great persecution was under Diocletian (304–11). One result of this was the Donatist schism in North Africa, where some Christians refused to accept the consecration of Caecilian as Bishop of Carthage in 311, because he had been a *traditor*, that is to say, he handed over copies of the Bible to avoid persecution. The rigorism of the Donatists, named after their second bishop, was not accepted by the majority, but the Donatist church survived into the eighth century, by which time North Africa had come under Muslim rule.

Mention of the Donatists is a reminder of the agonising choices that those who have faced persecution have had to make, as much in the twentieth century under Fascist and Communist regimes, as in the early centuries of the church. The persecutions caused severe suffering and many believers faced martyrdom with great courage. When the aged Polycarp (*c.*69–*c.*155), Bishop of Smyrna, was led into the arena, the proconsul urged him to 'Curse Christ' and then he would release him. 'Eighty-six years have I served him', Polycarp answered, 'and he has done me no wrong: how then can I blaspheme my King who saved me?'[5]

The Conversion of Constantine

The conversion of the Emperor Constantine (306–337) to Christianity was a dramatic change which had far-reaching consequences. Constantine's father, Constantius Chlorus, was governor of Britain, Gaul and Spain at the time of the Diocletian persecutions. He seems never to have had much stomach for the persecutions, which were half-heartedly enforced in his territories. When Diocletian and Maximinian abdicated, he became one of their successors. On his death in 306, his son Constantine was proclaimed emperor by his troops in York. Constantine then had a long struggle to become sole emperor, which he only achieved in 323 with the defeat of Licinius.

It was in 312, as he marched toward Rome to face a formidable opponent called Maxentius, that Constantine took a first decisive step toward Christianity. It seems he had heard that Maxentius was relying on pagan magic. Years later, Constantine told his friend Bishop Eusebius (*c.*260–*c.*340), the most eminent of early church historians, that in the early afternoon, as he was praying, he had a vision of a cross of light in the heavens bearing the inscription 'Conquer by this'. Later, in a dream, he saw the same sign and ordered his soldiers to mark this sign on their shields. In the battle at the Milvian Bridge, near Rome, Constantine was successful and captured Rome. The next year at Milan, he met with Licinius, with whom he temporarily divided the empire. They issued an edict tolerating Christianity. The details are obscure. It seems that Constantine already tolerated Christianity in the provinces under his control, so the Edict of Milan may have extended this toleration to the Eastern Empire.

Constantine's policy was one of toleration. He did not make Christianity the official religion of the Empire. To his death, he kept the old pagan title *pontifex maximus* and was only baptised on his deathbed. Even so, he increasingly came to favour Christianity. He built and enlarged many churches. He exempted clergy from taxation, until the sudden influx of recruits for the priesthood meant that he had to limit this concession! He prohibited the repair of ruined temples. His mother Helena (*c.*255–*c.*330) visited the Holy Land in 326 and identified several of the holy places, including the birthplace of Jesus at Bethlehem, where she built the Church of the Nativity, which is one of the most ancient churches that pilgrims continue to visit to this day. Constantine's sons were more affirmative of the Christian faith and quite soon, despite a set-back under

Julian the Apostate (361–63), Christianity became the official religion of the Empire.

There continues to be debate about Constantine's motivation and indeed whether official recognition was a curse or a blessing. Was his action indeed inspired by a vision or based on shrewd political calculation? Constantine could see the strength of Christianity and hoped it could be a unifying force in the Empire. That is why he summoned the Council of Nicaea in 325 in the hope of uniting the church against Arianism. The emperors, however, found there were frequent disputes in the churches and their efforts to enforce uniformity soon led to the persecution of so-called 'heretics', some of whom fomented discontent in the Empire or from beyond its boundaries.

In 324, Constantine defeated Licinius at Chrysopolis and became sole emperor. Almost immediately he chose as the site of his new capital Byzantium, a Greek city that had had a Christian community from at least the second century. When he inaugurated the city in 330, he named it Constantinople (modern Istanbul). The centre of imperial power had moved to the eastern Mediterranean. At its height, under Emperor Justinian I (527–65), Constantinople had a population of about half a million. In 381, the bishop of the city was given honorary pre-eminence after the Bishop of Rome. Despite a challenge from Alexandria, the Patriarch of Constantinople was by the sixth century, recognised as the Ecumenical Patriarch in the East. There was, however, gradual estrangement from Rome and the final breach is usually dated to 1054. Although in 1483 the city fell to the Muslim Turks, it remains the seat of the Ecumenical Patriarch of Constantinople who has a primacy of honour within the Orthodox churches.

Hardly anything survives from Constantine's city, but the great church of *Hagia Sophia*, 'Divine Wisdom', now a mosque, which was rebuilt on more than one occasion, is on the site of the church built by Constantine, which was itself built on the foundations of a pagan temple. The building is considered one of the world's most beautiful edifices.

Challenges and Conversions in the West

Whilst the Roman or Byzantine Empire in the East was at its height, the Empire in the West had begun to crumble under the onslaught of barbarians from the north. Their conquest is sometimes said to have begun in 378 when the Goths defeated and killed the Emperor Valens at the battle of Adrianople. The capture and sack of Rome by Alaric in 410 was an even more spectacular disaster, which prompted Augustine to write the *City of God*, although Rome recovered quite quickly.

Yet whilst the imperial power of Rome in the West was crumbling, Christianity was conquering the new rulers and the see of Rome was becoming the moral leader of the West. In 496, Clovis, King of the Franks, was baptised. This was a landmark in the conversion of the Germanic invaders and other rulers followed Clovis' example.

The Mission to England

The story of the mission to England, of which we have some detail, may serve as an illustration of the wider process. The mission to England, according to tradition, was inaugurated directly by Gregory, who was to become Pope Gregory the Great. In about 586, Gregory was in the slave market in Rome and noticed some slave boys with fair bodies and light hair. On enquiring about them, he was told they came from Britain, where the people were pagan, and that they were Angles. 'Right,' he said, 'for they have an angelic face and it becomes such to be co-heirs with the angels in heaven.' When he was told that they were from the province of Deiri, he exclaimed, 'Truly they are *de ira*, withdrawn from wrath and called to the mercy of Christ.'[6] Gregory offered himself to the Pope to go and convert them, but this was refused. When Gregory himself became Pope, he persuaded Augustine to lead a mission to Britain, which set out from Rome in 596, a century after the baptism of Clovis and thirty-nine years before A-lo-pen brought the faith to China.

On arriving in England, Augustine approached the King of

Kent, who had a Christian wife, and who allowed Augustine to establish his mission at his capital city of Canterbury. Before long, the king was baptised and many of his subjects followed his example. Pope Gregory kept in touch with the mission by letter and authorised Augustine to appoint twelve diocesan bishops and to place a bishop at York, who was to become an archbishop when the number of Christians increased. To this day, Canterbury and York are the English archiepiscopal sees and it was at York in 627 that St Paulinus baptised Edwin, King of Northumbria. Living close to the abbey at Dorchester-on-Thames, I am regularly reminded of the legacy of that early mission, because there in 634 one of the next generation of Christian missionaries, St Birinus, converted Cynegils, King of Wessex.

St Augustine, of course, was not the first to introduce Christianity to Britain. At Glastonbury in Somerset, there is a legend that Joseph of Arimathea came there. There is no solid evidence for this, although there were trading links between Syria and Britain, and another legend, referred to in William Blake's 'Jerusalem', claims that Joseph of Arimathea had brought Jesus as a child to the west of England. Certainly, Celtic Christianity had been flourishing for some centuries before Augustine arrived and he caused some resentment by his lack of tact. An attempt to reconcile the two traditions was made at the Synod of Whitby in 664, but it was Theodore of Tarsus, who came to England as Archbishop in 668, who united the Christians in England and who was the first bishop whom all English Christians were willing to obey.

Irish Missionaries

Further west, Irish missionaries were winning people to Christ. The apostle of the Irish was St Patrick (*c*.390–*c*.460), who was born in Britain of a Romanised family and brought up as a Christian. When he was sixteen, he was captured by Irish pirates and spent six bleak years as a herdsman in County Mayo, during which he turned with fervour to Christ. Eventually he escaped back to Britain and was reunited with his family. But, in a dream, as we know from his *Confessio*, which he wrote in his old age, one Victoricus handed Patrick a letter headed 'The Voice of the Irish'. As he read it he seemed to hear a group of Irish people pleading with him to walk once more among them. 'Deeply moved', he said, 'I could read no more.' He trained to be a priest, probably in Gaul, and after a time he was sent to be 'bishop in Ireland' and seems to have established his see at Armagh.

Two hundred years later, missionaries from Ireland helped to spread the faith in northern Europe. The most famous Irish missionary to the Frankish kingdoms was St Columbanus (*c.*543–615), who was a contemporary of Gregory the Great. St Columba (*c.*521–97), who was slightly older than both Columbanus and Gregory, was another Irish missionary. In about 562, moved 'by the love of Christ', he left Ireland and with twelve companions established a base on the rocky island of Iona, off the Scottish coast, from where he evangelised the mainland of Scotland and Northumbria. In modern times, the Iona Community was founded in 1938 by George MacLeod (1895–1991) to express the theology of the incarnation in social terms. His plan was that members should spend three months each year in community preparing for work in industrial areas of Scotland or in the mission field. The abbey has been restored and to the many pilgrims who visit it each year, Iona is a centre of spiritual renewal.

Continental Europe

A century after Columba, missionaries from England were going to the continent. St Willibrord (658–739), from Northumbria, worked in the Netherlands whilst the greatest successes of Wynifrith (*c.*680–754), who is better known as St Boniface, who came from Crediton in Devon, were in Germany. The Saxons continued to resist the gospel and their conversion in the latter part of the eighth century followed their conquest by Charlemagne. It was another 150 years before most of Scandinavia was converted.

By the year 1000, almost all of western Europe was Christian and during the previous centuries the popes in Rome had been increasing their authority and power, as well as accumulating land. In the year 800, it was the Pope who crowned Charlemagne as Roman Emperor in Rome, although Charlemagne was too forceful a character to be overshadowed by the Pope. Charlemagne's successors were less powerful and as they became unable to hold overbearing archbishops in check, bishops appealed to the Pope for support and this increased papal authority. Some of the popes, such as Nicholas I (858–67) were very able men, although in the early tenth century there was a succession of ineffective popes, most of whom held office only for a very short time. In the period between 897 and 955, there were seventeen popes.

The Rise of Islam

Whilst in western Europe Christianity had been expanding, in the east large areas of Christendom surrendered to Islam The power of Byzantium, as we have seen, was at its height under Emperor Justinian I (527–65). He built many churches; he issued the Justinian legal code, which profoundly influenced Western canon law and he tried to uphold orthodoxy by calling the Fifth Ecumenical Council, which condemned the Monophysites, who held that Christ had only a divine and not a human nature. The Monophysites refused to comply with Justinian's demands and found allies amongst those in Egypt, Ethiopia, Syria and Armenia who resented control from Constantinople. Theological and regional opposition to the emperor weakened the Empire and made it less able to withstand the attacks of Muslims, especially as heretical Christians were likely to be treated more leniently by Muslim than by Byzantine rulers.

The early seventh century saw a resurgence of Persian attacks on the Empire. In 611, the Persians took Antioch and then seized control of Syria and Palestine, pillaging Jerusalem and killing hundreds of Christians. The Persians also captured Alexandria in about 618 and took control of Egypt. At the same time, the Empire was being attacked by the Avars and Slavs from the north. In the 620s the situation was reversed. Emperor Heraclius bought off the Avars and reasserted the imperial power in the eastern Mediterranean, recapturing Syria, Palestine, including Jerusalem, and Egypt. The struggle, however, had drained the Empire's resources so that it was not able to withstand a new threat.

The Prophet Muhammad (570–632) had a deep respect for Jesus, who is mentioned several times in the Qur'an. The Qur'an, however, denied that Jesus was crucified, because God would not allow any servant of his to meet such a fate. The Qur'an, with its insistence on the Oneness of God, also denied Christian claims that Jesus was the Son of God. For some centuries, many Christians regarded Islam as a Christian heresy, but Muslims believed that Muhammad had received a fresh revelation from God and that Islam was a restatement of the eternal religion, which had also been proclaimed by Moses and Jesus, although their message had been corrupted by their followers.

In the years after Muhammad's death, Islam expanded rapidly. Under the leadership of the Caliphs, Arabs captured Damascus in 636. In the following year, all Syria came under their control and in 638, after a two-year siege, Jerusalem was captured by Omar (634–44), who treated the Christians honourably. Jerusalem became the third most holy city of the Muslim world, as it was from Jerusalem that Muhammad began his night journey to heaven. The so-called 'Mosque of Omar', the beautiful Dome of the Rock, was not in fact built by Omar, but by Abd el Melek Ibn Merwan. An inscription says it was built in AH 72 (691 CE). Alexandria was captured in about 642, whilst by 650 Mesopotamia and much of Persia was under Muslim control, as was some of North Africa. In 697, Carthage, the centre of Byzantine power in North Africa, fell to the Arabs and then early in the eighth century the Muslims crossed the Strait of Gibraltar and took control of much of Spain until their advance was halted at the battle of Tours or Poitiers in 732.

Muslim conquests did not mean the immediate end of Christianity in those areas. Islam regarded both Jews and

Christians as 'people of the book'. They were given a second-class status as *dhimmi*, but allowed some freedom, although they were subject to quite heavy taxation. Many Christians, however, fled. Catholics from North Africa took refuge in Sicily and southern Italy, whilst Greeks retreated to areas under the control of Byzantium. It was virtually impossible for the church to recruit new members and some Christians converted to Islam, either from conviction or for convenience.

Monophysite Churches

Several of the Monophysite churches, however, have survived under Islam. One example is the Coptic Church of Egypt. Prior to the Arab conquest, the people of Egypt identified themselves and their language in Greek as *Aigyptos*, which in Arabic is *qibt*, which is westernised as Copt. The term came to be the distinctive name of the Egyptian Christian minority. According to tradition, the church in Egypt was founded by St Mark. Alexandria was one of the chief sees of the early church, but Christians in Egypt suffered severely under the Diocletian persecutions. Then at the Council of Chalcedon in 451, Dioscorus (d.454), the Patriarch of Alexandria, was condemned. The Egyptian church became formally Monophysite and increasingly isolated. The Orthodox, or so-called 'Melchite church', comprising those Christians who remained in communion with Constantinople, received little support from the local people.

The Coptic church has survived long centuries of Arab rule. It was to their favour that they too opposed the Byzantium rulers. Under Arab rule, they started to use Arabic versions of the Bible and to use some Arabic in the liturgy. There are some Coptic dioceses outside Egypt, for example in Jerusalem and the Sudan. The Coptic church adopted a democratic form of government in 1890. It has a number of schools. In recent years, the church has been under some pressure with the rise of fundamentalist Muslim groups in Egypt and a hostile regime in the Sudan. The Coptic church is in communion with the Ethiopian, Armenian and Syrian Orthodox churches. There is also a small Uniat Coptic church dating from 1741 when

Athanasius, the Coptic Bishop of Jerusalem, joined the Roman Catholic church.

Another Monophysite church is the Syrian Orthodox church, whose members are sometimes called Jacobites, which descends from the Monophysite movement in the patriarchate of Antioch. Its numbers have declined with the difficulties of being a minority and because of severe losses during the Mughal invasions in the fourteenth century and by massacres in Turkish territory in the twentieth-century. They number about 300,000 in the Middle East and about 50,000 in North and South America. There are various Syrian churches in South India.

The fascinating stories of other Eastern churches, such as the Armenian or Nestorian churches, are too little known in the West. The Nestorians, who were keen missionaries, reached China in the Tang period (618–907).[7]

Monasticism

Amidst this numerical ebb and flow of the Church in the centuries from the conversion of Constantine to the end of the first Christian millennium, the most significant spiritual development was the growth of the monastic movement.

With official favour and even wealth, it was no longer a sacrifice to become a Christian. This led some of the more devout to escape the temptations of public life and go into the desert, either as hermits or to live in communities.

It was in Egypt in the third century that Christian monasticism first developed. Neoplatonism, which stressed the value of contemplation, was influential in the area. Egypt was also at the time a country with political and economic disorders and this may have encouraged spiritually minded people to withdraw from the world.

There is an ascetic strand in the New Testament with its emphasis on poverty and sacrifice. Renunciation might include family ties (Mark 10:29). In Matthew's gospel there is a verse which says 'others have renounced marriage because of the kingdom of heaven', although an alternative reading says 'others have made themselves eunuchs because of the kingdom of heaven' (Matt. 19:12). Paul was celibate, but he did not appeal to a direct command from the Lord to support his position. Peter and other apostles were married. Jesus, although it is presumed he did not marry, was spoken of as a 'wine-bibber' compared to his austere cousin John the Baptist.

Celibacy

Celibacy came quickly to be prized by the church. The second-century text *The Shepherd of Hermas*, whilst accepting that Christian widows and widowers might remarry, said that 'they would gain great honour and glory of the Lord' if they refrained from doing so. In 305, the Synod of Elvira in Spain demanded celibacy of bishops and other clergy, and this came to be the rule in the Western church. In the Eastern church, those who were married before ordination could continue to live with their wives, except for a bishop who was expected to find a nunnery where his wife could live.

At the Reformation, the Protestant churches repudiated the requirement that clergy should be celibate. The Roman Catholic church during the Catholic Reformation reaffirmed the rule, although as an ecclesiastical institution which, at least in theory, is open to the possibility of change. The Roman Catholic church continues to insist that clergy should be celibate, although a number of clergy renounce their orders as they are unable to meet this requirement. Celibacy occasions considerable debate. Some feel it reflects a negative valuation of human sexuality based on the dualism of Hellenistic thought, which saw salvation as a freeing of the soul from the body, rather than the biblical tradition which affirms the goodness of the whole creation.

Antony

The most famous of the early monks was St Antony (*c.*251–356). His parents died when he was about eighteen, leaving him to care for his sister. One day in church he heard a reading of Jesus' command to the rich young ruler, 'If you would be perfect, go, sell what you possess and give to the poor and you will have treasure in heaven; and come, follow me' (Matt. 19:21). Antony did just this, keeping only enough to provide for his sister. When he was about thirty-five, Antony retired completely to the desert. A number of other hermits gathered round him and in 305 he came out of his solitude to organise his disciples into a community of hermits living under a rule, although with much less common life than later orders. Antony foreshadowed two types of monasticism: one, the life of complete solitude and the other a way of life whereby monks continued to live in isolation, but with some opportunity for fellowship.

A third type of monasticism, known as the coenobitic (from the Greek 'for living together'), provides for monks to live together in a community with rules and a head monk. The pioneer of this approach was St Pachomius (c.290–346), a younger contemporary of Antony and another Egyptian.

The Growth of Monasticism

In the fourth and fifth centuries monasticism spread quickly and widely. Some of the monks practised extreme austerities, including those, like St Simeon Stylites (c.390–459), who lived on the top of a pillar. The majority lived in community, and the rule worked out in 358 by St Basil the Great (c.330–79), the brother of St Gregory of Nyssa and one of the Cappadocian fathers, was widely influential. It remains the basis of the way of life still followed by monks in the Eastern Church.

The patriarch of Western monasticism was St Benedict of Nursia (c.480–c.550), who in c.500, because of the licentiousness of Roman society, withdrew to a cave at Subiaco, forty miles to the east of Rome. Twenty-five years later, he moved to Monte Cassino, which became the chief monastery of the Benedictine Order. The buildings were destroyed in 1944 but have been rebuilt. At Monte Cassino, Benedict planned the reform of monasticism and drew up his rule, which became the basis of the way of life followed by many Western monastic orders, such as the Carthusians and Cistercians. The rule consists of seventy-three terse chapters, which deal with spiritual matters and questions of organisation, liturgy and discipline. Stability and obedience are paramount. 'Obedience is a blessing to be shown by all, not just to the abbot, but to one another, since we know that it is by the way of obedience that we go to God.' The main work is the divine office (*opus dei*), the regular worship of God, together with private prayer, reading and work. It was a simple, regulated life. The monasteries were places of stability in a disorderly world and became important centres of scholarship and Christian mission.

A New Millennium

Although the start of the second millennium is a convenient date to mark the new vigour of the Christian world, the renewal probably began some fifty years earlier. The next centuries were to see the spread of Christianity into north-western and central Europe, the recapture of the Iberian peninsula and the attempt, through the Crusades, to regain the Holy Land. The period was also marked by new vigour in the Byzantine Empire.

In 962, Otto I, who had been king of the Germans since 936, was crowned Holy Roman Emperor and brought stability to much of western Europe. Just over one hundred years later, William the Conqueror created the foundation of a strong state in England. The period saw the emergence of Christian monarchies in Spain and in Scandinavia. It was a period also of economic expansion, although China of the Sung Dynasty (960–1279) was far richer, more populous and more sophisticated. India, too, although politically divided, was probably richer and more advanced in civilisation.

Scandinavia

Denmark, Sweden and Norway all became Christian in the latter half of the tenth century. Harald Bluetooth (*c.*910–*c.*985),

King of Denmark, was baptised just before 950 and his son claimed that he had made the Danes Christian. There was, however, a reaction and it was under Canute (1016–35), King of Denmark and England, that the faith became firmly established. Canute, a devout Christian, made a pilgrimage to Rome and ordered his subjects to learn the Lord's Prayer and to go to Communion at least three times a year. In Norway, Haakon the Good (r. c.946–c.961), who had been reared at the English court, tried to win his people to Christianity, but was thwarted by the landowners. It was left to St Olave (Olaf) (995–1030) to spread the faith. The conversion of Sweden was rather later, but in 1164 it was given its own archiepiscopal see at Uppsala.

Russia

Vikings and Norsemen also took news of the gospel to Iceland, Greenland and North America. At the same time, Christianity was spreading eastwards to Russia, along both a northern and a southern route. It was under St Vladimir I (c.956–1015) that the mass conversion of the people of Kiev began. By the end of his reign in 1015, there were three bishoprics. It is said that Vladimir was visited by representatives of Islam, Judaism, Latin Christianity and Greek Christianity and that it was the Greek delegation which made the greatest impression. The church adopted the Byzantine rite in the old Slavonic language. Despite his choice, Vladimir was determined to assert his political independence of Constantinople. In the fourteenth century the leadership of the church moved from Kiev to Moscow and independence from Greek Orthodoxy was established.

Eastern Europe

The early years of the second millennium saw Christianity established in Poland and Hungary and other parts of Eastern Europe and by 1350, except for Lithuania, where mass baptisms were ordered in 1386, and Finland, most of Europe was Christian, at least in name, although pagan practices survived in secret in some areas.

Spain

Gradually Spain was won back from Muslim rule. For a time there was a flowering of Spanish culture, for example at Toledo, to which Muslim, Jewish and Christian influences contributed, but this Golden Age was not to last. Increasingly, Christian kingdoms, despite their rivalries, asserted control. In 1034, the Caliphate of Cordoba came to an end and the only Muslim foothold was the small state of Granada, which was eventually captured by King Ferdinand of Aragon (r.1474–1516) and Queen Isabella of Castille (r. 1474–1504), in 1492, the same year in which Columbus set out for the Americas and in which the Jews were expelled from Spain.

The Crusades

The use of force against those who did not share the Christian faith, be they pagan, Muslim or Jewish, was taken for granted by almost all Christians at the time. Religion was also closely related to political power and it was used by rulers to bind their states together. Christians today deplore the persecution of Jews and the attacks on Muslims, both of which have left a painful legacy that only now members of the three faiths are starting to address.

Although the Crusades were in the name of Christianity, their causes were to a considerable extent economic and political. The Byzantine Empire was threatened by Muslim power. The Pope, whilst wanting to give assistance to Christians in the East, also hoped to restore unity between the two branches of the Church and to strengthen his authority. Religious motivation was also significant. Many Christians travelled to Jerusalem on pilgrimage and at the time difficulties were being put in their way. Clearly, when in November 1095 Pope Urban II (1088–99), in a stirring sermon at a Synod in Clermont in France, appealed for a crusade to free the holy places, he caught the popular mood. The congregation shouted out '*Deus vult*', 'God wills it'. The Pope promised a 'plenary indulgence' – a pardon for all sins – to those who enlisted for the crusade. Popular preachers, such as Peter the Hermit, whipped up support of the people, often by maligning Jews and Muslims.

The First Crusade captured Antioch in 1098, with great slaughter, and in the following year took Jerusalem, killing many of its inhabitants. For a time Christian rule was established in the Holy Land, but after a crushing victory at Hattin in 1187, Muslims recaptured Jerusalem and most of the Crusaders' centres. A Third Crusade was launched in 1189, in which King Richard of England (r.1157–99), the so-called 'Lion-hearted', took part. In 1202, when papal power was at its height, Pope Innocent III launched the Fourth Crusade, which was diverted into storming and plundering Constantinople in 1204. A Latin Patriarch was established and for a time the church was united under the Pope. The Byzantine Empire, however, survived with its headquarters at Nicaea and in 1261 won back Constantinople, putting an end to Latin rule there. Neither Christian control of the Holy Land nor a united church could be achieved by force. Constantinople was fatally weakened by the Latin attack and eventually, in 1453, it fell to the Muslim Ottoman Turks.

The external expansion of Christianity in the period from the middle of the tenth century to the middle of the thirteenth century was matched by a period of vigorous growth in church life, followed by a period of stagnation or decline.

Monks and Friars

There was a renewal of monastic life, led by the monastery of Cluny, north of Lyons in France, and its abbots, of whom its founder Berno and his successor Odo (abbot 926–42) and the fifth abbot, Odilo (abbot 994–1084), were especially influential. In the twelfth century the leadership in creative monastic life passed to the Cistercians, of whom perhaps the best-known was St Bernard of Clairvaux (1090–1153). A vigorous and influential personality, he had a deep mystical devotion to Jesus, as is shown in the hymn ascribed to him, *Jesu, dulcis memoria,* of which the best-known English translation begins 'Jesus, the very thought of thee with sweetness fills the breast.'

A new development in the thirteenth century was the coming of the Friars or mendicant orders, namely, the Franciscans, the Dominicans, the Carmelites and the Augustinians.

St Francis of Assisi (1181–1226) is one of the most attractive figures in Christian history. He was born in Assisi in Italy. His father was a prosperous cloth merchant and as a youth Francis was a lively member of the young aristocracy. In late adolescence he began to take his religion more seriously, partly because of illness. He gave time to helping the poor and, despite his loathing for the disease, to the care of those with leprosy. His father was increasingly annoyed and eventually took him to the bishop, saying that he wished to disinherit Francis, who stripped off the clothes his father had provided and standing naked before the bishop declared that henceforth he would only serve 'our Father who art in heaven'. He started to restore some ruined chapels, but in 1209 he heard the call to become an itinerant preacher, proclaiming the kingdom of God and calling on people to repent. He lived in complete poverty, surviving on whatever food he was given. He radiated the love of Christ.

Soon others joined him and Francis sought the permission of Pope Innocent III for their preaching mission. The friars also conveyed their message by song, and Francis' *Canticle of the Sun* is still sung. Francis had a love of nature and of all living things. His disciples told of a sermon that he preached to the birds, urging them to praise their Creator. On another occasion when he was preaching, the swallows made so much noise that he asked them to be quiet until he had finished, which they did. In 1212 an order for women, the Poor Clares, was established and in 1221 a tertiary order, for those living in the world who aspired to the Franciscan ideals.

Francis wished to present the gospel to the Muslims and in 1219 met with the Sultan. By the time Francis approached the end of his life, his order had outgrown him and soon needed clear organisation, but there were divisions in the movement.

The Dominicans, founded by St Dominic (1170–1221) in 1215, like the Franciscans, date from the early thirteenth century. From the start they were dedicated to teaching and scholarship. Many outstanding scholars were Dominicans, including the greatest Catholic theologian, St Thomas Aquinas.

The vitality of the Christian faith was evident also in various lay movements, such as confraternities and singing guilds and the Flagellants, who in penance for their sins scourged themselves and ran in the streets half-naked. Other groups were to be regarded as heretical, such as the Waldenses, who stressed poverty and simplicity, and the Cathari or Albigensians, whose asceticism derived from a dualism which despised the body.

The Papacy

This period also saw the papacy, after reforms early in the eleventh century, reach the height of its power. St Gregory VII (*c.*1021–85), or Hildebrand to give him his original name, had already exercised great influence under Leo IX. As pope, Gregory issued decrees against simony and enforced the celibacy of the clergy. He had an exalted view of the papacy, whether or not the *Dictatus Papae* are by him. He held that the Roman church was founded by God and that the Roman Pontiff alone deserved the title 'universal', and that he could depose or reinstate bishops. He even humbled the Emperor Henry IV, forcing him to submit at Canossa, in north Italy in 1077, and to do penance. The Emperor is said to have stood for three days in the snow outside the Pope's lodgings before being granted absolution from his excommunication. This, however, was only the start of the struggle. In 1084, Henry captured Rome. Gregory was rescued by Norman soldiers, but their behaviour provoked great antagonism against Gregory, who fled to Monte Cassino and thence to Salerno, where he died. His last words were, 'I have loved justice and hated iniquity, therefore I die in exile.'[8] Historians who are critical of the centralisation of papal power would, however, question Gregory's verdict.

There were other strong popes. It was Innocent III, who

reigned from 1198 to 1216, who brought the papacy to the apex of its power. His ideas were not new, but he expressed them with clarity. He wrote that Christ 'left to Peter the governance not of the church only but of the whole world' and he had no hesitation in interfering in the affairs of the various European kingdoms. He insisted on high moral behaviour by the clergy and dominated the Fourth Lateran Council, which was held in 1215. He also laid down that all Christians were to make their confession to a priest at least once a year.

Decline

After Innocent III, the papacy began to decline, although there were some capable popes in the thirteenth century. The popes were caught up in political struggles of the age and internal divisions. From 1309 to 1377, the popes resided in Avignon, which although not actually in France, was overshadowed by that nation. Several of the popes lived in great luxury, but their influence was declining.

The vigour of European life was slackening. The feudal system was declining and it was a time of much fighting in western Europe. The major disaster, which slowed down economic life, was the devastation caused by the Black Death (1347–51). This was a series of bubonic plagues that reduced the population of Europe by a third and that of England by about a half. The religious orders felt the full effect of the plague and were unable to recruit enough new members to fill the gaps.

English Mystics

Even so this was a period which produced some fine mystical writing such as the fourteenth-century *Theologia Germanica*, which profoundly influenced Martin Luther, and the works of the English mystics. This period also saw some of the most splendid examples of Gothic architecture, such as King's College chapel at Cambridge.

The Cloud of Unknowing, whose author remains anonymous, was written in the fourteenth century. It teaches that God cannot be known by human reason. In contemplation, the soul is aware of a cloud of unknowing between itself and God, which can only be penetrated by 'a sharp dart of love'. The author encouraged people to repeat a short phrase or single word to foster loving attention on God.

Walter Hilton (d. 1396) in his *Ladder of Perfection* traces the soul's ascent to God. He insisted that a bodily turning to God 'without the heart following' is of no value. Both the author of *The Cloud of Unknowing* and Walter Hilton appear critical of Richard Rolle's (*c.*1300–49) emphasis on affective mystical experiences of 'heat', 'sweetness' and 'song'.

Perhaps the most popular of the English mystics today is Julian of Norwich (*c.*1342–*c.*1413), partly because there are a number of contemplative prayer groups called Julian groups. She probably lived as an anchoress close to St Julian's church in Norwich. In May 1373, Julian, while suffering from a severe heart attack, had a series of visions relating to the Passion of Christ, which she recorded in the shorter text of her *Showings*. Some fifteen years later she had a further revelation, after which she recorded a longer version of her writings. She stressed that 'Love is our Lord's meaning'[9] and her words of confidence, 'Sin is behovely, but all shall be well, and all shall be well and all manner of things shall be well'[10] are often quoted. Like an earlier woman mystic, Hildegard of Bingen (1098–1179), Julian stressed the motherly character of God's love and said that God is really a Mother as well as a Father.

Churches in the East

In the east, the Byzantine Empire was under increasing pressure from the Ottoman Turks, who, as we have seen, in 1453 captured Constantinople, where the great cathedral of Saint Sophia (Holy Wisdom) was converted into a mosque. In central Asia, the Mongols had become Muslims and Timur (Tamerlane) (1336–1405), from his capital at Samarkand conquered large areas of central Asia, making life very difficult for the small, mainly Nestorian, Christian minorities. In China the Mongol Dynasty, which had been welcoming to foreigners, was replaced by the Ming Dynasty, which was xenophobic and expelled small foreign communities, including presumably the Christians.

New Life

Yet amidst the decline, new life was growing, for example in the economic activity of Genoa and Venice and the desire to increase trade with Asia. The invention of printing by movable type in the mid-fourteenth century was preparing the way for the spread of knowledge. The Renaissance renewed interest in the intellectual heritage of antiquity, whilst the new learning encouraged fresh study in their original languages of the scriptures, which as the source of faith were to be the inspiration of the Reformers.

For this chapter and the next, Kenneth Scott Latourette, *A History of Christianity* (Eyre and Spottiswoode), the six-volume *Pelican History of the Church*, and John R. H. Moorman, *A History of the Church in England* (A. & C. Black, 1953), are useful.
Hans Lietzmann, *A History of the Early Church* (1951, James Clarke, 1993), covers the first four hundred years in some detail. M. D. Knowles, *Christian Monasticism* (1969), and E. A. Bowman, *Western Mysticism: A Guide to the Basic Works* (1978), are good introductions to their respective subjects.

6

A Changing Church in a Changing World

The sixteenth century brought new life to the church in western Europe but also division and conflict. The Reformation and the Catholic (or Counter-) Reformation were related movements, which both sought to bring the church nearer to the Christian ideal, but which ended up by shattering the unity of the Western church.

The Reformations

The causes of the Reformation are complex. Indeed, scholars today speak of Reformations, because there were a variety of movements for change and protest. We might compare the Reformation to the 'peace' or 'environment' movements of recent years which have been a loose coalition of groups with very varied aims and ideologies. In part, the Reformation was a protest against abuse in the Catholic church, and the movements which come under this label all repudiated the authority of the papacy, asserting instead the supreme authority of scripture. They also rejected monasticism. Those belonging to the Catholic Reformation believed that change was possible within the existing structures.

There were also socio-political and economic causes of the Reformation. It is broadly true to say that those countries which had for many centuries been part of the Roman Empire and

143

which had long before assimilated Latin culture – Italy, Spain, Portugal, France and Austria – remained loyal to the Catholic church, whereas the countries of northern Europe broke away. The emergence of Protestantism has been seen as the reaction of Teutonic peoples against religious control from the Latin south. Another generalisation is that Protestant movements tended to spring from lower social strata, whereas the Catholic Reformation was led by members of the aristocracy.

Late Medieval Movements for Reform

The Cathars

There were in the later Middle Ages a number of movements regarded as heretical. The Cathars or 'the Pure' in northern Italy and southern France, where they were often known as Albigenses, were a serious threat to the Catholic church in the thirteenth and fourteenth centuries. They were dualists, believing that there were two eternal powers, the one good and the other evil. The inner circle of Cathars were 'the perfects', who followed a life of strict asceticism, living as celibates and eating only a vegan diet. Admission to this inner circle was by the rite of *consolamentum*, after an arduous probationary period. Those thus 'consoled' saw themselves as the only true Christians and denied the title to Catholics. The decline of the movement was partly because of internal divisions and partly because of repression by the Inquisition.

Wycliffe

In the fourteenth century John Wycliffe (*c.*1330–84), a Yorkshireman who became a don at Oxford, voiced views which challenged the offical teachings of the Church. For example, he said that popes might err and that salvation did not depend on membership of the Church, but on election by God. He wished to make the faith more available to the people and had the Latin Vulgate version of the Bible translated into vernacular English. He also sent out travelling preachers, whose adherents became known as Lollards (from the old French word for 'mumble'). As his thinking became more radical,

Wycliffe, who was in the service of John of Gaunt and the Black Prince and therefore in part protected, lost support at Oxford and in 1382 many of his teachings were condemned by Archbishop Courtenay (*c.*1342–96), a great-grandson of King Edward I, whose name is remembered in the name of the village of Nuneham Courtenay, which is one of my parishes.

Hus

There are different views about whether Wycliffe and the Lollards had a lasting influence in England, where under Henry V (1413–22) severe measures were taken against Lollardry. Certainly, Wycliffe's writing had a strong influence on John Hus (*c.*1373–1415), who studied at the newly founded and famous university of Prague. In 1402, Hus became rector and preacher in the chapel of the Holy Innocents of Bethlehem in Prague and his preaching attracted a wide following from all classes. Besides preaching in Latin, he also used Czech, thereby encouraging the growing Czech patriotism. His reforming views provoked opposition and excommunication by the Archbishop of Prague. Hus appealed to the Pope, who reinforced his excommunication. In 1412 Hus left the city of Prague and started to preach in the open air. The church authorities continued to pursue him and on 6 July 1415, he was burned at the stake. His last audible words were, 'Lord, into thy hands I commend my spirit.' The movement continued and the Hussites were to become the spiritual ancestors of the Moravians, who in turn influenced the Wesleys. John Hus has also remained a Czech hero, especially to those opposed to foreign domination of their country.

Mention of Wycliffe and Hus is a reminder that the Reformation should not be seen in isolation. At the popular level, religion had become ritualised and stylised. Many priests offered the mass in a mechanical way and only very occasionally gave the people Communion. Most priests had few books and gave little teaching. Devotion to the Virgin Mary was encouraged and prayers and masses were offered for the dead – often for a fee, by which an indulgence could be purchased which was supposed to free a loved one from the punishments of purgatory. The preacher Johann Tetzel (*c.*1465–1519) was alleged to have claimed that:

> *So soon as the coin in coffer rings,*
> *the soul from Purgatory springs.*

The popular religion has been described as 'a cult of the living in the service of the dead'.

Humanist Learning

In the universities, the scholastic teachers struggled to reconcile Aristotle's writings to the traditional teachings of the church. A new approach was adopted by the humanists, who concentrated on the study of classical languages, including Greek and Hebrew, and sought to get back to biblical sources of the faith.

Erasmus

The best-known of the humanists was Desiderius Erasmus (*c.*1466–1536), who was born in the Low Countries, probably at Rotterdam. He studied at Paris and travelled to Oxford, Louvain and Italy and he became the first Lady Margaret Professor of Greek and Theology at Cambridge. Erasmus spent most of his later years in Basle.

A very able linguistic scholar, Erasmus sought to base the faith on the biblical text. His crowning achievement was his edition of the Greek New Testament, which showed up certain inaccuracies in the Vulgate or official Latin version of the scriptures. Alongside the Greek text he placed his own elegant Latin version. He also appended some notes, some of which were biting comments on contemporary abuses. His prefatory essay was a fine plea for the study of the scriptures. He wrote:

> I could wish that every woman might read the Gospel and the Epistles of St Paul. Would that these were translated into each and every language so that they might be read and understood not only by Scots and Irishmen, but also by

Turks and Saracens . . . Would that the farmer might sing snatches of Scripture at his plough, that the weaver might hum phrases of Scripture to the tune of his shuttle, that the traveller might lighten with stories from Scripture the weariness of his journey.[1]

Erasmus was a master of satire. In his *Praise of Folly* (1509) he showed up how remote ecclesiastical and scholarly debate was from pastoral concern. He mocked the abuses in some monasteries.

Although some of Erasmus' critics complained that he was the real author of schism and worse than Martin Luther, Erasmus remained a Catholic. Reluctantly he was drawn into some public controversy with Luther. To Luther's amazement, Erasmus when he was dying did not ask for the last sacrament, but his heir, who was with Erasmus at his death said, 'As was his life, so was the death of this most upright of men. Most holy was his living, most holy his dying.' His last words, which were in Dutch, his mother tongue, were '*Lieve God*' or 'Dear God.'[2]

Martin Luther

It was Martin Luther who was to take this new humanist approach of a return to the original sources (*ad fontes*) from the universities to the parishes. Luther is often remembered for his outspoken protests against the selling of indulgences in his *Ninety-Five Theses* (1517) but his main concern was with 'justification by faith', which he claimed was based on scripture, of which the interpretation in his view had been obscured by medieval scholasticism.

Martin Luther (1483–1546) understood justification in Paul's letter to the Romans (3:21–6) as the instantaneous realisation that sinners are forgiven and made righteous by the work of Christ crucified. Justification is the unmerited grace of God conveyed to sinners by the atoning work of Christ. He rejected the Augustinian view that justification was the gradual accumulation of righteousness. Human beings could not earn

147

justification, but could only be put right with God by faith in Christ's work of atonement.[3]

It was Luther's attack on indulgences that caught public attention and brought him into trouble with the authorities. In the summer of 1518, the Pope summoned Luther to Rome to answer charges of heresy and contumacy, but the hearing was transferred to the next Imperial Diet or Parliament of the Holy Roman Empire. Eventually, Luther appeared at the Diet of Worms. Called upon to recant, he replied, 'Here stand I. I can do no other. God help me.'[4] Already threatened with excommunication, the Edict of Worms (May 1521) outlawed him and placed him under a ban, but he was saved by his ruler, Friedrich, Elector of Ernestine Saxony (1486–1525), who smuggled him into exile to Wartburg.

Luther's attacks on the Pope continued, but besides the public controversy, he also worked to make his teaching known to 'common people' and set about translating the New Testament into German, which was a brilliant piece of work and one which had a deep influence on the German language. Luther wrote numerous Bible commentaries, hymns and tracts against various opponents, including the Jews.

Zwingli

Luther had the protection of his prince. Ulrich Zwingli (1484–1531), another leading reformer, had to win over the people of the Swiss city state of Zurich. Zwingli's father was a village bailiff and his uncle a village priest. He was a bright student and was fluent in Latin and Greek, reading the church fathers in the original. Like Luther, he was impressed by Augustine and was also attracted by the Christian humanists, especially Erasmus. In 1519, Zwingli became people's priest in the Great Minster at Zurich. Influenced by Luther's writings, he stressed the authority of the Bible and questioned any doctrine or practice that did not have scriptural support. However, he broke with Luther over the significance of the Lord's Supper. Luther defended belief in the 'real presence' of Christ at the Eucharist and insisted that when Jesus said of the bread 'This is my body', his words were to be taken literally. To Zwingli, Jesus' words, 'Do this in memory of me' were the key. Although he believed Christ to be present and to be discerned by faith, he regarded the rite primarily as a memorial which bound worshippers together in loyalty to Jesus.

Calvin

Another leading reformer, John Calvin (1509–64) also based himself in a Swiss city, Geneva. Although Calvin was of humble ancestry, he was reared in aristocratic society. He was born at Noyon, sixty miles north-east of Paris, and at fourteen went to the University of Paris. From boyhood he was deeply religious and critical of moral laxity. He was influenced by the new humanism and had a good knowledge of Latin, Greek and Hebrew. In 1534, he left Paris and settled in Basle, where, in the same year, the first edition of his *Institutes of the Christian Religion* was published. Soon afterwards Calvin was persuaded by Guillaume Farel (1489–1565), a fiery Reformation preacher, to join him in Geneva, but in 1538, the authorities turned against the reform party, so Calvin moved to Strasbourg. But in 1541 the Magistracy of Geneva invited him back and for twenty-five years his influence was dominant in church and state. John Knox (*c.*1513–72), the leader of the Reformation in Scotland, said of Geneva under Calvin that it was the most perfect school of Christ that ever was in earth since the days of the apostles. Calvin's influence also spread throughout Europe from his College of Geneva, founded in 1559, which trained pastors to promote biblical theology throughout the continent. Calvin's writings, especially his *Institutes* and his biblical commentaries were also widely influential.

Calvin's writings are not particularly novel and he did not engage in much argument with Catholic or other Protestant thinkers. He claimed that he was reiterating what the church had always taught, although this message had been obscured by Roman Catholic innovations. His work won attention because of its clarity and systematic arrangement. He insisted that his teachings were all based on scripture.

The final edition of the *Institutes* had four books. The first dealt with God as creator, preserver and governor of the universe. The second outlined the redemption won by Jesus Christ. The third dealt with the Holy Spirit, and the fourth with the church and its relation to civil governments.

Calvin held that although the essence of God transcends all human thought, some knowledge of God is possible from the beauty and orderliness of the universe. Because of sin, however, man was totally depraved and his only hope of salvation was the pardon offered to those who believed in Jesus Christ. By his sufferings and death Jesus satisfied the righteous judgment of God and took upon himself the punishment for sin that man deserved. Those who experienced this salvation were chosen or elected by God. The church, Calvin held, was not identical with any visible institution, but its true members are known only to God.

The Reformation in England

Henry VIII

The Reformation in England was initially political. Henry VIII (1491–1547; ruled 1509–47), who was six feet tall, powerfully built and, as a young man, a fine athlete, married Catherine of Aragon, who was the aunt of the Emperor Charles V. Catherine had previously been married to Henry's brother, Arthur, who was fourteen at the time. Six months later Arthur died and the marriage had not been consummated. It was against church law for a man to marry the wife of his deceased brother, but a papal dispensation permitted Henry, who had just become king at the age of eighteen, to marry her. The marriage was primarily political in purpose and intended to gain for England a powerful ally.

By 1527, Henry and Catherine had been married for eighteen years. Catherine had borne him three sons and two daughters, but except for Mary, all had died as infants. Henry wanted a male heir. Also at this time he fell in love with Anne Boleyn, a lady of the court who had some ambitious relations. Henry wanted to persuade the papacy to annul the marriage, but the Pope was afraid of offending the Emperor Charles. Thomas Cranmer (1489–1556), who became Archbishop of Canterbury in 1532, suggested that the legality of the marriage be put to the universities. As the Pope refused to give the required annulment, Henry eventually pushed the English Parliament into declaring that the English church was competent to decide its own cases, and in 1534 Parliament declared that the king 'is and ought to be the supreme head of the English Church'. The authority of the papacy had been repudiated. The Dissolution of the Monasteries (1536 and 1539), some of which were in need of reform, was also primarily because the king wanted their wealth.

Henry VIII did not want any doctrinal or liturgical change. Indeed, for writing a book against Luther[5] he had been given by the Pope the title 'Defender of the Faith' – a title still claimed by the British monarch. Archbishop Cranmer, however, was a reformer at heart. Henry initially resisted attempts to translate the Bible into English and William Tyndale (c.1494–1536) was executed for his efforts. None the less, the Great Bible, which was based on the work of Miles Coverdale (1488–1568) and Tyndale, was produced in 1538 and gradually found its way into the churches. Cranmer also, before Henry's death, produced a Litany in English.

Cranmer and The Book of Common Prayer

It was during Edward VI's short reign (1547–53) that Thomas Cranmer produced the Prayer Book (1549, revised 1552), which is the lasting memorial to his learning and liturgical skill. Its use was required by the Act of Uniformity.

The Book of Common Prayer, written in unforgettable English and with melodious cadence has, until the last quarter of the twentieth century, been the hallmark of English Christianity and of the Anglican Communion. Its use was forbidden by Queen Mary in 1553 but, with slight modifications it was reinstated by Queen Elizabeth I. During the Civil War, Parliament abolished the Prayer Book in 1645, but after the restoration of the monarchy it was again reinstated with some changes in 1662 and is sometimes known as the '1662 Prayer

Book'. An attempt to revise it in 1928 was rejected by Parliament, although some of the revised material came to be quite widely used. In 1980, the Church of England introduced the *Alternative Service Book*, often known as the ASB. Further revision is now in progress. Similar new Prayer Books have been produced by other churches of the Anglican Communion, although the 1662 Prayer Book, which is essentially Cranmer's work, is still used in a number of churches.

Cranmer's *Book of Common Prayer* contains services for Morning and Evening Prayer, an order for Holy Communion and services for rites of passage. The Baptism service was much simplified and in the funeral service all prayers for the dead were omitted. Ceremonies emphasising the priestly functions of the clergy were omitted. The most significant change was in the Eucharist. The emphasis was moved from the concept of sacrifice and real presence to commemoration and communion. It is the offering of the worshipper's 'souls and bodies' in obedience to God which is a 'reasonable, holy and lively sacrifice', not the self-offering of Christ. In the 1549 book, the priest says to the communicant, 'The Body of Our Lord Jesus Christ which was given for thee . . .', whereas in 1552, the priest says, 'Take and eat this in remembrance that Christ died for thee . . .' Under Elizabeth, the two sentences of administration were joined together.

Mary

The move for reform in England was checked by Queen Mary (1516–58, ruled 1553–58) who married the Catholic King Philip of Spain and who tried to restore the old order. Leaders of the Reformation were tried and some, including Cranmer, Latimer and Ridley, were put to death. Hugh Latimer (*c.*1485–1555), who for a short time was Bishop of Worcester, and Nicholas Ridley (*c.*1500–55), who was Bishop of London from 1550, were burned to death in Oxford on 16 October 1555. In the midst of their agony, Latimer called out, 'Be of good comfort, Master Ridley, and play the man; we shall this day light such a candle by God's grace in England as I trust shall never be put out.'[6]

Great pressure was put on Cranmer to recant and he did repudiate some of the doctrines which he had taught, but in the end he died for his beliefs and as he faced martyrdom, he first put the hand which had signed his recantations into the flames, saying, 'This hand hath offended.'[7]

Elizabeth I

During the long reign of Elizabeth I (1533–1603, ruled 1558–1603), the Reformation in England became more settled, especially after the defeat of the Armada in 1588 removed the Spanish peril.

Her first Parliament met in January 1559 and passed two acts of great importance. The 'Act of Supremacy' and the 'Act of Uniformity' together form what is known as the 'Elizabethan Settlement'. Henry's legislation against Rome was revived, although Elizabeth chose to be called 'supreme governor', unlike Henry who called himself 'supreme head' of the church in England. The 1552 Prayer Book was reintroduced, with only minor alterations.

In time, English people became used to the Prayer Book, to receiving the cup as well as the bread and to clergy who were married. There were some who maintained the Catholic faith and had to go into hiding. As time went by, there was increasing pressure for a more radical reformation and Elizabeth's last years found her resisting Puritan demands for change. John Jewel (1522–71) and Richard Hooker (1553–1600), however, provided a theological justification for the *via media* or middle way of the Church of England.

James I and Charles I

Pressure from the Puritans for further change continued under the early Stuart monarchs. During the reign of James I (1566–1625, ruled 1603–25), the 'Authorised' or 'King James' English version of the Bible, with its incomparable English, was published in 1611. During the reign of his son Charles I (1600–49, ruled 1625–49), who backed the introduction of greater ritual by Archbishop William Laud (1573–1645, archbishop 1633–45), religious differences became embroiled with the political differences. These culminated in the Civil War and the beheading of Charles I.

The Commonwealth and the Restoration

During the Commonwealth and the Protectorate of Oliver Cromwell (1599–1658, 'Lord Protector' 1653–8), the Puritans, although divided amongst themselves, were dominant. The use of the Prayer Book was made illegal and episcopacy was abolished. Under Cromwell, the Jews, who had been expelled in 1290, were allowed to return to Britain.

With the restoration of Charles II (1630–85, ruled 1660–85), the Church of England was re-established and the Prayer Book and episcopacy reintroduced. Within a few months some seven hundred Puritan clergy were ejected from their livings. They and others who could not accept the Act of Uniformity (1662), despite civil disabilities, preserved the Puritan inheritance in what became the 'dissenting' or 'non-conformist' chapels of the Baptists, Presbyterians and Congregationalists.

John Bunyan

One of the best-known Puritans was John Bunyan (1628–88), whose *Pilgrim's Progress* has become a spiritual classic. Bunyan was born into a poor home at Elstow in Bedfordshire. He served for a period in the Parliamentary army. In 1657 he became a preacher of the Bedford Independent church, but was partially silenced during the Restoration period and spent nearly twelve years in prison.

Pilgrim's Progress tells of the dangers and distractions, such as Vanity Fair, Doubting Castle and Giant Despair, that Pilgrim had to overcome on his journey to the Celestial City. There are many memorable passages, not least the account of Mr Valiant-for-Truth crossing the river of Death.

> Then said he 'I am going to my Father's: and though with great difficulty I am got hither, yet now I do not repent me of all the trouble I have been at to arrive where I am. My sword I give to him that shall succeed me in my pilgrimage, and my courage and skill to him that can get it. My marks

and scars I carry with me to be a witness for me, that I have fought his battles who will now be my rewarder.' When the day that he must go hence was come, many accompanied him to the river side, into which as he went he said, 'Death, where is thy sting?' And as he went down deeper, he said, 'Grave, where is thy victory?' So he passed over and all the trumpets sounded for him on the other side.[8]

James II and William and Mary

Charles II's brother, James II (1633–1701, ruled 1685–8) became a Roman Catholic in about 1670 and his attempts, as king, to improve the position of his co-religionists led to his downfall.

He was succeeded by William and Mary, during whose reign the so-called 'Toleration Act' affirmed the position of the Church of England, but, without removing any of their civil disabilities, allowed Dissenters freedom of worship. Such toleration was not extended to Roman Catholics or Unitarians. Although from Elizabeth's time there had been a continuing underground Roman Catholic church, it was not until the nineteenth century that the Roman Catholic church was readmitted into England and the civil disabilities of those who were not members of the Church of England were removed. Even today, the Church of England remains the established church and twenty bishops sit in the House of Lords.

The Catholic Reformation

In many other European countries, the sixteenth and seventeenth centuries saw swings of power between Roman Catholics and Protestants, often as a result of fighting. The initial Catholic response to Luther and other reformers was to condemn their teaching. Soon the Catholic church itself engaged in major reform. This spontaneous movement to reform the religious life, to re-evangelise Protestant countries, and to convert the newly discovered peoples of America and the East, was associated particularly with the new religious Order of Jesuits under Ignatius of Loyola and the reform of existing orders. The attempts of the Council of Trent failed to heal the rifts in the Western church, but reached new definitions of justification and revised the liturgy. During this period, papal authority became more entrenched, the Inquisition was given a permanent status (1542) and the Index of prohibited books was set up (1557).

Loyola

It was in Spain that the Catholic Reformation had its earliest development. Ignatius (of) Loyola (c.1491–1556), who was born in one of the Basque provinces, was its most influential leader. Of a noble family, in 1521 he was severely wounded in battle. A cannon ball broke his leg, and during the long tedious convalescence he read a life of Christ and a book of the lives of the saints. On his recovery, he dedicated himself to become a soldier of Christ and imposed on himself the strictest of disciplines. He also, from his own spiritual experiences, developed a pattern of meditation, contemplation and prayer which he set out in his very influential *Spiritual Exercises*.

The Ignatian way of prayer moves religion from the head to the heart in absolute devotion to God. This is expressed in his prayer:

> *Take, Lord, and keep all my freedom, my memory, my understanding, and all my will, whatever I have and possess. You gave them to me, and I restore them to you . . . Give me your love and your grace: that is enough for me.*[9]

Another of his prayers also expresses this offering of his whole life to God:

> *Dearest Lord, teach me to be generous;*
> *Teach me to serve thee as thou deservest;*
> *To give and not to count the cost,*
> *To fight and not to heed the wounds*
> *To toil and not to seek for rest,*

To labour and not to seek reward,
Save that of knowing that I do thy will.[10]

Gradually, Ignatius gathered a small group of followers. Despite the suspicions of the Inquisition and others, in 1540, papal permission was given for the establishment of a new order, known as the Society of Jesus, which was like an army, whose members were soldiers of God. The Society's growth was phenomenal. When Ignatius died, some sixteen years after its establishment, there were about one thousand members. The numbers continued to increase and Jesuits became active in many countries. St Francis Xavier (1506–52), one of the earliest Jesuits, travelled to India and Japan to make the gospel known. Jesuits made a special appeal to young people.

Teresa of Avila and John of the Cross

Spain was also the setting for new growth of mysticism, associated especially with St Teresa (or Theresa) of Avila (1515–82) and St John of the Cross (1542–1605). For many years Teresa remained an obscure nun, often troubled by ill health, but in her forties she began to have ecstasies and visions of Christ. She also came to feel the need of a stricter discipline than that practised at her nunnery. In 1562, she founded the convent of St Joseph at Avila, where the primitive rule was observed. There she wrote *The Way of Perfection*, having just completed her spiritual autobiography. Even in her lifetime she was revered as a saint and was canonised only forty years after her death.

John of the Cross, the son of an aristocrat, was deeply influenced by Teresa. She chose him to initiate men's houses of her reform movement. He believed that to be filled with God, the soul had to empty itself. He wrote of this in his *Ascent of Mount Carmel, The Dark Night of the Soul* and the *Living Flame of Love*. John of the Cross was canonised in 1726.

There was spiritual renewal in other Catholic countries. In Italy, for example, the Oratory of Divine Love came into being as early as 1497. Gradually the papacy became affected by this

157

renewal and in 1555 a member of the Oratory of Divine Love became Pope as Paul IV (1555–9), and his successor but one, Pius V (1566–72), was eventually canonised.

The Council of Trent

An earlier Pope, Paul III (1534–49), in a vain attempt to halt the divisions in the church, convened a council at Trent. There were three periods when the Council met. The first was from 1545–7, when the Nicene creed was reaffirmed and scripture and tradition were recognised as the source of religious truth. Only the church, the Council said, had authority to interpret scripture. The second period was from 1551–2, when the doctrine of Transubstantiation was reaffirmed and the teachings of the Lutherans, Calvinists and Zwinglians were condemned. The third period of the Council's work, from 1562–3, sealed the divisions within Christendom. The denial of the chalice to the laity was upheld, as was the teaching about the sacrifice of the mass.

What Divided Catholics and Protestants?

In less than fifty years the unity of the Western church had been shattered. Although relations between different churches are now more friendly, the legacy of the divisions continues to this day. The Protestant world was and remains fragmented. Many factors contributed to the making of the Reformations. Even so, certain key issues stand out.

Perhaps most important is the question of authority. All Christians accept the authority of scripture, but which interpretation of scripture is authoritative? Catholics linked the tradition of the church with scripture and gave the final authority in interpretation to the church. Roman Catholics located the church's authority in the papacy, which came to be regarded as 'infallible'. 'Infallibility' is a negative term signifying preservation from error rather than inspiration. The term applies properly to people or institutions rather than to the statements which they make. The First Vatican Council in 1870 proclaimed that the pope is infallible when speaking *ex cathedra* (i.e. from his throne) and defining a matter of faith or morals to be held by the universal church. The Second Vatican Council (1962–5) extended this claim to the body of bishops as a whole united with the pope, for example at an ecumenical council. It also said that the church as a whole is preserved from error by the Holy Spirit when there is universal agreement within it on its fundamental beliefs. It is sometimes said, at a more popular level, that if God wanted to make his purposes known, God would not only need to provide authoritative Scriptures, but also a way of knowing with certainty what they meant. For the Protestant, the ultimate authority for the interpretation of scripture is the individual's reason and conscience. At the Diet of Worms, Luther insisted that he would not renounce his beliefs unless 'convicted by scripture and plain reason'. 'My conscience', he continued 'is captive to the Word of God. I cannot and I will not recant anything, for to go against conscience is neither right nor safe.'[11] Cranmer eventually reached a similar position, recognising in his martyrdom, that conscience is superior to the authority of the monarch, even if the monarch holds authority from God.

The emphasis on the individual is, of course, a recipe, for division. People often differ about the plain meaning of scripture. In the sixteenth century and subsequently, there have been many divisions amongst Protestant churches. At one time there were at least four different Methodist churches. On the other hand, Protestantism affirms the 'priesthood of all believers'. Salvation, or justification, is by faith, which is the faith of the individual. It is supposed that each believer is in personal relationship with God. Some modern theologians would say that Christian belief is primarily in the Word who is Christ and only secondarily in the Word of Scripture, which points beyond itself to Christ. At the heart of faith is a personal relationship between God and the believer of love, trust and obedience.

In their return to scripture, many reformers questioned practices of the church. If, for example, the believer has a direct relationship with God, priests are no longer required as mediators. The individual can confess his or her sins and know in his or her own heart the assurance of God's forgiveness. Again, if the believer has been justified by faith and has the knowledge of God's favour, he or she does not need to seek indulgences nor to offer masses nor beg for pardon. The Communion, instead of pleading the sacrifice of Christ, became a remembrance of God's love shown in Christ's willingness to die for the sake of sinners. The Eucharistic Prayer in Cranmer's *Book of Common Prayer* begins, 'Almighty God, our heavenly Father, who of thy tender mercy didst give thine only Son Jesus Christ to suffer death upon the cross for our redemption . . .' The service also expresses the depth of communion between Christ and believers, who pray 'that we may evermore dwell in him and he in us'.[12] The expression of such communion requires participation in the bread and cup. It was not sufficient just to attend mass at which only the priest communicated. It has to be said, however, that it is only in the twentieth century that many Protestant churches have taught the value of frequent Communion. For many, such loving communion was most real in prayer and the devotional reading of scripture. The Catholic Reformation, as we have seen, with its emphasis on the mystical, and later with growing devotion to the Sacred Heart of Jesus also emphasised the importance of personal relationship with God.

The differences between Protestants and Catholics in their understanding of the Communion service were reflected in arguments about the nature of Christ's presence. Catholics held to the doctrine of 'transubstantiation', which said that at the consecration the substance, or underlying reality, changed into the body and blood of Christ, although the accidents, that is the physical appearance of bread and wine, was unchanged. The doctrine of transubstantiation, which is dependent on a particular philosophical view of reality, was recognised at the Lateran Council of 1215 and was formally defined at the Council of Trent. The Eastern church has virtually the same teaching, although it avoids the word 'transubstantiation'. Amongst the reformers, Luther, although rejecting the idea of sacrifice, spoke of the 'real flesh and real blood of Christ' on the altar. His teaching is sometimes labelled 'consubstantiation', which means that the substances of both the body and blood of Christ and of bread and wine coexist on the altar. Zwingli, however, spoke of the communion service as an act of remembrance. Other reformers rejected the doctrine of transubstantiation, but said that Christ was spiritually present at the Eucharist. Calvin attempted a compromise between Luther and Zwingli; and the sixteenth-century Anglican theologian Richard Hooker (c.1554–1600), wrote:

> What these elements are in themselves it skilleth not, it is enough that to me which take them they are the body and blood of Christ, his promise in witness hereof sufficeth, his word he knoweth which way to accomplish, why should any cogitation possess the mind of a faithful communicant but this, 'O my God thou art true, O my Soul thou are happy.'[13]

A simpler way of putting this, sometimes attributed to Elizabeth I, is, 'What thy word doth make it, that I believe, and take it.'

In this century, Catholic and Protestant theologians have come much closer together in their understanding of the Eucharist. They recognise that some past disagreements were conditioned by different philosophical approaches and they now see Jesus' words and actions at the Last Supper in the context of the Jewish Passover, which makes present to every generation of the people of Israel the salvation experienced by their forefathers in the Exodus from Egypt.

Amongst the Protestant churches, there were considerable differences about church order. The Church of England and the Scandinavian Lutheran church retained bishops. Some Anglicans have made much of the importance of the 'apostolic succession'. This is the claim that the bishops of today can trace their ordination back through successive ordinations to the apostles, who were commissioned by Christ, from whom they receive their authority. In Scotland, under John Knox's (c.1513–72) leadership, a Presbyterian model was adopted, where authority rests with representative synods of presbyters (ordained ministers) and elders. Other radical churches such as the Anabaptists were more democratic. They also took a very negative view of worldly society and some of them were prepared to countenance rebellion against unjust and ungodly princes. By contrast, some Anglican divines in the first part of the seventeenth century taught that kings ruled by divine right or authority.

For some people, the most obvious difference between Catholic and Protestant churches was in the ornamentation. Some Catholic churches, especially the seventeenth- and eighteenth-century baroque churches of southern Europe, were very elaborate, whereas many Protestant churches were simple, even austere.

From the mid-sixteenth to the mid-seventeenth century, the rival Christian churches battled for supremacy in the different countries of Europe. Although the ostensible cause of hostilities was religion, political and economic factors were important. For example, many of the Protestant princes of northern Europe wanted to escape from the control of the emperor. It was also assumed that the cohesion of a state required religious unity and the principle that the country should accept its ruler's religion – *cujus regio ejus religio* – came to be quite generally accepted.

By the middle of the seventeenth century, Spain, Portugal, Italy, France, Belgium, Poland and much of the New World was obedient to the pope. In Ireland the people remained attached to Catholicism, despite the attempts of English monarchs to force Protestantism on to them. Northern Germany, the Netherlands, Scandinavia, England, Wales and Scotland were Protestant, although some countries were predominantly Lutheran and others Calvinist. England, as we have seen, had its own distinctive traditions. In the latter part of the seventeenth century, several Protestant groups established themselves in New England. Further east, the Orthodox church was rather static, although there was considerable vitality in the Russian church, where Moscow was regarded as 'the third Rome' and the Metropolitans, like the Tsars, increased their authority.

The Age of Enlightenment

By the late seventeenth century, much of Europe was drained and exhausted by internal conflict. Weariness with religious strife was reflected by changes to the intellectual and spiritual climate. The eighteenth century is sometimes called the 'Age of Reason'. The Dutch Jewish philosopher Baruch Spinoza (1632–77), whose views were repudiated by both Jews and Christians, set the tone. His approach to religion and the study of scripture was purely rational. He denied the miraculous. He foreshadowed the intellectual questioning of Christianity which has become increasingly strong in the West in the last three centuries.

With advances in the natural sciences and mathematics, the eighteenth century saw a new confidence in human reason and a rejection of what was considered superstitious. Deism, for example, based on J. Toland's (1670–1722) *Christianity Not Mysterious* (1696), propounded what was called 'natural religion', which consisted of universal truths which could be discerned by people everywhere. It left little place for revelation.

A better-known exponent of this approach was Voltaire, the pseudonym of François Marie Arouet (1694–1778). He advocated religious tolerance and was critical of the oppressive character of the French church. The Scottish philosopher David Hume (1711–76) was a through-going sceptic. He believed the argument for God as the primal cause was invalid. He, therefore, challenged both Deism and Christianity. He also attacked belief in miracles, which was at the time one of the main arguments used to support Christian claims. Meanwhile, Edward Gibbon (1737–94), in his famous *Decline and Fall of the Roman Empire* described that event as the triumph of barbarism and religion, by which he meant Christianity.

Instead of arguments between Christians, which continued, Christianity itself was now open to question, and especially the concept of revelation. In the nineteenth century, as we have seen, there were other attacks, especially on the literal accuracy of the Bible. David Strauss questioned the historical accuracy of the New Testament, whilst the findings of Charles Darwin seemed incompatible with the biblical description of the creation of the world in seven days. Feuerbach and Freud questioned the reality of God, seeing God as a human projection. Friedrich Nietzsche (1844–1900), a German philosopher, held that life is the will to power, as exercised by the great individual, the superman. The superman had to reject values derived from Christianity which encouraged humility and weakness. Karl Marx (1818–83) too was critical of religion, which obscured the struggle for power of the working classes. He described religion, in a famous phrase, as 'the opium of the people'.[14] His deterministic view of history had no place for God as Lord of history.

Many of the intellectual challenges to Christianity have already been referred to in the earlier chapters on Christian belief. The church was also challenged by political and economic change. The French Revolution and the rule of Napoleon over large parts of continental Europe shattered the old order, known as the *Ancien Régime.* Although, in the nineteenth century, the monarchy was restored in France together with the aristocracy and the church, their previous authority, wealth and privilege could not be re-established. In Russia, Catherine II expropriated the monasteries' vast holdings in land and serfs.

Economic and industrial change was also affecting church life. With the coming of the Industrial Revolution many people moved from the country to the cities. Conditions of life were different. People were required to work long hours and in many cities it was some time before the churches had the clergy and buildings to minister effectively to the new inhabitants.

The Evangelical Revival

Yet if the eighteenth and nineteenth centuries were a period of many challenges to Christianity, they were also times of significant growth. The nineteenth century was the great century of Christian mission and churches were established across the world. The work of Wesley and the Evangelical Revival brought personal faith to thousands and stirred up movements for reform, such as the abolition of slavery.

The Wesleys

The most famous leader of the Evangelical movement was John Wesley (1703–91), whom we have already met in chapter 1. He was ably assisted by his brother Charles (1707–88) and their friend George Whitefield (1714–70).

After their conversion, John and Charles started to preach widely about conscious acceptance of God's pardon and daily growth in holiness. In 1739, their friend George Whitefield started preaching in the open air to miners and soon John also started to preach out of doors. To do this, he needed the consent of the local vicar. When one refused, John declared, 'the world is my parish'. John travelled, mostly on horseback, hundreds of miles a year. Charles enriched the movement with his great gift of thousands of hymns, many of which are still widely used today.

Despite an enthusiastic response from many of those to whom they preached, the Wesleys also met heckling and abuse, as well as opposition from some clergy and church leaders. Methodist societies increased and at the time of John Wesley's death their membership was said to be 71,668. In 1744, a conference of local preachers was held and this became an annual event. John wanted to remain a member of the Church of England, but many of his followers became increasingly independent and Selina, Countess of Huntingdon (1707–91) registered the chapels which she built as 'dissenting chapels'.

Starting from 1760, Methodism grew quite quickly in North America. To ensure leadership there, John Wesley ordained Dr Thomas Coke (1747–1814) as Superintendent or Bishop. According to Church of England practice, only a bishop could consecrate another bishop. Charles was shocked and wrote to his brother, 'Before you have quite broken down the bridge, stop and consider.' John, however, persisted and in 1785 ordained some men for work in Scotland and a little later ordained three people to work in England.

Gradually Methodists drifted away from the Church of England. Wesley's influence, however, was felt in the Evangelical revival within the Church of England, led by Charles Simeon (1759–1836), for many years vicar of Holy Trinity church in Cambridge. In the early nineteenth century, a group of leading lay evangelicals, as we shall see,[15] who belonged to what was known as the 'Clapham sect', led the campaign for the abolition of slavery, which was ended in the British dominions in 1833. They were also active supporters of foreign missions and of Sunday schools. A little later, Lord Shaftesbury (1801–85), another outstanding evangelical, concentrated on efforts to improve the conditions of industrial workers, as well as being for many years president of the British and Foreign Bible Society.

Within the Methodist movement, by the end of the eighteenth century, there were divisions. Whitefield and the Wesleys drifted apart. George Whitefield believed in predestination, but the Wesleys followed the teaching of the Dutch Reformed theologian Jacobus Arminius (1560–1609) who held that Christ died for all people. There were other divisions in the nineteenth century. Even so Methodism grew rapidly, especially in the USA.

Following American Independence, several Protestant churches there set up national organisations. The Presbyterians formed a General Assembly and the Dutch and German Reformed churches became independent of their European parent churches. Anglicans drew together in the (Protestant) Episcopal church. In the nineteenth century, which was marked by a series of revivals, both the Baptist and Methodist churches grew rapidly. Methodism also spread in Canada and Australia and other places where people from Britain had settled.

The Missionary Era

Catholic Missions

The nineteenth century also saw sustained efforts by the churches of western Europe and of North America to spread the gospel in Asia and Africa. Already from the sixteenth century, Catholic missionaries, especially from Spain and Portugal, had preached the Christian faith in Asia and South America. In 1542, St Francis Xavier reached Goa, on the west coast of India. He went on to Travancore, Sri Lanka, and in 1549 landed in Japan. Other Jesuits followed, but in Japan, in the seventeenth century, their work was cruelly crushed.

In South America, the spread of Christianity was under the direction of the crown. The papacy had little real influence. The church was caught up in the struggles between Portugal and Spain and was often a pawn in oppressive exploitation of the people who were already settled there before the white invasion. Some of the missionaries, such as Bartolome de Las Casas (1474–1566), who worked with the Chiapas people of Mexico, had a deep, if paternalistic, concern for their people and tried to resist colonial exploitation. Even so, much of the history of the spread of Christianity in Latin America is one of oppression and suffering, although it remains a part of the world where the Catholic church is still strong. In recent years, several notable Catholic leaders, such as Archbishop Oscar Romero (1917–80), who was killed as he celebrated mass, have championed the rights of the poor, and it is in Latin America that radical Liberation theology has had its most outspoken exponents.

Australasia

White settlers, many of whom were convicts sent there involuntarily, started arriving in Australia in the late eighteenth century. From the mid-nineteenth century free settlers, mostly from the British Isles, arrived in large numbers. The churches were quite successful in maintaining the newcomers' loyalty, even though in the outback settlers might be very isolated. The twentieth century has seen the coming together of the major Protestant churches into the United Church of Australia while the membership of the Roman Catholic church has increased steadily, partly because of the growing number of immigrants from southern Europe. The abandonment of the 'whites only' settlement rule has led to an influx of immigrants from South East Asia, so that some of parts of urban Australia have become multi-ethnic and multi-faith. From the early days of the settlement, efforts were made by some Christians to reach out to the Aboriginals, whose numbers were drastically reduced in the nineteenth century. In recent years there has been growing appreciation of the Aboriginals' sense of sacred space and of their rich spiritual traditions of the 'dream-time'.

Africa

In sub-Saharan Africa, the island of Madagascar was one of the first areas of Protestant work. To South Africa, British and Dutch settlers each brought their respective forms of Christianity. There was also considerable missionary work amongst the African population, especially by the London Missionary Society. By 1914, it was reckoned that about thirty per cent of the African population was Christian. David Livingstone (1813–73), the greatest missionary to Africa, started his work in South Africa, but his urge to explore, together with his Christian faith, led him to make many journeys into the interior. The fame of his travels spread and encouraged others to take up the work. In 1857, in a lecture at Cambridge, he issued this challenge to his audience: 'Do you carry on the work which I have begun. I leave it with you.'[16] In response, the Anglican Universities' Mission to Central Africa was established in 1858.

A particular area of Christian growth was Uganda, which became a British protectorate in 1894, where Anglicans sent by the Church Missionary Society and the Roman Catholic Mill Hill Fathers both did much work. By 1914 there were some 200,000 Christians, about forty per cent of them being Anglican and sixty per cent Catholic. In the vast area known from 1914 as the Belgian Congo (now the Democratic Republic of Congo), Catholic missionaries were very active and the church's growth there was spectacular.

India

In Asia, numerical growth was very much smaller, despite the heroism and sacrifice of many missionaries. In India, where especially in the south there had been a small Christian presence from the earliest days of the church, the East India Company discouraged missionary activity. One of the most outstanding early Protestant missionaries, Christian Friedrich Schwartz (1724–98), therefore, did much of his work in the independent kingdom of Tanjore, where he became a chief adviser to the rajah or prince. Likewise, William Carey (1761–1834), a Baptist missionary, Joshua Marshman (1768–1837) and William Ward (1764–1823) established themselves at Serampore, a tiny Danish colony, some sixteen miles from Calcutta, where there is still an important theological college.

In the nineteenth century, British restrictions on missionary activity were lifted and there was a great deal of work, although the number of converts was small. It is probably true to say that the greatest missionary contribution was in terms of educational and medical work. Many schools and colleges were established and offered a good, albeit Western style of education. Alexander Duff (1806–78), of the Church of Scotland, which produced a number of scholarly missionaries who made a significant contribution to higher education in India, established a college at Calcutta in 1831. In 1832, John Wilson (1804–75) established Wilson College in Bombay and a little later John Anderson (1805–55) set up in Madras 'the Institution', which was to become Madras Christian College, which moved to Tambaram, a suburb of Madras in the 1930s. Another college, founded by Stephen Hislop, was at Nagpur, which has became an important Christian centre. At Vellore, Ida Scudder (1870–1959), daughter of an American missionary doctor, established a medical training centre for women, and later also for men, which, like the hospital at Ludhiana in the north, was to set standards for medical care. Other Christians worked with the poor and outcastes, where they gained most converts, and with the leprosy patients.

China

In the early nineteenth century, China was closed to foreigners, and Christians, who were descendants of those converted by earlier missionaries, were a tiny number. China's doors were levered open by the colonial powers, led by the British who forced the Chinese government to allow the importation of opium. In the second half of the century, there was an influx of both Catholic and Protestant missionaries. Many of the latter worked for the China Inland Mission, which was founded by James Hudson Taylor (1832–1905), who first went to China in 1853 and returned in the late 1860s, when he tried to adopt a Chinese style of life.

In the twentieth century, Christian missionary work in China has had to contend with the changing and difficult political situation. When the Communists won power, all foreign missionaries were expelled. Catholics were forced to reject papal authority, although some secret Catholics refused to do this. The Protestants of various denominations were forced together and the church launched the Three-Self Movement, based on self-administration, self-support and self-propagation, to rid it of imperialist influences. Christians, like many others, suffered severely during the Cultural Revolution, but in recent years there has been quite a rapid growth in numbers of both Catholics and Protestants.

The Missionary Heritage

It is fashionable today in some circles to disparage missionary work, but care is needed in judging a previous generation by contemporary standards. Missionary work is seen to represent Western paternalism. Too often the missionaries did impose a Western life style on their converts and in recent years African and Asian Christians have tried to recover their cultural heritage. Some missionaries identified too closely with the ruling powers, although others were critical of empire. In South Africa many Christians took the lead in opposing apartheid. It is also sometimes felt to be arrogant to presume that only one faith is true, and this has been a widespread Hindu criticism of missionary work. Yet, missionary activity has been at least a factor in the renewal of the ancient religions of Asia and some missionary scholars helped to make knowledge of these faiths available in European languages.

Whilst missionary efforts met with considerable success in the Americas, Australasia and Sub-Saharan Africa, Christianity, despite considerable support in the Philippines and South Korea, remains very much a minority religion in most Asian and North African countries, where the great faiths of Hinduism, Buddhism and Islam have been long established.

The Ecumenical Movement

It was in the mission field that the urgency of Christian unity was first most strongly felt. The term 'ecumenical' comes from the Greek *oikoumenikos*, which means the 'inhabited earth'. Although the word has come to be used of the search for Christian unity, there has been a parallel and now growing quest for understanding and co-operation between members of the world religions.

The denominational differences of Europe and America seemed irrelevant in the mission field where Christians, even if all were counted together, were still a tiny minority. In schools, colleges and hospitals Christians of several denominations might find themselves working together. Consultation between missionaries of different denominations who were working in the same or nearby areas began quite early in the nineteenth century. For example, the Bombay Missionary Union was formed in 1825, consisting of members of four societies and including Anglicans, Congregationalists and Presbyterians. By the 1850s, there were regional conferences in north and south India. In Japan the first conference for missionaries from all parts of the country was held in 1872. In China, missionaries of different churches joined in translating the Bible in 1843.

There was also from early days regular consultation between missionary societies. As early as 1819, the secretaries of foreign mission boards with headquarters in London formed an association for 'mutual counsel and fellowship'. In 1885, a Standing Conference of all German Protestant missionary societies was formed and the Foreign Missions Conference of North America was first convened in 1895.

Towards the end of the nineteenth century, international Protestant missionary gatherings began to be held, and in 1910 a significant and remarkable World Missionary Conference was held in Edinburgh. The preparatory papers give a fascinating picture of the progress of Christian missions and of the surprisingly sympathetic attitude of many missionaries to other faiths and cultures.[17] The conference, which was a landmark of the Ecumenical movement, appointed a Continuation Committee, which helped to start an influential missionary journal called *The International Review of Missions*. Eventually, from these developments, the International Missionary Council was formed in 1921, which in 1961 was integrated into the World Council of Churches (WCC) at the New Delhi Assembly.

The two movements which initially came together to form the WCC in 1948 were 'Life and Work' and 'Faith and Order'. Life and Work,[18] inspired by Nathan Söderblom (1866–1931), Primate of the Church of Sweden, was concerned with the relation of Christian faith to society, politics and economics. It held major conferences at Stockholm in 1925 and in Oxford in 1937. Faith and Order was concerned to address theological differences and questions of ministry. It held major conferences at Lausanne in 1927 and at Edinburgh in 1937.

The World Council of Churches

Plans for the formation of the World Council of Churches were well advanced before the outbreak of the Second World War, but only came to fruition in 1948. The Council is a 'fellowship of churches which accept our Lord Jesus Christ as God and

Saviour'. The headquarters were established at Geneva in Switzerland. Membership now consists of Protestant, Anglican, Orthodox and Pentecostal churches. The Roman Catholic church sends observers to many meetings. Assemblies have been held every seven or eight years in different continents: at Amsterdam in 1948; Evanston, USA, in 1954; New Delhi, 1961; Uppsala, Sweden, 1968; Nairobi, 1975; Vancouver, 1983; Canberra, Australia, 1991; and in Harare, Zimbabwe, in late 1998.

The WCC, which we shall discuss more fully in a later chapter[19] has been a source of renewal and has stimulated a great deal of contact between member churches, but it has not been without its tensions. From Africa and Asia, a growing number of independent churches, free of foreign missionary control, have taken their place at the Council. The views of their delegates have often challenged the more conservative outlook of representatives of the churches from Europe and North America, for example in persuading the WCC to establish the Fund to Combat Racism. The Council has in part reflected the political divisions of the world, especially when it met in Canberra during the Gulf War. The theological approaches of member churches are often very different. The Council also seems distant to many members of local congregations. The churches have been reluctant or unable to find the funds necessary for the Council to achieve its full potential.

Church Unions

The World Council of Churches does not itself negotiate unions between particular churches. This is a matter for the respective churches themselves. A number of unions have taken place – some, as with the Methodists, within the same family of churches. Others brought several churches together, as for example the pioneering Church of South India, which was inaugurated in 1947 and which united Methodists and most Anglicans in the area with Presbyterians, Congregationalists and Dutch Reformed bodies which had already come together. The number and pace of unions has, however, been much slower than the pioneers of the ecumenical movement would have hoped for. Some other churches, whilst not agreeing to unite, now allow some inter-communion with other churches, which means that members of one church can receive Communion if they attend a service at a church of another denomination.

Evangelical Protestants have often thought of the church as a spiritual fellowship of all believers, rather than as an organised institution. To them questions of church order and discipline have been of little importance. From at least the middle of the nineteenth century, such Protestants, from a number of denomi-nations, have been ready to work together in the Sunday school movement, in Bible Societies, in the Young Men's and Young Women's Christian Associations and through a variety of other bodies. Many Anglicans, however, who have insisted that clergy should be ordained by a bishop in the apostolic succession[20] have not been willing to receive Communion from clergy not so ordained, although Anglicans now seem more relaxed about this. The divisive issue recently has been whether women should be ordained.

Roman Catholics, until the Second Vatican Council (1962–5), insisted that theirs was the one true church. They denied the validity of the orders of other clergy. The Council, convened by Pope John XXIII, gave an enormous impetus to a new attitude of friendship towards members of other Christian churches. Although communion with members of other churches was never approved, in the 1970s it happened inform-ally in several countries, but in recent years the authorities have severely discouraged this. The willingness of many Protestant and Anglican churches to ordain women, of which the Orthodox churches also disapprove, has added to the tensions. Even so, there is much practical co-operation between Roman Catholics and members of other churches.

The Interfaith Movement

The Second Vatican Council also marked a turning point in the Catholic attitude to other religions. The initial concern was with

Catholic relations with the Jews, but the decree on this subject was eventually widened to refer to all religions. It stresses that 'all peoples comprise a single community' and that from ancient times 'there has existed among diverse peoples a certain perception of that hidden power which hovers over the course of things'.[21] Reference is made to the contemplation of the divine mystery in Hinduism and to Buddhism's acknowledgment of the 'radical insufficiency of this shifting world'. The Declaration then says that 'the Catholic Church rejects nothing which is true and holy in these religions' and encourages dialogue with members of other religions and co-operation on social and moral concerns.

There is then a special section on relations with Muslims and another on relations with Jews, *Nostra Aetate*, which rejects long centuries of Christian anti-Jewish teaching and preaching. Although various pressures led to the watering down of the text on relations with the Jews, it affirmed the great 'spiritual patrimony common to Christians and Jews' and expressed the Council's wish to foster mutual understanding.

Since Vatican II, the Catholic church, both at international and national levels, has actively pursued dialogue with people of all faiths, whilst continuing to proclaim Christ as 'the way, the truth and the life'. Pope John Paul II, on his travels, has regularly met with leaders of other faith communities. In 1986, he invited leaders of all religions to join him for a Day of Prayer for Peace at the Italian town of Assisi, which was the birthplace of St Francis. He has also made a historic visit to the synagogue in Rome.

The World Council of Churches has also been concerned to foster dialogue and co-operation with people of living faiths and decided in 1971 to set up a sub-unit for this purpose.

The relationship of the Christian faith to other faiths has been a controversial matter. Traditionally Protestants have claimed that salvation was only possible through faith in Jesus Christ and Catholics have said that 'outside the church there is no salvation'. This view, which is often labelled 'exclusive' has been challenged by those who adopt an 'inclusive' position, which recognises the saving presence of God within other faith communities, but which insists that the full and final revelation of God is in Jesus Christ. Others have argued for a 'pluralist' approach, suggesting that no religion can claim a preferential position, but that the Divine Mystery, who is revealed in each religious tradition, is never fully apprehended and that each faith tradition witnesses to aspects of the divine glory.

While in recent years churches have given more attention to dialogue with people of other faiths, much of the initiative has come from individuals and unofficial organisations.

In this century also, there has been a considerable growth in the study of religions as an academic discipline and courses on the world religions are taught in some schools. Many books and videos about the world faiths are now available. At the same time interfaith organisations, often initially viewed with suspicion by religious leaders, have encouraged people of different religions to meet and get to know each other, in the hope that they can work together for peace and to uphold moral values.

The 1893 World's Parliament of Religions

The beginnings of the 'interfaith movement' are often dated to the World's Parliament of Religions which was held in Chicago, in connection with the World Fair, in 1893. The idea came from Charles Bonney (1831–1903), a lawyer, who was a member of the Swedenborgian church, which derived its distinctive teachings from the extensive writings of the Swedish scientist, philosopher and theologian, Emanuel Swedenborg (1688–1772). Bonney, described at the time in the *Catholic World* as 'the bearded patriarch of the Cosmic religions'[22] hoped that the Parliament would unite religions on the basis of the Golden Rule and in good deeds. As people of faith came together as brothers and sisters, so he believed that the 'nations of the earth would yield to the Spirit of concord and learn war no more'.[23]

During the course of the twentieth century, a number of interfaith organisations have been established. One of the first was the World Congress of Faiths, which was convened in London in 1936, by Sir Francis Younghusband (1863–1942), an explorer and mystic. Whilst sharing Bonney's concern for moral values and peace, Younghusband, from his own spiritual experience, believed that the meeting with the Divine transcended the particularities of individual religions. This view has been held by a number of those who have advocated inter-religious fellowship; others, however, stress the very real differences between religions.

Some interfaith organisations, such as The World Conference on Religion and Peace, and the Peace Council, have focused on work for peace. Others have devoted their energies to human rights or environmental issues. Since the special events held in 1993 in India, Britain, Japan, the USA and some other countries to mark the centenary of the World's Parliament of Religions there has been growing emphasis on the practical work that people of different faiths can do together to address the critical issues of today, such as violence, poverty and pollution. Others, however, remain more interested in intellectual discussion, some believing that the teachings of the great faiths are eventually convergent. Others are more concerned to explore the various spiritual paths and suggest that the true meeting is in the 'cave of the heart'.

Interfaith activity is very various. Some attempts have been made to co-ordinate this work on a national basis through the Inter Faith Network for the United Kingdom, which was established in 1987 and the North American Interfaith Network (NAIN). Efforts to ensure world-wide co-operation through, for example, the International Interfaith Centre at Oxford, are still in their infancy. There are also efforts to co-ordinate dialogue between members of two religions. For example, the International Council for Christians and Jews links those engaged in Christian–Jewish dialogue, and the Christian–Buddhist society is for those involved in that relationship.

Threats of Secularism, Communism and Fascism

Despite these efforts, religious and ideological differences have aggravated the many conflicts of the twentieth century. Although, at times, voices have been raised to suggest the withering away of religion as 'man has come of age', the closing years of the twentieth century have seen an increase of religious extremism and conflict. For much of the century, however, the greatest threats to Christianity in Europe and North America were secularism, Communism and Fascism.

Secularism

Secularism is a term used in different ways and which covers several phenomena. In part it indicates an assertion of the autonomy of daily life, thereby excluding the interference of religious authorities in the government or political and economic life of a country. In the USA, there has always been a clear separation of church and state, although church membership is higher there than in western Europe. In this sense, the word 'secularism' is used in contrast to a theocratic regime, such as Iran under the ayatollahs, where religious leaders exercise political control. The term can also suggest that individual citizens do not have any moral pattern of behaviour imposed upon them by the state. For example, in many countries until recent years, homosexual acts, which were regarded as immoral by the dominant religion, were illegal and punishable by law. Today in some Western countries this is a matter for the individual. In the same way, in most Western countries abortion, with some restrictions, is no longer illegal. Beneath this is the question of whether a society needs some shared moral values. If so, should the government by education and legislation seek to encorage or impose these values?

Secularism may also describe a change of mood by which people no longer seek to explain life by reference to religious beliefs. For example, there was a time when if a child was ill, the parents would ask the priest to say special prayers and they perhaps would make a vow. Now, the expectation is that medical science and skill will provide the way to recovery. Illness is not seen as a punishment from God. Believers will, of course, still pray for those who are ill, but even some believers do not expect a miracle but see prayer as a way of attuning their will to God's will.

A Changing Church in a Changing World

Awareness of God seems absent from the consciousness of many people. Religion is regarded as a private or 'leisure' activity, which some people engage in at weekends, whilst others play golf, go sailing or take up yoga. This may be in part because of the dramatic changes to people's way of life. Industrialisation and now the information revolution have changed the way people work. It has increased mobility, offered some people more leisure and destroyed tight-knit local communities. At the same time, the horrors of war and genocide together with the various intellectual challenges to Christianity have undermined belief. Many people are not convinced by the Christian claim that the world is made and governed by a God who is Love.

Communism

If the acid of secularism has eroded belief, Communism attacked it. In 1917 the tsar's regime in Russia collapsed and very quickly the new Soviet authorities declared all land to belong to the nation and took over the church's extensive properties. Soon afterwards, it was declared that only civil marriages would be legally recognised. Quickly religious schools were forbidden and religious life drastically curbed. Religious life was largely restricted to offering the liturgy in the few churches which were allowed to remain open. Many Christians, some of whom showed great courage, were imprisoned or killed and the career prospects of anyone known to be a Christian were small. The pressure on the church was severe, although it was eased during the Second World War so as to enlist her support against the Germans.

The countries in eastern Europe, having already suffered from German occupation, which came under Communist control after the Second World War, experienced the same hostility to religious life.

Fascism

Fascist rule in Italy and Spain seemed at first to favour the Roman Catholic church against often atheistic socialist groups. In 1929, the Pope signed a concordat with Mussolini, who had taken power in Italy. Almost immediately, however, church youth organisations were absorbed into Fascist youth movements and the government asserted more control over church schools. When Italy invaded Ethiopia in 1935, Pope Pius XI declared wars of conquest to be unjust, and during the Second World War Pope Pius XII worked for peace and tried to protect the suffering. There has, however, been considerable criticism of Pope Pius XII for not being more vigorous in his condemnation of Fascism. Why, it has been asked, was Hitler never excommunicated, despite the atrocities of his regime and the pressure he put on Catholics in Germany?

In Spain, the republican regime, which came to power in 1931, nationalised ecclesiastical property, disestablished the church, expelled the Jesuits and restricted church schools. It is not surprising that the church supported General Franco (1892–1975), under whose regime the church was again made the state religion and was given back its property. In Portugal too under the long rule of Prime Minister Salazar (1889–1970), who was a devout Catholic, the church had government support. It is questionable, however, whether the church's alliance with Fascist rulers was in its long-term interest and it has clouded its record on human rights.

The Nazis

In Germany, some Christians initially gave their support to Adolf Hitler (1889–1945). The nation's defeat in the First World War was a shock and it was followed by severe economic difficulties. Some Christians hoped that Hitler could provide the strong government which they felt was needed. Even those opposed to Hitler were weakened by the divisions amongst Protestants. Soon after the First World War many of the regional Protestant churches – *Landeskirchen* – had united in the German

Evangelical Federation. Even so, Protestants were divided and these divisions were increased by Hitler's advent to power. Some supported the German Faith Movement, led by Jacob Wilhelm Hauer, which wanted to accommodate Christianity to the 'German spirit'. Others joined the less extreme Faith Movement of the German Christians, which confined its membership to those of Aryan descent, cut off all connections with Freemasons and vigorously denounced Communism, whilst supporting Hitler. Others, led by the courageous Pastor Martin Neimüller (1892–1984), who opposed the new regime's interference in church affairs and discrimination against Christians of Jewish background, came together in the Confessional Synod or Church. From different Protestant churches, they declared their opposition to Hitler at the Synod of Barmen in 1934.

Like many others who opposed Hitler, those Christians who did so suffered severely. Some were killed, including Dietrich Bonhoeffer (1906–45), a brilliant theologian who was implicated in a plot to assassinate Hitler. Others were imprisoned, like Neimüller himself, who was sent to Dachau concentration camp. After the war, Neimüller did much to restore the German church and to bring it into the ecumenical movement. He was a president of the WCC from 1961 to 1968. He became a pacifist and was active in the Christian peace movement and in opposition to nuclear weapons.

Although the Nazis were defeated in 1945, their regime and particularly the horror of the Holocaust in which some eleven million people were killed, of whom six million were Jews, was a traumatic shock to German Christians. How could such barbarity happen in the heart of Christendom? This question has prompted a purging of anti-Jewish elements from Christian teaching and, as we have seen,[24] led to theological rethinking.

From the Second World War to Today

The division of Germany immediately after the Second World War into two countries, East Germany, under Communist control, and West Germany, which was democratic, weakened the rebuilding of the churches, although several kept pan-German structures. The churches in East Germany in the 1980s were to play an important part in bringing about the demise of Communist power, but churches throughout Germany face the problems of loss of faith common to much of Europe, which have been particularly notable in France, where a large number of people seem to have lost all real contact with the church.

The Christian churches in Europe have survived the onslaught of Fascism and Communism. In Russia, the Russian Orthodox church is regaining some of its old prestige. In Poland, the Catholic church commands considerable support. Elsewhere in much of Europe churches of all denominations struggle to slow down the decline in membership, although conservative Christian groups, perhaps meeting as house-churches, have increased their following. In part the churches' decline reflects changes in European society. The church's economic and political power in the world has declined. Many European societies have become ethnically, culturally and religiously plural. Christianity no longer provides the world view or moral framework to be a cohesive factor in European society. Perhaps most significantly, in a changed intellectual climate and in societies that are rapidly changing both econo-mically and culturally, the Christian faith does not command the intellectual and personal assent and conviction of as many people as it did.

None the less, many churches have been vigorous in their efforts to address contemporary concerns. The wealth of religious books published each year reflects active theological debate. Liturgical revision, new hymns and changing patterns of worship reflect vibrant Christian communities. There is new interest in prayer, meditation and contemplation. Many Christians are actively engaged in social action and campaigning. There is far greater awareness of environmental problems, while feminist theology is bringing new insights to the whole church.

In North America, church attendance has not seen the same decline as in Europe, partly perhaps because churches play a larger part in people's social life. In Africa and Latin America, there are areas of vigorous church growth. The resurgence of Islam and the revival of Hinduism and Buddhism have restricted church growth in areas where those religions are dominant, but the churches are growing in South Korea and the Philippines.

It is a mixed picture. Some people anticipate a continuing decline in church membership with a decreasing importance for organised church authorities and institutions. This may not, however, mean a decline in faith, as a growing number of people who see themselves as followers of Jesus do not attach great importance to church structures. Others hope that the profound rethinking of the Christian faith and reshaping of church life will make it more relevant to people today. Yet it may be that, fast as the church has been changing, society continues to change even more quickly.

The general histories of the church mentioned at the end of the previous chapter also deal with the period covered in this chapter.

On the Reformation, see Roland Bainton, *The Reformation of the Sixteenth Century* (1953, Hodder and Stoughton, 1963); E. Cameron, *The European Reformation* (1991); and H. O. Evennett, *The Spirit of the Counter Reformation* (1968).

B. M. G. Reardon, *From Coleridge to Gore* (Longmans, 1971), and A. M. Ramsey, *From Gore to Temple* (1960), are useful for Anglican thinking during the period covered.

On the Church in the twentieth century, a stimulating book is David L. Edwards, *Religion and Change* (Hodder and Stoughton, 1969).

For the Ecumenical Movement, see *Dictionary of the Ecumenical Movement*, ed. N. Lossky *et al.* (1991).

On Christian–Jewish relations see my *Time to Meet* (SCM Press, 1990); and *Christian–Jewish Dialogue*, ed. Helen Fry (University of Exeter Press, 1996).

On the history of the Interfaith movement, see my *Pilgrimage of Hope* (SCM Press, 1992), and *Faith and Interfaith in a Global Age* (CoNexus Press and Braybrooke Press, 1998). On the theological issues see Alan Race, *Christianity and Religious Pluralism* (SCM Press, 1983).

7

Love God

Jesus told his followers, 'Love the Lord your God with all your heart and with all your soul and with all you strength and with all your mind and love your neighbour as yourself' (Luke 10:27). These words from the Hebrew Bible sum up the disciple's calling to grow in the love of God and the service of others. In a well-known prayer, St Richard of Chichester (1197–1253) asked, 'May we know thee [Jesus] more clearly, love thee more dearly, and follow thee more nearly.'

Christian discipleship can be characterised as the desire to know and love Jesus better and to serve him in the world. In this chapter, we shall try to look at the ways in which the disciple comes closer to his or her Lord. In the next, we shall look at how faith in Jesus affects the way a disciple lives.

The devotional life of the Christian is so varied that only a few impressions can be given here. In fellowship with Christ, the disciple both senses more vividly the love of God in Christ and in response is deepened in his or her love for God. Prayer is perhaps the most obvious way of seeking fellowship with God, but some Christians value highly the devotional reading of the scriptures and for others their spiritual life centres on the sacrament of Holy Communion. Special occasions in a Christian's life are usually marked by religious ceremonies, which are often called rites of passage.

Many Christians also celebrate festivals to mark the main events in the life of Jesus, thereby giving significance to the different seasons of the year, which in Catholic churches are indicated by the colour of the altar frontal and the priest's vestments. Christmas, which marks Jesus' birth, and Easter which celebrates Christ's resurrection, are times of joy. The liturgical colour is white and gold. Both festivals are preceded by penitential seasons: Advent comes before Christmas and Lent, which recalls the forty days that Jesus spent fasting in the wilderness, comes before Easter. The colour for both is mauve. For Pentecost or Whitsun, which celebrates the coming of the Holy Spirit, the liturgical colour is red. Other events in Jesus' life, such as his circumcision or transfiguration are remembered on special days, as are the apostles and evangelists and other saints and martyrs.

Prayer

Jesus himself was asked by his disciples to teach them how to pray. His reply, 'the Lord's Prayer', has become a model and is used in almost all Christian services. The version in St Matthew's gospel (cf. Luke 11:2–4) is:

> *Our Father in heaven,*
> *Hallowed be your name,*
> *Your kingdom come,*
> *Your will be done*
> *on earth as it is in heaven.*
> *Give us today our daily bread.*
> *Forgive us our debts,*
> *As we also have forgiven our debtors.*
> *And lead us not into temptation,*
> *But deliver us from the evil one.*

Usually the doxology, which appears in some ancient manuscripts, is added: 'For yours is the kingdom and the power and the glory for ever, Amen.'

Traditionally prayer is addressed to God the Father, through Jesus Christ the Lord, in the power of the Spirit. There are few hymns and prayers addressed to the Holy Spirit, but many which address Jesus directly.

Prayer at its simplest might be described as talking to God, or perhaps better being with God, because words are not always necessary. In one sense, a believer is always in the presence of God, but this may not at all times be consciously remembered. Lovers do not forget each other, but may not be the whole time consciously thinking of the other. This is why many Christians set aside time each day and especially on Sundays to concentrate on their awareness of God. A widespread custom or perhaps reasonable expectation for a Christian, would be to pray every morning and evening and to pray together with other Christians on every Sunday. Members of religious communities may pray together several times each day. The mother of small children may not have the time and quiet for formal prayers, but even as she cares for her family may remember God's goodness. In Victorian Britain, many households, at least of a certain social standing, assembled together each day for prayer. There was also regular worship in church on Sunday. Today, even committed Christians may be less regular in their worship. Some shops are open on Sunday, many sporting events take place and people use the day to visit families or for recreational purposes.

Adoration

There are many types of prayer. Children are sometimes taught the mnemonic 'ACTS'. 'A' stands for 'Adoration' or praise or worship. It is easy even in prayer to be self-centred, either by spending all the time telling God what is wanted or by cultivating spiritual experiences. Praise and adoration centre the believer on the glory of God. Christians hope that the ultimate destiny of the believer, perhaps of all people, is to see God and to be in the presence of the One who is Light and Love, Beauty and Holiness. The sense of God's holiness carries with it for the worshipper an awareness of unworthiness and sin. Sin is often thought of as wrongdoing or bad thoughts and actions, but the Greek word comes from archery and originally meant a falling short of the target. Paul said that all people have fallen short of the glory of God. Sin can signify a person's failure to reach their full potential. The letters to the Ephesians and Colossians (Eph. 4:13 and Col. 1:28) speak of the believer growing up into the full stature of Christ himself. Rather as an amateur sportsman or woman may go to watch a star and feel his or her own game is inferior, so the worshipper as she or he senses the glory of God and the holy sacrificial love of Jesus Christ, recognises her or his own shortcomings.

In the book of Isaiah, the prophet tells how, after worshipping in the Temple, he had a vision of the Lord, 'seated on a throne, high and exalted'. He heard the seraphs calling, 'Holy, holy, holy is the Lord Almighty; the whole earth is full of his glory' – words still used by many churches at the Communion service. Then the prophet cried out, 'Woe to me . . . For I am a man of unclean lips and I live among a people of unclean lips and my eyes have seen the King, the Lord Almighty' (Isa. 6:1–8). Isaiah's lips were then touched by a live coal from the altar. Then, when the prophet heard the Lord asking, 'Whom shall I send? And who will go for us', he replied, 'Here am I. Send me.'

Confession

Sometimes, there has been such heavy emphasis on human sin and wrongdoing that it has produced too negative a view of human life. Indeed, it has sometimes been exaggerated so as to magnify the greatness of God's pardon. God, at times, has been pictured as a mighty emperor and the worshipper as the most humble subject. The traditional prayers of confession in many churches, often dating from the time of the Reformation, seem today to be too grovelling. Jesus' own picture was of God as the Father welcoming home the prodigal son.

The purpose of Confession (the 'C' of ACTS) is to be set free from the burden of sin. It leads into absolution, which is God's assurance of pardon through Jesus Christ. In some churches people make a private confession of their sins to a priest, who claims the authority of God to pronounce pardon. Most Christians would expect to find the assurance of forgiveness through their own private prayers. The concept of forgiveness by God may seem alien to many people in the modern world and there are those who feel that guilt is an unhealthy reaction. Certainly some people may feel inappropriate guilt, but if a person is conscious of having done something wrong, a sense of guilt is natural. In part this can be taken away by saying sorry to the person who has been hurt and trying to make amends, and this is expected of the penitent, but the Christian gospel offers a promise of inner peace. Indeed, after a private confession, the priest having pronounced absolution may say, 'Go in peace, your sins are done away.' A person's conscience, whatever he or she has done, can find forgiveness and peace. In the words of a much-loved hymn by Charlotte Elliott (1789–1871):

> *Just as I am, thou wilt receive,*
> *Wilt welcome, pardon, cleanse, relieve.*
> *Because thy promise I believe,*
> *O Lamb of God, I come.*[1]

Thanksgiving

The experience of being forgiven leads into expressions of Thanksgiving (the 'T' of ACTS) to God, although there is much else for which to be grateful to God. Indeed, the central prayer of the church is often called the Prayer of Thanksgiving and one of the names for the Communion service is Eucharist, from the Greek word for thanksgiving. Thanks are offered to God for his being, for the creation and redemption of the world and for the guidance of the Spirit.

One example from the early centuries of the church of the opening part of the Eucharistic prayer is that of St Chrysostom, which is still the normal Eucharistic prayer of the Orthodox church:

It is meet and right that we should laud thee, bless thee, praise thee, give thanks unto thee, and adore thee in all places of thy dominion: for thou art God ineffable, incomprehensible, inconceivable; thou art from everlasting and art changeless, thou, and thine Only-begotten Son, and thy Holy Spirit. Thou from nothingness hast called us into being; and when we had fallen away from thee, thou didst raise us up again; and thou hast not ceased to do all things until thou hadst brought us back to heaven and hadst endowed us with thy kingdom which is to come. For all which things we give thanks unto thee, and thine Only-begotten Son and thy Holy Spirit; for all things whereof we know, and whereof we know not; for all thy benefits bestowed upon us, both manifest and unseen. And we render thanks unto thee for this ministry which thou dost deign to accept at our hands . . .[2]

The beautiful opening of the Third Eucharistic Prayer of the Church of England's *Alternative Service Book* (1980) draws its inspiration from the Eucharistic prayer found in the *Apostolic Tradition* of Hippolytus of Rome (*c.*170–*c.*236), which is thought to represent a tradition of the early third century.

> Father, we give you thanks and praise
> through your beloved Son Jesus Christ, your living Word
> through whom you have created all things; Who was sent
> by you, in your great goodness, to be our Saviour;
> by the power of the Holy Spirit he took flesh
> and, as your Son, born of the blessed Virgin,
> was seen on earth
> and went about among us;
> He opened wide his arms for us on the cross;
> he put an end to death by dying for us
> and revealed the resurrection by rising to new life;
> so he fulfilled your will and won for you a holy people.[3]

Self-Offering

Thanksgiving leads into self-offering. The prophet Isaiah, as we have seen, having had his sin atoned for, offered himself to the Lord's service, with the words, 'Here am I. Send me.' The classical expression of this is in the General Thanksgiving, which was included in the 1662 revision of the Prayer Book. It was written by Bishop Reynolds, a Presbyterian leader who was prepared to accept the bishopric of Norwich, to which he was consecrated in 1661 and where he served until 1676. After mentioning the many reasons to give thanks to God, the prayer continues:

> And, we beseech thee, give us that due sense of all thy mercies, that our hearts may be unfeignedly thankful, and that we show forth thy praise, not only with our lips, but in our lives; by giving up ourselves to thy service and by walking before thee in holiness and righteousness all our days.[4]

Supplication

The 'S' in the mnemonic ACTS is usually taken to stand for 'Supplication', although it could stand for 'service'. In either case, it suggests the movement from adoration, confession and absolution, and thanksgiving to the disciple's concern for God's world. Supplication is a word for asking humbly for something. Sometimes the word 'intercession' or 'petition' is used.

Jesus said, 'Ask and it will be given to you; seek and you will find; knock and the door will be opened to you' (Matt. 7:7). Jesus also told the parables of the Unscrupulous Judge (Luke 18:1–8) and of the Importunate Friend (Luke 11:5–8) to encourage the disciples to be persistent in prayer.

Intercession is a central feature of Christian prayer and of prayer in many religious traditions. It is natural that in times of need and difficulty people who believe in God ask for divine help. But does prayer really change God's mind? If God is indeed best pictured as a loving Father, does he not in any case seek the good of his children? Jesus said, 'When you pray, do not keep on babbling like pagans, for they think they will be heard because of their many words. Do not be like them, for your Father knows what you need before you ask him' (Matt. 6:7–8). Human parents encourage their children to say 'please' so that they learn not to take things for granted, but to appreciate others who provide for them. In the same way, prayer develops a sense of dependence on and gratitude to God. But does God hear prayer? At times the Psalmist wondered, and many in the concentration camps must have asked, if God listened to their cries. It has been said that every gravestone is a memorial to an unanswered prayer.

Sometimes it is pointed out that it should not be assumed that the only answer to a prayer is 'Yes'. It may be that looking back a person can see the hand of God in what happened, even if at the time she had hoped for a different answer to her petitions. Sometimes a person who has an incurable illness, may find that his feelings of bitterness or resentment are changed, or that the concern of those who care is itself an answer. Indeed, prayer may change the attitude of the pray-er, and intercession for the suffering may inspire action to help them.

The universe, to the theist, operates according to divinely ordained laws. Does God at times suspend those laws? Does God sometimes overrule human freedom that seems to be so precious to God? Is it perhaps that whilst God always wills the best for people, God so respects human freedom that the divine will is not imposed on people? Prayer, however, may help to make available the divine reservoirs of grace and guidance. Certainly human lives are intertwined, and we know as yet little about the power of thought transference.

Probably most Christians through the ages have believed that God is able to answer prayer. If God does not, they blame their own unworthiness. In the past, a major disaster, such as flood or famine, might be met by a National Day of Prayer. Some Christians would still see this as an appropriate response, but others would have problems with it. Today, some Christians, because of difficulties with traditional concepts of prayer will, in practice, speak of its effect on the person who prays. There is an interesting passage in the hymn 'Turn back, O Man, forswear thy foolish ways' written by Clifford Bax (1886-1962) at the end of the First World War, which reads,

* * *

Yet thou, her child, whose head is crowned with flame
Still wilt not hear thine inner God proclaim –
'Turn back, O Man, forswear thy foolish ways'.[5]

Is 'the inner God' the voice of conscience? Is the appeal to peoples' higher nature rather than to the divine being? As we have seen,[6] some modern Christian thinkers believe God's power in the world is exercised through the appeal to conscience.

Contemplative Prayer

The intellectual difficulties that some Christians have with intercessory prayer may partly explain the increased contemporary interest in contemplative prayer or the prayer of silence. Such a way of prayer was until recently adopted only by those who were well advanced in the spiritual life. Today, it may be suggested to those who are quite new in faith. Essentially, it is a learning to be quiet in the presence of God. It is a stilling of the body and the mind. Unlike other forms of prayer which are discursive and use words, contemplative prayer, which is also sometimes called centring prayer, tries to discover an inner silence. Such a form of prayer does not need to grapple with the intellectual difficulties that intercessory prayer presents for some people. It is also free of traditional religious language and images. For example, those whose father abused them in childhood will have real difficulties with the image of a Heavenly Father. Not everyone finds it easy to think of God as 'King of Kings and Lord of Lords'. Those who enter into the prayer of silence may discover God's presence or Spirit in the depth of their being, whereas much traditional worship pictures an external and transcendent God.

The attraction of this way of prayer may be similar to the appeal of Taizé devotional worship. Taizé is an ecumenical monastic community founded in 1940 by Roger Schutz. The worship includes many simple repetitive chants, such as 'Lord hear my prayer and let my cry come unto you', or *'Laudate omnes gentes'* (Praise, all you people), which are reminiscent of an Eastern mantra or indeed, in terms of the repetitive simplicity of the words, of some of the entries for the European Song Contest! Like the prayer of silence, the Taizé chants help to still the mind and open the worshipper to the presence of God.

In the Orthodox church, the practice of the Jesus Prayer has been taught since the seventh century. It is an attempt to fulfil St Paul's injunction to 'Pray continually' (1 Thess. 5:17). The words of the prayer are usually 'Lord Jesus Christ, Son of God, have mercy upon me.' They should be repeated so regularly that they become part of the rhythm of breathing.

Reading the Bible

For some disciples, it is in devotional study of the word of God that they sense most vividly the divine presence. The scriptures are read by Christians both in public worship and privately. The Bible used by many of the first Christians was the Greek translation of the Hebrew Bible, which is known as the Septuagint (sometimes abbreviated as LXX) because tradition says that it was translated by seventy-two people.

Following the practice of the synagogue, passages from the Septuagint were read out in Christian worship, along with a sermon. This often formed the first part of the Eucharist and was sometimes known as the mass of the catechumens, who were people preparing for baptism. In the early years of the church, teaching about Jesus was by word of mouth. The work of the twelve apostles was prayer and the ministry of the word (Acts 6:2). From the sixties of the first century, accounts of Jesus' life began to be written down (Luke 1:1) and presumably the letters of St Paul were collected. Christians started to add to their services readings from these writings. There are quotations from them in the writings of Clement of Rome (*fl.c.*96) and St Polycarp (*c.*69–*c.*155). Eventually those writings which were thought to be by apostles were collected in the authoritative canon of scripture, although for several centuries the gospels or letters appeared in separate volumes. Even when printing made the production of whole Bibles much easier, many churches continued to include a selection of set readings in their mass or prayer books.

In the Church of England, it is customary for the Bible to be left permanently on the lectern. In the French Reformed church it lies open continually on the holy table, and in the Church of Scotland the Bible is carried in at the beginning of the service. In Catholic churches, it is carried in procession for the reading of the gospel, for which it is customary to stand. Respect is shown to the Bible as a holy book. Some Christians would make sure that no other book is placed on top of it.

During the Middle Ages, readings from the Bible were often very brief. A concern of the Reformers was to make scripture widely available to the people and the Bible was translated into the vernacular tongues. Many people, however, were illiterate and depended upon hearing the scripture read aloud.

In recent years, the Catholic church has given renewed emphasis to reading the Bible and to preaching. Other churches, such as the Anglican church, have increased the variety of readings at the Eucharist and now include regular lections from the Hebrew Bible. There have also, especially over the last fifty years or so, been a number of new translations of the Bible.

The faithful have, in most centuries, had the opportunity to hear scripture read in public worship. Traditionally, Christian schools would also have given time to the reading of the Bible. Protestants especially have also been encouraged to read the Bible privately. Some have read it without notes or commentary, but others have made use of the various aids for Bible study which are available. Some of these concentrate on helping to place a passage in its original context so that the reader can be aware of the concerns of the author; others apply the passage to contemporary life; others, following the teaching of St Ignatius Loyola, encourage the reader to use her imagination to picture the scene described and thereby come close to Jesus. The believer trusts that through reading the Word of God, he or she may hope to hear God speak.

The Holy Communion

' "Do this in remembrance of me." Was ever another command so obeyed?' asked Gregory Dix (1901–52), a great liturgical scholar. 'People have found no better thing than this to do for kings at their crowning and for criminals going to the scaffold; for armies in triumph or for a bride and bridegroom in a little country church; for the wisdom of a Parliament or for a sick old woman afraid to die . . . tremulously, by an old monk on the fiftieth anniversary of his vows; furtively by an exiled bishop who had hewn timber all day in a prison camp; gorgeously for the canonisation of St Joan of Arc.'[7]

In most Christian traditions, the Eucharist, known perhaps as the Communion, the Mass, or the Lord's Supper, is central to Christian worship. Here the worshipper believes he or she is in the presence of God.

H. Bonar (1806–89) expressed it like this in one of his hymns:

Here, O my Lord, I see thee face to face;
Here faith would touch and handle things unseen;
Here grasp with firmer hand the eternal grace,
And all my weariness upon thee lean.[8]

The Communion service includes readings from scripture, the saying of the creed, often a sermon and prayers, including confession, absolution and intercession. It may include the 'peace', when worshippers greet each other and wish each other 'the peace of the Lord'. This is an ancient practice which has been revived in recent years in several churches. I first encountered it in the Church of South India, where it affirmed the Christian rejection of caste barriers.

The Eucharistic Prayer will, as we have seen above, include thanksgiving and also remembrance of Jesus' words and actions on the night he was betrayed. At his last supper with his disciples, Jesus took bread and broke it and said to them, 'Take, eat, this is my body given for you.' He also took wine and gave that to them, saying, 'This is my blood which is shed for you.

Drink this in remembrance of me' (Mark 14:22–5). As we have noted, the exact meaning of these words has been a matter of dispute, but worshippers believe that in making a memorial of what Jesus said and did, they share in his death and resurrection.

Four Eucharistic actions may be distinguished: the taking of the bread and wine; the giving thanks; the breaking of the bread and, fourth, the sharing of the bread and cup. These actions repeat what Jesus himself did at the Last Supper.

Jesus who is remembered is both Man and God. There are those who emphasise that he was the perfect man who made the one complete offering of himself in obedience to the Father. The worshipper seeks to unite his weak offering with Christ's. To quote from another Eucharistic hymn, written by William Bright (1824–1901):

> We here present, we here spread forth to thee
> That only Offering perfect in thine eyes,
> The one true, pure, immortal Sacrifice.
> Look, Father, look on his anointed face,
> And only look on us as found in him.[9]

For others, Jesus as God assures the believer of God's pardon and peace. This can be seen in the beautiful poem 'Love', written by the seventeenth century English poet and country parson George Herbert (1593–1633):

> Love bade me welcome; yet my soul drew back,
>   Guilty of dust and sin.
> But quick-ey'd Love, observing me grow slack
>   From my first entrance in,
> Drew nearer to me, sweetly questioning
>   If I lack'd any thing.
>
> 'A guest', I answer'd, 'worthy to be here'.
>   Love said, 'You shall be he'.
> 'I the unkind, ungrateful? Ah my dear,
>   I cannot look on thee'.

Love took my hand, and smiling did reply,
*   'Who made the eyes but I?'*

'Truth Lord, but I have marr'd them; let my shame
*   Go where it doth deserve.'*
'And know you not', says Love, 'who bore the blame?'
*   'My dear, then I will serve.'*
'You must sit down', says Love, 'and taste my meat.'
*   So I did sit and eat.*[10]

The Communion not only binds the believer to the Lord, but to other worshippers. This is expressed in the chorus of a modern hymn by Bob Gillman (b.1946):

Bind us together, Lord,
bind us together
with cords that cannot be broken.
Bind us together, Lord,
bind us together,
O bind us together with love.[11]

It is this that makes so tragic the divisions of the church which stop Christians of different churches sharing in Eucharistic fellowship. A number of churches now practice inter-communion with other churches, which means that a member of one church, say, the Church of England, can receive Communion at a Swedish Lutheran church, but the Roman Catholic church does not allow its members to receive Communion at churches which are not in communion with the Pope, nor, except in very special circumstances, does it invite others to receive at Catholic altars.

The Communion service should strengthen the disciple for witness and service to the world and it may end with the dismissal, 'Go in peace to love and serve the Lord.' This self-dedication is beautifully expressed in a hymn based on the Liturgy of Malabar in South India:

Strengthen for service, Lord, the hands

That holy things have taken;
Let ears that now have heard thy songs
To clamour never waken.

Lord, may the tongues which 'Holy' sang
Keep free from all deceiving;
The eyes which saw thy love be bright,
Thy blessèd hope perceiving.

The feet that tread thy hallowed courts
From light do thou not banish;
The bodies by thy body fed
With thy new life replenish.[12]

There are many differences in Eucharistic practice from church to church. Some Protestant churches still only have Communion quite infrequently, whilst others encourage the faithful to share in the Lord's Supper on every Lord's Day. Many priests and some lay people will receive the sacrament daily.

Some churches use special unleavened wafers, which recall the manna or 'bread from heaven' which God provided for the children of Israel as they wandered in the desert. Others prefer ordinary bread, which suggests that God redeems and transforms our everyday life. Some Protestant churches use unfermented grape juice instead of wine and may have individual little cups rather than a common chalice.

Besides the celebration of the Eucharist, many churches hold services which concentrate on the reading of scripture, preaching, prayer and singing psalms and hymns. In some churches, such as the Anglican, there is a set structure for Matins and Evensong, whereas in other churches the services will be more dependent on the minister who is leading them.

The Arts

Music

Music, both vocal and instrumental, plays an important part in church worship. Hymns continue to be popular, as is shown by the large audience in Britain for the television programme *Songs of Praise.* This is why I have quoted from a number of hymns, as they convey the devotion of the worshipper. Ideally, there would have been a tape cassette to accompany this book, so that one could listen to the hymns being sung!

Luther encouraged hymn singing, but there are Greek and Latin hymns dating from the early centuries of the church. Methodism is known especially for its hymn singing, and as we have seen Charles Wesley wrote some six thousand hymns. Whilst they invite personal trust in the forgiveness offered in Christ, they are rich in doctrinal teaching. A good example is the second verse of the well-loved Christmas hymn, 'Hark! The herald-angels sing':

> *Christ, by highest heaven adored,*
> *Christ, the everlasting Lord,*
> *   Late in time behold him come,*
> *Offspring of a virgin's womb.*
> *   Veiled in flesh the Godhead see!*
> *Hail, the incarnate Deity!*
> *   Pleased as man with man to dwell,*
> *Jesus, our Immanuel.*[13]

Classical hymns are a medium of teaching and they usually speak of God. Many hymns of the American revivals say more about the worshipper's spiritual experience. An enormous number of hymns continue to be written and some recent hymns have focused on Christian social responsibility, such as 'When I needed a neighbour' by Sydney Carter (b.1915). In India, some of the churches have adapted *bhajans* or devotional songs to Christian use and some African churches now use African traditional music in worship.

At a High Mass, besides the chanted readings and the celebrant's prayers, the music of the Mass falls into two categories known as the 'proper' and the 'ordinary'. The proper denotes those parts of the service which vary according to the day or the season, such as the introit or gradual. The ordinary or invariable parts of the service include the *Gloria, Sanctus* or *Agnus Dei.* There are many settings, especially for the ordinary – some of the finest of which were composed by the great European musicians of the sixteenth and seventeenth centuries, such as Johann Sebastian Bach (1685–1750), who wrote the noble *Mass in B Minor.*

The *Missale Romanum* contains music dating back to the time of Pope Innocent II and even the seventh-century Gregory the Great. The modern *Missa Normativa* of Pope Paul VI is now the official Mass of the Catholic church and is usually celebrated in the vernacular of each country.

The particular contribution of the Church of England has been its chanting of the Psalms, known as Anglican chant, heard at its best in a cathedral Choral Evensong. This consists of a tune in barred music, harmonised, in which the first part of each half-verse is sung on a reciting note and the concluding words fitted to a tune in metrical rhythm. At the Reformation, French and Swiss Reformed churches introduced metrical psalmody, although it was in Scotland that the metrical Psalter became a characteristic feature of national worship.

Besides the wealth of choral music, there is an enormous repertoire of church organ music, although quartets used to be more common, and today the guitar and other instruments are sometimes used in worship. Campanology, the ringing of church bells, is also associated with Christian worship. Most often bells are used to call the faithful to worship, but they may be rung to celebrate a great festival, a wedding or major national occasion. For example, the bells of many churches will be rung to welcome the new millennium.

Art and Architecture

There is not room to write adequately of the contribution of other arts to Christian worship. Architecture provides the buildings in which that worship takes place and churches and cathedrals have been spoken of as 'sermons in stone'. The various styles each in their own way point to God, and the consecrated building or sacred space even today challenges the secular assumptions of society.

Churches have been richly adorned with stained glass, great paintings, sculptures and other decoration. Some of the plate used for the Holy Communion is exquisite work in gold and silver. Medieval manuscripts were often written in beautiful calligraphy and richly decorated. Many of the vestments of priests and bishops are splendid. Week by week new flower arrangements are placed in churches across the world and at special seasons, such as harvest, the decoration will be more elaborate, with sheaves of corn, fruit and vegetables.

Nothing less than the best is good enough for God. Through the centuries Christians have offered the best of their artistic skills to God. Some Christians today, as in every generation, question this extravagance and think the money would have been better used for the poor. Yet the artistic and cultural wealth of Europe and some other areas of the world is part of the Christian heritage.

Rites of Passage

So far, we have considered the regular pattern of Christian devotion which includes, prayer, Bible reading and sharing in the Communion. Most churches also provide for the special occasions in a person's life, such as birth or marriage.

Sacraments

The term 'sacrament' may be used of the ceremonies to mark these occasions, although there is some dispute between churches on the number of sacraments. The word 'sacrament' is Latin in origin and meant an 'oath'. It was used to translate the Greek word *mysterion*. Augustine defined a sacrament as a 'visible form of invisible grace'. According to the Catechism in the *Book of Common Prayer* a sacrament is 'an outward and visible sign of an inward and spiritual grace given unto us, ordained by Christ himself, as a means whereby we receive the same, and a pledge to assure us thereof'. Protestant churches recognise two sacraments which they claim were ordained by Christ himself: baptism and Holy Communion. Catholics, since at least the time of Peter Lombard (c.1100–60) have recognised seven sacraments: baptism, confirmation, the Eucharist, penance, extreme unction, orders and marriage. In Catholic theology a valid sacrament requires the right matter, for example bread and wine at the Eucharist, and the right intention. Further, the recipient needs to be in a state of faith.

Baptism

Baptism is the rite of admission to the church, practised by almost all denominations, most of which recognise the validity of baptism by whichever church it is performed. Its origin is probably to be found in the Jewish practice of baptising gentiles who were attracted to Judaism and in John the Baptist's baptism 'for the forgiveness of sins' (Mark 1:4). Jesus himself was baptised by John (Mark 1:9) and the church claimed that the Risen Christ had commanded the apostles 'to make disciples of all nations, baptising them in the name of the Father and of the Son and of the Holy Spirit' (Matt. 28:19).[14] Various themes were linked with baptism, such as the washing away of sins, dying with Christ, rebirth or the gift of the Spirit.

The first Christians were adults, although Acts 16 says that a jailer 'and all his family' were baptised. Did the family include infants? We do not know, but it seems that quite early parents wanted to have their children baptised with them. This is understandable at a time of intense persecution, especially when baptism was seen as removing the stain of original sin and as guaranteeing entry to heaven. Thus by the early Middle

Ages, infant baptism became the norm.

The difficulty was that baptism was originally administered to those who had declared their faith in Jesus. Could the faith of the parents or godparents or of the church suffice? The issue was re-opened at the Reformation and the radical Anabaptists saw baptism only as the response of faith, not as a means of grace, and rejected infant baptism. This is still the position of the Baptist churches and of some Pentecostals and Brethren, who practice 'adult or believer's baptism', insisting that candidates must themselves confess their faith in Christ. The Salvation Army has no sacraments and has a service of dedication for children.

In the early church, a person would be baptised, perhaps in a river, by immersion, and Baptists continue to dip the whole body under water. In other churches water is poured or sprinkled over the infant. The child is named at the ceremony, signed with the sign of the cross, welcomed as a member of the church, which is the family of God, and his or her parents are perhaps given a lighted candle, which symbolises Christ, who is the Light of the world.

Confirmation

Churches which administer baptism to infants have a ceremony, often confirmation, at which, when old enough, the child makes his or her own confession of faith, although in the Orthodox church confirmation is administered as part of the baptism ritual. In the Catholic church, confirmation today is normally conferred shortly after the seventh birthday. In the Church of England, the candidate is more likely to be in the teens. Confirmation is administered by the bishop laying hands on the candidate. Candidates used to be expected to wear white, and as confirmations often took place at Pentecost, that festival acquired the name 'Whitsun'. In the Church of England and some other churches, it is expected that a person will have been confirmed before receiving communion, although in the Roman Catholic church 'first Communion' may precede confirmation. In the American Episcopal church quite young children may be welcomed to receive the bread and the wine.

There is considerable discussion today about rites of admission. It is widely agreed that baptism is the full rite of initiation and should be all that is required before a person receives Holy Communion. Yet, it is also said that a person should understand the meaning of the sacrament before partaking of it. There are also questions about the most appropriate age. The view taken depends in part whether the emphasis is put upon God's grace given in baptism and confirmation or whether the stress is on the individual's expression of personal faith and commitment to Christ.

Marriage

Christians have a high doctrine of marriage. They are expected to practice monogamy. Marriage is believed to be a gift of God in creation, which means that it is God's will for all people, not just Christians. Jesus blessed marriage by his presence at the wedding in Cana of Galilee (John 2).

The reasons for marriage are the procreation of children and their nurture, sexual relations in a context of love and security, and the couple's mutual help and support for each other. Many Anglican and Protestant churches have recently reversed the order of the reasons for marriage, although Catholics, in their opposition to artificial means of contraception, insist that intercourse should always be open to the possibility of procreation. At times the church, with an emphasis on the virtues of celibacy, has seemed to have a negative view of human sexuality. Indeed, the 1662 Prayer Book spoke of marriage as 'a remedy against sin and to avoid fornication'. Today the emphasis is on the physical union as expressing and strengthening the, as it were, sacramental union of two whole persons. This is why, besides being forbidden in scripture, the church has opposed pre-marital and extra-marital sexual intercourse. Casual relationships separate the physical from the giving of the whole person to the other. In Western society today, however, many people, including Christians, live together before marriage. Some Christians would now put the emphasis on the quality of the relationship rather than its legal status.

Divorce

In Catholic theology, the sacrament of marriage creates an unbreakable metaphysical bond. This, therefore, means that divorce is not possible, although it may be possible to annul a marriage on specific grounds which mean that it was never a true marriage.

The discipline of different churches on divorce varies, partly because according to Matthew's gospel (Matt. 19:3 and 9), Jesus allowed divorce on the grounds of adultery, whereas according to Mark's gospel (Mark 10:2–12), he did not allow it in any circumstances. Some Christians recognise that the marriage relationship, as well as one or other partner, may die. It is also acknowledged that while lifelong union is God's intention for marriage, not everyone lives up to the ideal. The gospel speaks of forgiveness and a new start. As a result, a growing number of Protestant and Anglican churches allow those who have been divorced to receive Communion and will bless a second marriage or perhaps celebrate it in church. A recent question is whether, if the couple request it, a marriage should be celebrated in church if one partner belongs to a religion other than Christianity.

A wedding is often a great family day of celebration and the preparations and cost will be considerable. Traditionally the bride wears white and is given away by her father. The couple's promises to each other make a valid marriage. The priest is there to bless, and in some countries also acts in a legal capacity. The couple have to declare their willingness to marry and their lifelong commitment to the other. A ring or rings are exchanged as a sign of the union. There will be prayers, perhaps a mass is celebrated and there will be hymns and music and a reception.

Homosexuality

Today in a very few churches there may be a celebration of gay marriage, but even the blessing of homosexuals and lesbians who enter into a long-term relationship is rare. Traditionally, following Leviticus 18:22 and some passages in the Pauline epistles (e.g. Rom. 1:26-7) the church has condemned homosexuality. The Roman Catholic church maintains this position, recently describing the homosexual orientation as an 'objective disorder'.[15] In Protestant and Anglican churches, a distinction is now often made between a homosexual orientation and homosexual genital acts; the orientation is part of some people's God-given make-up and not something for which they should be condemned. The churches, however, tend to counsel chastity, especially for the clergy. There is, in my view, some inconsistency in the position of some churches. If homosexuality is part of people's God-given nature, it seems hard to deny them the physical expression of their love. Further, if something is wrong for clergy, it should be wrong for laity, otherwise a false separation is introduced into the people of God.

For centuries the church discriminated against those who were illegitimate, for example in not allowing them to be ordained, thus punishing children for the sins of their parents. This is no longer the case.

A Matter of Debate

Attitudes to sexuality have changed so much in the so-called 'permissive West' in recent years, that it is difficult to have a clear picture of Christian teaching on the subject. Some churches, especially the Roman Catholic church and Conservative Evangelical churches, maintain the traditional teaching that sexual intercourse should take place only between a married couple. They condemn pre-marital and extra-marital sexual relations, as well as homosexuality, lesbianism and masturbation. More liberal churches acknowledge many of the insights into human sexuality resulting from scientific research in this century. They also recognise that Christian teaching has often taken a negative view of human sexuality, thus reflecting Greek and Gnostic views that salvation consisted in the soul escaping from the body, rather than the Hebrew picture of the human being as a psychosomatic whole. It is also admitted that Christian teaching on the subject has mostly been propounded by men, many of whom seemed afraid of women. At last, feminist insights are helping the church to a more balanced view. Further, if the emphasis is put on the loving quality of the relationship, rather than the status of those involved, the church can be more welcoming to people of different lifestyles.

Parenthood

The church has always recognised the importance of family life and stressed the responsibilities of parents in the physical, mental, moral and spiritual upbringing of children. In many countries, churches have provided care for orphaned children. They have also established schools and made a significant contribution to the development of the educational system, although in several countries in recent years church schools have been taken over by the state. In some countries, Christian schools and colleges, which offer a high standard of education, seem to minister to the privileged classes.

In the nineteenth century, some churches established Sunday schools to offer children who were working in factories or on the land the chance to learn to read and be instructed in the Christian faith. Today, Christian charities continue to express a similar concern by opposing unfair trading practices which condemn young children in parts of Asia to spend hours weaving carpets or making toys and sports equipment for the developed world. Churches are active too in the campaign against sex tourism and the sexual exploitation of children.

Most churches encourage responsible parenthood and today, apart from the Roman Catholic church, regard the use of artificial contraceptives as a matter for the couple to decide. The Roman Catholic church seemed to be moving in this direction, until Pope Paul VI issued the encyclical *Humanae Vitae* in 1968, in which he went against the advice of the majority of those on the commission which he had set up to examine the issue. The encyclical reaffirmed the Catholic church's condemnation of artificial measures to prevent contraception.

The Catholic church is also resolutely opposed to abortion. Since 1869, the Catholic church has regarded the embryo as having the status of a human being from the moment of conception. Abortion is therefore tantamount to deliberate killing or murder. It is recognised that efforts to save a mother's life, as in the removal of a cancerous but pregnant uterus, which may result in an abortion, are morally acceptable if that was not the intention. Other churches are not clear about the stage at which an embryo becomes a human being. St Thomas Aquinas held that ensoulment occurred in a male after forty days and in a woman after ninety days. Many churches, while recognising that abortion and the taking of life is an evil, accept that there are circumstances in which it may be a lesser evil, for example if a mother's physical or mental health is put in jeopardy. Few Christians endorse 'abortion on demand'.

The Sick

Among the seven sacraments recognised by the Catholic church are penance and holy unction. Catholics, as we have seen, have traditionally been encouraged to make private confession to a priest, who offers them absolution. Laying on of hands and anointing with holy oil are part of the ministry to the sick, bringing special assurance of God's blessing. In some churches, the laying on of hands is part of a ministry of faith-healing and claims are made for miraculous healings. In almost all churches, there will be regular prayers for those who are ill and ministers or members of the congregation will visit those who are sick at home or in hospital. Regular communicants will also be offered the chance to share in the sacrament. In some churches, some of the bread and wine is 'reserved' or kept after a Communion service and taken at a later time to those who are ill. The aumbry in which the reserved sacrament is kept in a church may be marked by a nearby light and be a focus of devotion. In other traditions, the minister will celebrate Holy Communion at the bedside.

Death

Prayers, confession and absolution, holy unction and Holy Communion may all be part of the ministry offered to those who are dying.

Funeral customs vary from church to church and country to country. Traditionally, Christians have practised burial, although cremation has become common in the twentieth century. The Roman Catholic ban on cremation was not lifted until 1963.

Some Protestant churches object to prayers for the dead. The Church of England's *Book of Common Prayer* funeral service, for example, has no prayers for the soul of the departed and focuses attention on those who have been bereaved. The objection to praying for the departed derives from Reformation objections to Catholic teaching about purgatory. According to Catholic teaching, as defined at the Councils of Lyons (1274) and Florence (1439), those who die in the grace of God expiate their unforgiven venial or pardonable sins by undergoing due punishment before being admitted to the beatific vision. Some late medieval preachers claimed that prayers and masses offered for their souls, for which the priests expected a fee, could speed up the process. Luther, as we have seen,[16] regarded this sale of indulgences as an abuse. Further, Protestants with their emphasis on God' s justifying grace held that the believer was assured of entry into heaven at death.

Today prayers for the souls of the departed are quite common. Indeed, the focus of a funeral or memorial service seems to be becoming a remembrance of the departed's life rather than a proclamation of the gospel of the resurrection. Churches offer pastoral sympathy and support to the bereaved, but there seem now in the West to be no agreed rituals of mourning, as for example in most Orthodox Jewish families.

Ordination

Catholics regard ordination as one of the seven sacraments and it is held to impart an indelible character. The ministry of the church traces its origins to Jesus' commissioning of the Twelve (Matt. 10:1–5) and of the seventy (Luke 10:1), although critical New Testament scholars question whether either occasion goes back to Jesus himself, who may not have had plans for the founding of the church. According to Acts 13:1–3, Paul and Barnabas were commissioned for their missionary journey by prayer and the laying on of hands.

In the early church there seems to have been a distinction between the apostolic or itinerant ministry and the local ministry. The three major orders of bishop, priest and deacon emerged quite early, although in the Middle Ages other minor orders were recognised. At the Reformation, some churches rejected the idea of priesthood and moved the emphasis of ministry from the offering of the sacrifice of the mass to the preaching of the word of God. In the Church of England at the Reformation, the priest at his ordination was given a Bible instead of a paten and chalice. Some churches, such as the Church of England, retained the traditional three-fold pattern of ministry, but this was abandoned by the Lutheran church in Germany and by Calvinists. The Quakers have abandoned the idea of an ordained ministry.

In episcopal churches, ordination is by a bishop and usually takes place at a Eucharist. A new bishop is consecrated, which makes him (or now very occasionally her) a bishop. He is then enthroned when he takes charge of a diocese. In the same way there is in many churches a ceremony when a new clergyman takes charge of a church or parish. In the Church of England, this is called an 'induction' and 'installation'. It is perhaps worth adding that the terms 'priest' or 'deacon' or 'minister' refer to a clergyman or clergywoman's status, whereas terms such as 'rector', 'vicar', 'curate' or 'chaplain' refer to the actual job. Rectors and vicars have exactly the same spiritual status. The difference harks back to the days when clergy received tithes or offerings from the laity. A vicar did not receive tithes directly. Instead they were paid to a monastery and he received a payment or stipend. A 'dean' is the senior priest in charge of a cathedral, sharing responsibility with the other members, who are usually called 'canons'. The term 'reverend' is an epithet of respect applied to clergy since the fifteenth century, and from the seventeenth century it was used as a title. Archbishops are styled 'Most Reverend'. Catholic priests are commonly called 'Father'. Clergy in some traditions wear distinctive everyday dress, of which the clerical collar, popularly known as a 'dog-collar' is the most common. Catholic and Orthodox priests wear special clothes – vestments – when they celebrate Mass.

For some, these traditions add to the dignity of church life and enhance the sense of worship. For others, they are a deterrent, setting the clergy apart and appearing to make the church irrelevant to contemporary life. It is unhelpful to make generalisations, as the traditions of different churches and countries are so varied. It is also important not to allow the external, which in unfamiliar traditions may seem strange and even comic, to obscure the life-giving mystery which can never be contained in human words or artefacts. As Sydney Carter wrote:

> Catch the bird of heaven,
> Lock him in a cage of gold;
> Look again tomorrow,
> And he will be gone.
>
> *Ah the bird of heaven!*
> *Follow where the bird has gone*
> *Ah! The bird of heaven!*
> *Keep on travelling on.*
>
> Lock him in religion,
> Gold and frankincense and myrrh,
> Carry to his prison,
> But he will be gone.
> *Chorus*
>
> Temple made of marble,
> Beak and feather made of gold,
> All the bells are ringing,
> But the bird has gone.
> *Chorus*

Bell and book and candle
cannot hold him any more,
For the bird is flying
As he did before.
Chorus. [17]

Of the many books on prayer, H. E. Fosdick, *The Meaning of Prayer* (1915, Fontana, 1960), and Evelyn Underhill's *Worship* (1936, Fontana, 1962), are classics; and Archbishop Anthony Bloom, *Living Prayer* (Libra Books, Darton, Longman and Todd, 1966), is helpful.

Olive Wyon, *The Altar Fire*, is a devotional introduction to the Eucharist which has considerable theological content. *Liturgy and Worship*, eds. W. K. Lowther Clarke and Charles Harris (SPCK, 1959), is a thorough introduction to the worship of the Church, with special reference to the Anglican Communion.

8

Love Your Neighbour

'Faith by itself, if it is not accompanied by action, is dead', said James in his epistle (Jas. 2:17). John said the same, 'Dear children, let us not love with words or tongue but with actions and in truth' (1 John 3:18). Jesus himself linked the commands to love God and to love the neighbour.

In Matthew's gospel, Jesus' final parable is of the Last Judgment when the sheep and goats will be separated. To those on his right hand, Jesus said, the king will say:

> Come you who are blessed by my Father; take your inheritance, the kingdom prepared for you since the creation of the world. For I was hungry and you gave me something to eat, I was thirsty and you gave me something to drink, I was a stranger and you invited me in, I needed clothes and you clothed me, I was sick and you looked after me, I was in prison and you came to visit me.

The righteous in astonishment asked when they had seen the king hungry or naked or as a stranger and the king replied, 'I tell you the truth, whatever you did for one of the least of these brothers of mine, you did for me' (Matt. 25:31–46).

Love of the neighbour is shown not only by the way a disciple lives, which we shall consider first, but also, as we shall see in the second section of the chapter, by the combined efforts of the followers of Jesus to meet human need and, third, by attempts to change the structures of society.

A Christian Way of Life

'The greatest of these is love'

Paul in his letter to the Galatians describes the fruits of the Spirit as 'love, joy, peace, patience, kindness, goodness, faithfulness, gentleness and self-control' (Gal. 5:22). In his first letter to the Corinthians, Paul speaks again of spiritual gifts of which love is supreme: 'Love is patient, love is kind. It does not envy, it does not boast, it is not proud. It is not rude, it is not self-seeking, it is not easily angered, it keeps no record of wrongs . . .' (1 Cor. 13:4–8).

Love is the characteristic way to sum up the quality of life expected of the follower of Jesus. It is a selfless, sacrificial concern for the other and mirrors the love shown to the believer by God in Christ. Christians recognise that they cannot show this love in their own power, but only if their lives are transformed by Christ. The Sermon on the Mount (Matt. 5–7) sums up Jesus' ethical teaching, but it has been said that the gospel comes first. The Sermon describes the new way of life of those who live in loving recognition of God as their Father. People, of their own will, cannot live free from anxiety about the future nor turn the other cheek when someone hits them.

Love is not sentimental and it does not have sexual overtones. Indeed, the Greek word used in the New Testament, *agape*, distinguishes this love from the sexual associations of *eros*.

Traditional teaching speaks of four cardinal virtues of prudence, temperance, fortitude and justice, on which all others depend. Ambrose (*c.*339–97), the Bishop of Milan who baptised Augustine and who is one of the four Doctors of the Church, said the cardinal virtues were derived from the four virtues listed by Plato. They were extended by the medieval scholastics to seven by adding the three theological virtues of faith, hope and charity, which are mentioned by Paul (1 Cor. 13:13).

Love Your Neighbour

The Complexity of Moral Decisions

It is difficult always to be loving and to be as concerned for the other as for the self. It is often equally difficult to know the most loving thing to do. Is it always right to tell the truth, even if that would cause pain? Corrie ten Boom (1892–1983), whose home in Haarlem was a sanctuary and hiding place for Jews during the Second World War and who herself survived imprisonment in Ravensbruck concentration camp, told how she lied to save Jews from the Nazi death camps. Is it always right, as Jesus suggested, to turn the other cheek, or is the use of violence on occasion the lesser of two evils?

Although the basic command to love your neighbour as yourself seems simple, its application is very complex. Christian teachers have struggled with the many moral decisions that a person has to make in day-to-day life. Paul's letters already show examples of this, when he discussed the question of food offered to idols or questions of marriage and virginity (1 Cor. 6–8).

Christian teaching has veered between two extremes. On the one hand there is the approach of Situational Ethics which emphasises the importance of determining in each situation what is the most loving thing to do. Augustine's words, 'Love and do what you will'[1] are often quoted to justify this approach. The disciple relies, in the end, on the inner guidance of the Holy Spirit, but it is easy to mistake one's own opinion for the voice of God! On the other hand, papal teaching as expressed through encyclicals has an almost infallible authority. No longer does the individual need to resolve the complexity of a moral decision, instead the individual is required to obey the teaching of the church. The difficulty is that any rule has a certain inflexibility and its application may not always be the best response to human need. For example, in teaching on abortion, the Roman Catholic church says it is always wrong, because murder is forbidden, whereas liberal Protestants may accept that it is the lesser of two evils.

Christians' moral judgments are informed by the teaching of the Bible and especially the New Testament, although decisions should not be made by merely quoting a text. The biblical teaching should be weighed together with the traditions of the church, the present-day teaching of the church, and the best contemporary expert opinions. In the end, the believer's conscience is sacrosanct. Cardinal Newman (1801–90) said, 'Conscience is the first of all the Vicars of Christ.'[2] Conscience should be informed, but it should not be coerced.

The question of whether there are absolute values is one which is a subject of debate amongst moral philosophers. Many Christians see God as the guardian of the moral law, but some thinkers recognise the autonomy of morals and hold that people can discern what is right and wrong independently of their basic beliefs about the universe.

It is understandable that there has been and still is considerable disagreement between Christians on many ethical matters. The differences affect both the Christian's own lifestyle and his or her attitude to the behaviour of others.

Food and Drink

Some Christians, for example, object to the use of alcohol, whilst others see nothing wrong in its enjoyment in moderation. The latter point to biblical texts in which wine is extolled as part of the bounty of God (Ps. 104:15) and to Paul's advice to Timothy, 'Stop drinking only water and use a little wine because of your stomach and your frequent illnesses' (1 Tim. 5:23). The former can point to warnings about wine leading to debauchery (Eph. 5:18) and to the social abuses which alcohol can produce. It was this latter which led members of the Temperance movement in Britain in the nineteenth century to campaign against the use of alcohol and to set up alcohol-free clubs. Until recently the Methodist church was known for its temperance, and William Booth (1829–1912), the founder of the Salvation Army, campaigned against alcohol. In the USA, the Temperance movement grew in strength during the nineteenth century and by 1916, nineteen states had entirely forbidden the sale of alcohol.

Most Christians are prepared to eat meat, although there have been some, in every generation, who were vegetarian because of the wish to avoid taking life. Clement of Alexandria wrote, 'It is far better to be happy than to have your bodies act as graveyards for animals. Accordingly the apostle Matthew partook of seeds, nuts and vegetables, without flesh.'[3] Tertullian and John Chrysostom seem to have been vegetarians and Jerome advocated a meat-free diet, although he did not entirely follow his own advice. Some of the Celtic saints had a close relationship with animals. John Wesley was a vegetarian and campaigner for animal rights. Today a number of Christians are active in animal welfare movements. Some churches hold animal or pet services, usually in early October to mark the saint's day of St Francis of Assisi.

In the Middle Ages monks and nuns kept a number of fasts, when they abstained from meat as an exercise in self-discipline. The observance of regular fasting began with weekly fast days on Wednesdays and Fridays, to which were added the forty days of Lent. In the Eastern and Oriental churches, fasting meant the abstinence from all food, or at least from all animal food products. In the West it meant only one chief meal a day, although Ash Wednesday and Good Friday, which were also observed by the laity, were kept as complete fasts. In England, after the Reformation, Queen Elizabeth I insisted that the custom of eating fish on a Friday should be continued, not for religious reasons but to preserve the fishing industry. This in turn meant that there would be enough ships to protect the country in the event of war.

Medical Advances

We have seen in the previous chapter that Christians disagree on questions such as divorce, homosexuality, contraception and abortion. Medical advances are creating new dilemmas. Most Christians accept the transplantation of human organs, provided there is no coercion. Efforts to assist fertility are usually welcome, including artificial insemination by the husband (AIH). A few Christians object to artificial insemination by a donor (AID) because the husband would not be the real father. There seems to be no objection to the sex detection of a foetus, but there would be if it became a means of sex-selection. Christians would disagree about the abortion of a child who is expected to be severely handicapped. Some would insist that each life is valuable, others might question whether some children with very severe brain damage are in any real sense capable of human life.

Many Christians resist the idea of human cloning. It is theoretically possible to produce a 'carbon-copy' of a human being. Yet this might seem to be a human usurpation of God's right to create. Cloning would create very considerable identity and psychological problems and the process by-passes the mother's womb. These are matters on which there will be more debate.

The weight of Christian opinion is against euthanasia, believing that to God alone belongs the power to give life and to take life. The Christian, however, believes that death is not the end but the gateway to another life. Christians, therefore, may be critical of over-strenuous efforts to keep a patient, as it were, artificially alive. They would encourage spiritual preparation for death and have in recent years taken a lead in the hospice movement, which seeks to provide for the terminally ill a loving, caring environment where pain is controlled as much as possible.

War

There have been sharp disputes about recourse to arms. The early Christians were pacifist and in every century some Christians have upheld this position. When Christianity became the religion of Empire, the doctrine of the just war was developed. Augustine tried to draw together the threads of a just war theory, although the first systematic account of this teaching appeared in the *Decretum* of Gratian (d. no later than 1159) which is the major source of Roman Catholic canon law. The theory requires, first, that there is a just cause, which may be to regain something that was wrongfully taken or to punish evil or in defence against planned or actual aggression. Second, it requires that war is initiated by a legitimate authority; third that there is a right intention on the part of those involved. Fourth, the use of force must be proportional, that is to say, relevant to the issue and not doing more harm than good. Many Christians have not been able to see how a nuclear war could meet this requirement, although those Christians who have supported nuclear disarmament have not necessarily been total pacifists. Traditionally, a just war also had to be for the sake of peace and have a reasonable hope of success. The teaching also tried to limit the cruelties of war.

Whilst many of the Reformation churches took over this teaching, the radical churches, such as the Mennonites, followers of Menno Simons (1496–1561), who in 1536 left the Catholic priesthood and joined the Anabaptists, preached non-resistance to evil. The Quakers also taught non-violence. Pacifists claim that non-violence is to follow the way of Christ crucified. Only love can transform and reconcile the enemy. Yet, while it is true that violence can never produce lasting peace, which requires the reconciliation of those opposed to each other, some Christians think that violence can hold evil in check. Nuclear weapons have shown, however, the enormous danger of violence, whilst acts of genocide have made clear the deadly potential of evil tyrants.

Penal Policy

At the Reformation, there was disagreement whether a Christian should submit to unjust rule, and some radical Christians upheld the right to rebel against a tyrant. Paul had said that 'there is no authority except that which God has established . . . [The one in authority] does not bear the sword for nothing. He is God's servant, an agent of wrath to bring punishment on the wrongdoer' (Rom. 13:1–5). The Book of Revelation, on the other hand, produced by a community suffering persecution, took a less sanguine view of civil authority. None the less, Christians have recognised the need to check crime, forcibly if necessary, and to punish the offender.

Wrongdoing creates a corruption of character and destroys human relationship. An adulterer, for example, is likely to destroy his marriage. The suffering of oneself or others is the necessary consequence of the wrongdoing. In John's gospel, punishment is self-inflicted by those who reject the offer of light (John 3:16–21) – it is not inflicted by God because his majesty has been offended. There are, however, passages in the New Testament and in later Christian writing in which God is pictured like a king who punishes those who rebel. In human society such deliberate punishment is, in a sense, artificial and dramatic. It is not directly produced by the wrongdoing. It is retributive, but many Christians have argued that retribution, which is akin to legalised revenge, is not an adequate motive for punishment. Punishment needs further aims. It may be to deter the wrongdoer from evil ways; it may be to discourage others from following a bad example; it may be to declare society's abhorrence of the crime. Many would argue that punishment should be remedial – not only to frighten the criminals from further wrongdoing but to show them the error of their ways and to educate them into a new way of life.

This is not the place for a discussion of penal policy, but the picture a person has of how God acts will affect his or her view of how society should act. If the picture is of a God who rejoices over one sinner who repents or who welcomes the penitent just as the father welcomed his prodigal son, then the emphasis is on the wrongdoer's rehabilitation. Certainly, society needs to be protected from criminal action, but the criminal continues to be a person made in the image of God and one for whom Christ died. Further, the Christian hesitates to judge another, partly because of the warning of Jesus (Matt. 7:1), but also because of an awareness that any virtue is not his or her achievement, but the result of God's grace in his or her life. The English Protestant martyr John Bradford (*c.*1505–55) when he saw a group of criminals being led to their execution said, 'But for the grace of God there goes John Bradford.'[4] Those Christians who emphasise the remedial purpose of punishment usually oppose capital punishment.

Conscious of the suffering of prisoners and well aware that through the centuries many faithful Christians have been wrongfully imprisoned and put to death, Christians have emphasised the importance of visiting prisoners, have campaigned for prison and penal reform and have supported organisations such as Amnesty International that campaigns for prisoners of conscience. One example is the Quaker Elizabeth Fry (1780–1845), who became a 'minister' in 1811. In 1813 her interest was roused in the state of prisons and she devoted herself to the welfare of female prisoners in Newgate. She campaigned for the separation of the sexes, classification of criminals, female supervision of women and the provision of secular and religious instruction. She gave evidence to a committee of the House of Commons and travelled in Europe, promoting prison reform. She was also concerned about the treatment of the insane.

Meeting Human Need

The recognition that God created human beings in his image and that Christ died to show that every single person is precious in God's sight has inspired many Christians to practical service of others, especially through educational and medical work. Christians in Europe have played a major part in the development of schools and universities, the provision of medical care and the relief of the poor. Such service of others was also a hallmark of much missionary work in Africa and Asia.

Today, because many of these responsibilities have been assumed by governments, it is worth while to recall the Christian legacy in these fields. Still today, many Christians are motivated by their faith to devote their lives to medical, educational and caring professions. Other Christians are actively engaged in voluntary bodies which seek to meet special needs.

The Church and Education

Most of Christianity's first converts were poor and illiterate (1 Cor. 1:26). During the second century, a growing number of educated people were attracted to the faith. They naturally wanted their children to have as good an education as they had

had themselves, but the only schools available were the grammar and rhetoric schools which offered an education based on Greco-Roman non-Christian culture. Clement of Alexandria and Origen, as well as Augustine and Jerome, encouraged Christians to use secular schools, because they recognised the value of Hellenistic culture, provided it was subservient to Christian teaching. Tertullian was more suspicious of Hellenistic culture. He admitted the necessity of using secular schools, but deplored the situation.

Many Christians continued to use secular schools even when, after the conversion of the Emperor Constantine to Christianity, Christians also established catechetical schools, particularly for adults who wished to be baptised. The most famous catechetical school was in Alexandria in Egypt, where the syllabus included the best in Greek science and philosophy as well as Christian studies.

In western Europe, the invasions from the north gradually broke up the Roman educational system, although grammar and rhetoric schools survived in France and Spain into the eighth century. Slowly the church began to provide its own education, especially for the clergy. Even in the dark days from the fifth to the eighth century there were Christian scholars, such as Boethius (c.480–c.524) and Cassiodorus (c.485–c.580) in Rome, St Isidore (c.560–636), who was Archbishop of Seville in Spain, and the Venerable Bede (c.673–735), who has been called the 'father of English church history'. Monasteries offered some education and a few became centres of learning, especially in Ireland, where, as in other Celtic regions, there had been a tradition of education dating back to pre-Christian times.

Bishops too founded schools, usually in their cathedral city. These are sometimes regarded as the successors of the Roman rhetoric schools and as the precursors of grammar schools. Whilst initially mainly for those intending to be ordained, they quite quickly started to welcome other young people. Sometimes provision was made for those who needed to board. These schools too were influenced by the syllabus and the style of teaching in the monastic schools. Children were expected to be dutiful. As Bede said, 'a child does not contradict the professors'.[5] The discipline was strict.

Under the Emperor Charlemagne (742–814), who built on the monastic and episcopal schools, there was further development. Charlemagne was a lover of learning, and when he came to the throne he was distressed to find how poor was the Latin of many of his correspondents, including bishops and abbots. He recognised that the correct interpretation of Holy Scripture required a fluent knowledge of Latin. He gave orders that 'in each bishopric and in each monastery let the psalms, the notes, the chant, calculation and grammar be taught and carefully corrected books be available'.[6] He also set up a school at his palace at Aachen and imported talent from different parts of Europe, including Alcuin (c.735–804), who had been master of the school at York, and the grammarian Paul the Deacon (c.720–c.800) from Italy.

There were far more extensive educational developments during the cultural awakening of the eleventh and twelfth centuries, including the organisation of universities, such as the University of Paris, which formally came into being between 1150 and 1170. The universities of Oxford and Cambridge are slightly later and other ancient universities of Europe date from the thirteenth to fifteenth centuries. Most of the students were in holy orders and theology was regarded as the 'queen of the sciences'.

The development of universities led, in turn, to an increase of schools of various kinds. Besides the ones run by ecclesiastical authorities, some of the trade guilds started their own schools. It has been estimated that toward the close of the Middle Ages, England and Wales, with a population of about two and a half million, had 400 grammar schools – a rather better provision than in Victorian England.

In the sixteenth century, the Renaissance, with its New Learning, broke the dominance of scholastic studies and helped to broaden the syllabus while at the same time the spread of printing increased the availability of books. The dissolution of the monasteries and the upheavals of the Reformation period, however, caused considerable disruption. The Reformers were committed to the importance of education. Calvin in Geneva, where the theological academy under Theodore Bees (1519–1605) reached high standards of scholarship, advocated 'universal' education. In the Netherlands, which were Calvinist, free public schools were set up in every village and town by the early seventeenth century. John Knox, another Calvinist, had tried to do the same in Scotland but was prevented by the Scottish nobility.

In countries which remained loyal to the Catholic church there was also a development of education, in part thanks to the enthusiasm of the Jesuits.

The eighteenth century saw important changes to the pattern of education. Teaching in mother languages grew in importance and rivalled Latin; the exact sciences were brought into the curriculum and the correct method of teaching became a pedagogic question. The dominant religious motivation for education was beginning to be replaced. In the nineteenth century, this change was further developed, especially in those countries most affected by the French Revolution. Almost everywhere the aristocratic control of society was fading and a new commercial class wanted education to fit the needs of an industrial society.

In nineteenth-century Britain, the churches took a leading role in the development of elementary education. This, however, was marked by denominational rivalries. From 1870, the state has taken increasing control, although the Church of England and Roman Catholic churches still have a significant role, and religious education, which now includes teaching about the other major world religions as well as Christianity, is still required, as well as a daily act of collective worship. Christian influence was also dominant in the establishment of the so-called English 'public' or fee-paying schools. Thomas Arnold (1795–1842), who was appointed headmaster of Rugby in 1828, set the pattern for producing Christians, gentlemen and scholars – in that order. It has to be said that despite their good quality of education, public schools have been socially divisive.

Elsewhere, the role of the churches in education today depends upon political history. In France, for example, the law of 1886 enacted that only lay persons should teach in public schools and that there should be no distinctive religious teaching. Private fee-paying schools continue to offer a religious education. In Spain, state schools co-exist with private, almost exclusively church schools. In the USA, there has been a clear separation of church and state, so that no religious education is allowed in state-funded schools. Protestant churches, therefore, invested heavily in well-organised Sunday schools, whilst the Roman Catholic church developed an extensive network of 'parochial schools', which are wholly financed and administered by the Catholic church. In most eastern European countries Communist governments ended the churches' involvement in education and often made any instruction in the faith, even at home, very difficult.

While sometimes church involvement in education has seemed to be self-interested and seen as a way of propagating the faith, at its best it represents a Christian concern for the full dignity of the human being. Christians have therefore resisted schooling which is just training for a job and seen its role as developing each person's full potential as a physical, mental and spiritual being.

The Church of England's *Durham Report on Education* (1970) puts the matter like this:

[Do human beings] differ as socially acceptable citizens at all significantly from house-trained dogs? Or are human beings anything more than extremely elaborate computers whose major distinction is that they are comparatively cheap to come by? If this is our view of the nature of man, then the educational process need plainly be no more than a process of individual and social conditioning . . . [Christians] believe in the intrinsic worth of each individual . . . whether bright or stupid, beautiful or ugly, good or bad . . . For Christians it derives from a certain conception of man as created in the image of God, redeemed by Jesus Christ, and destined for eternal life. Each individual as an object of the love of God has a unique value. Against tendencies to depersonalise and to dehumanise which are prevalent in society the Christian will want constantly to emphasise the importance of personal relationships . . . The development of the person in all his aspects, religious and moral, as well as physical and mental, is therefore a matter of the deepest importance to him.[7]

The Care of the Sick

The church has also played an important part in the development of medical care in the West. In Greek and Roman times, temples were used as hospitals. After the conversion of Constantine, the establishment of hospitals became an integral part of church organisation. Following a decree that Constantine issued in 335, hospitals were developed in Rome, Constantinople, Ephesus and other parts of the Roman Empire. The Hôtel-Dieu of Lyons in France was opened in 542 and the Hôtel-Dieu of Paris in 660. It has to be admitted that more attention in these hospitals was given to the well-being of the patient's soul than to his or her bodily ailments.

The monasteries also set a new standard in their care for their sick members. Monasteries had an *infirmitorium* or place to which sick monks were taken for treatment. Monasteries also possessed a pharmacy and often a garden with medicinal plants. The monasteries also opened their doors to pilgrims and other travellers and no doubt offered them medical care when it was required, as well as to the lay people who served them.

The growth of hospitals accelerated during the Crusades, especially as more people were killed by disease than by the Muslim enemies. Military hospitals were set up along the routes which the crusaders travelled. The Knights Hospitallers of the Order of St John in 1099 established in the Holy Land a hospital that could care for 2,000 patients. The Order has survived through the centuries as the St John's Ambulance.

Most hospitals in the later Middle Ages were associated with monasteries, although some were built by cities, and this practice increased in those countries where the monasteries were disbanded. In the nineteenth century great advances took place in medical care and hospital provision, associated with

Florence Nightingale (1820–1910) and her reform of nursing, Louis Pasteur (1822–95) and his work in the development of germ theory, and Lord Lister's (1827–1912) advances in surgery. While many Christians were still motivated by their faith to become doctors and nurses, the Christian hegemony in medical care was fast disappearing. Even so, the nineteenth century, as we have seen, was a period in which missionaries established Western-style hospitals and medical care in many parts of Asia and Africa. Now, there is a new interest in the West in the traditional healing practices of the East.

Some Christians may appear to regard faith-healing as an alternative to orthodox medicine. Most Christians do not see the church's ministry to the sick as a rival to orthodox medicine. The majority of Christians are likely to think that God's gift of healing is normally mediated through the skill and dedication of doctors and nurses. It is also widely recognised that religious faith is no protection against depression and mental illness and that Christians should have no feelings of guilt in seeking psychiatric help. It was a Christian clergyman, Chad Varah, who in 1953 took the lead in setting up the Samaritans, an organisation with no particular religious affiliation, which offers counselling to the suicidal.

Poverty, Aid and Development

Alms-giving has always been expected of faithful Christians and care for the poor has been a continuing Christian concern. In medieval Europe the monasteries offered relief to the destitute. After the Reformation, in Protestant countries, other provision had to be made, but it was often still the responsibility of the church.

In sixteenth-century England, the Elizabethan Poor Laws were administered by parish overseers, who were sometimes the same people as the churchwardens. The alms collected at the Communion service and some of the tithes were used for the relief of the poor. In the nineteenth century, pauperism amongst the able-bodied came to be regarded as a moral failing, and the New Poor Law of 1834 made the provisions of the workhouse so unattractive that they were meant to force people back to work.

Growing humanitarian concern and the recognition of the complex causes of unemployment led in the twentieth century to the development of the Welfare State in Britain. Most developed countries now make basic provision for the unemployed and destitute, although mounting costs are leading several countries to re-examine their welfare provision.

In poorer countries, the destitute have to depend on begging. Civil war and famine have created terrible conditions for many people. Millions of people never get enough to eat or have an inadequate diet. This has troubled the consciences of Christians and others in richer countries and the churches have shared in the voluntary efforts to send aid to victims of emergencies and to assist small-scale development projects. Although the amounts given by churches are tiny compared to the aid budgets of governments, the money has usually been well spent. The churches have also tried to help mobilise public opinion in favour of overseas aid.

Christian Aid

An example of this concern is the work of Christian Aid, as recalled by its pioneering first Director, Janet Lacey. Born in Sunderland in County Durham, Janet Lacey's first interest was the theatre. In 1946 she went to Germany to work for the YMCA (the Young Men's Christian Association), but she was soon asked to join the Youth Department of the British Council of Churches and from there moved to Inter-Church Aid, which later became known as Christian Aid.

The agency's first task was to try to help the legacy of refugees and displaced persons in Europe created by the Second World War. This was a slow business, partly because several governments were reluctant to admit them. In 1959, four young English politicians wrote an article in *Crossbow* called 'Wanted, a World Refugee Year', which drew attention to the 200,000 people in Europe who were still refugees. Within a year, ninety-seven nations responded to the challenge. During the year, £30 million was donated, of which two-thirds came from the public and the rest from governments. Many countries agreed to relax their rules and let in a few more refugees. The World Council of Churches opened thirty-four refugee homes. In Britain, the UK World Refugee Year Committee set a target of £2 million, but ended up with over £7 million and nearly £2 million worth of clothing and houses.

The Year did not solve the problem and subsequently many more millions of people have been made refugees. The last fifty years have seen massive numbers of refugees in many parts of the world, for example the Palestinians in the Middle East, or refugees from Tibet, or recently in Rwanda. I recall visiting a Palestinian camp, where a very tall hedge was pointed out to me. I was told that in 1947 several people had said that it was a waste of time to plant the bushes. The refugees would soon be going home. In fact, some have been refugees for their whole life.

Even before the end of World Refugee Year, however, attention was also turning to the desperate poverty of many people. In 1961, the Director of the UN Food and Agricultural Organisation launched the Freedom from Hunger Campaign, which lasted for ten years and then became the UN Development Decade. In the 1960s, I was working in the Medway towns and was chair of the Freedom from Hunger and Christian Aid Committee. One project was to raise money for a Halco Tiger drilling machine which could make available supplies of clean water. I vividly recall visiting a village where a well had just been installed, providing for the first time a pure water supply, which it was hoped would reduce illness and infection and provide some water for irrigation. This was only one of many projects which encouraged people to help themselves and which brought real improvement to some villages.

Christian Aid, with other agencies, has also tried to respond to the immediate impact both of natural disasters and those caused by fighting and violence. For example, when the Mau Mau rebellion erupted in Kenya in 1952, the local churches tried to organise relief. Janet Lacey recalls how the churches in Britain were bombarded with demands for help, which were way beyond the money Christian Aid had available. Janet

Lacey then went to see for herself the situation and describes a visit to some of the detainee camps and prisons:

> It was pouring with rain. I'll never forget those detainee camps. Hundreds and hundreds of African men huddled together in groups in large wire netting compounds, with grey blankets held tightly round their bodies. The grey sky, the grey faces and the grey blankets made them all look like L. S. Lowry's paintings, almost 'stick' men, unhappy and lost. I found it hard to take. They were men. What were they feeling and thinking? Guards with guns were at every entrance.[8]

Christians in many countries have tried to bring assistance to refugees, victims of disasters and those condemned to a life of poverty. They have also tried to prod governments into doing more to help. Many people have been given relief and renewed hope. Through this work Christians of different denominations have discovered a unity in service. They have recognised also that there can be no restriction on compassion and that aid should not be used to recruit converts for the church. The criterion for receiving help is need, not creed. After one earthquake disaster, Christian Aid gave money to help the villagers rebuild their mosque. As Janet Lacey wrote, 'Christian Aid is not just another charity but should be a reconciling factor in the Church and the world, between nationality, classes and between Christian and non-Christian.'[9] Those Christians, however, who see the urgent need of the world's poor are likely to be impatient with the priorities of the institutional churches and their reluctance to let their prayers for unity be translated into effective action.

Campaigning to Change Society

Relief of those in need – sometimes called 'ambulance-work' – is not enough. Many Christians recognise the importance of changing the conditions in society that cause the distress. Critics complain of what they call 'meddling' in politics. The Christian, however, believes that Jesus came that people 'might have life and have it to the full' (John 10:10). The church, therefore, is concerned with social conditions as well as with spiritual matters. The belief that every single person is precious in God's sight has inspired some Christians to work for social changes such as the abolition of slavery, an end to the exploitation of factory workers, the removal of racial discrimination and apartheid, and the prevention of cruelty to and the sexual abuse of women and children.

Abolition of Slavery

The name forever associated with the campaign to abolish slavery is William Wilberforce (1759–1833), a member of the Clapham Sect, who became a member of Parliament in 1780 – the same year as the future Prime Minister William Pitt the Younger, who was a friend of Wilberforce, entered Parliament. Wilberforce was not the first to denounce slavery. The Quakers had already protested against it. Then Granville Sharp (1735–1813) formed the Abolition Society, and Thomas Clarkson (1760–1846) several times risked his life collecting evidence of the terrible conditions in which the trade was carried on.

Ships set out from England to Africa, loaded with cheap cotton goods which were bartered for slaves. The slaves were then transported to America and sold for raw cotton, sugar and tobacco, which was shipped back to England. The conditions in the ships were often terrible. The men and women were herded together in much discomfort and many died in the course of making the so-called 'middle passage'. Even with these losses, the trade was profitable and in 1771, for example, 50,000 slaves were transported.

William Wilberforce and his colleagues knew the strength of the vested interests which they had to tackle and the indifference of public opinion. Their only weapon was the appeal to conscience. Wilberforce ended a three-and-a-half-hour speech in the House of Commons with these words, 'What is there in this life that should make any man contradict the dictates of his conscience, the principles of justice and the laws of God?'[10] The campaigners used every means possible to arouse public feeling. They held meetings, issued pamphlets and even had anti-slavery slogans painted on their soup bowls. As their guests ate their soup, they would gradually discern the words 'Abolish all slavery' or find a picture of a black man with the words, 'A man and a brother'.

Victory came on 23 February 1807 when, by a very large majority, the House of Commons declared the slave trade illegal. In 1833 all slavery was abolished throughout the British Empire. In the United States of America, where both black rebellions and religious revivals helped create opposition to slavery, it was only completely abolished after the Civil War (1861–5).

Factory Reform

Members of the Clapham Sect were also concerned about the underprivileged in Britain, but the most famous campaigner was the Seventh Earl of Shaftesbury (1801–85), known as Lord Ashley from 1811 to 1851. He campaigned on many issues. He favoured the political emancipation of Roman Catholics. He secured the passage of the Lunacy Act of 1845, which for the first time treated the insane as a 'person of unsound mind', rather than as a social outcast. He led the campaign to shorten the hours worked by those in the textile mills to ten per day. By the Mines Act, Ashley, who had found boys as young as five working in the mines, excluded all women and girls and boys under thirteen from work in coal mines. He urged the government to sponsor low-cost housing for urban workers. For thirty-nine years he was President of the Ragged Schools Union, which during that time provided education for some 300,000 poor children. He was, however, accused of neglecting the conditions of rural workers, including those on his own estate.

The concern for the plight of workers continues to exercise the Christian conscience. Christians have been active in campaigns about working conditions in Asia, for example, on tea plantations and in sports and toy factories. Christian Aid has also drawn attention to the effect making carpets for the Western market has on the eyesight of children who have to do the work.

The Basis for Social Action

While the Evangelicals' concern for the social problems of their day was mainly practical and philanthropic, trying to effect change through Acts of Parliament and by giving relief to those in need, the response of the Church of England's High Church party, known as the Tractarians or Oxford Movement, was more theological. Their answer was a high doctrine of the church and the provision of priests to work in slum areas.

The Christian Socialists

A third approach was articulated by a group who came to be known as Christian Socialists, who were led by F. D. Maurice (1805–72), who was Professor of Theology at Kings College, London, from 1846 until he was dismissed when his *Theological Essays* (1853) provoked a crisis because he questioned the teaching of eternal damnation. Maurice was interested in the application of Christian principles to social reform. Maurice said that Christ came not to establish a religious sect, but a kingdom which should embrace all people. In such a kingdom there could be no class-distinctions, no rich or poor and no oppressor or oppressed. This approach has had a lasting influence on the Anglican church and on other churches, for example through William Temple and his contribution to the Life and Work Movement, which as we have seen, became part of the World Council of Churches.

The Social Gospel Movement

Maurice's writings also influenced the leaders of the 'Social Gospel' movement in the USA. In part this Protestant movement reiterated the dream which had brought Independents, Puritans and Quakers to North America who hoped to build an ideal Christian society in the New World. They also were influenced by the writings of the German theologian Albrecht Ritschl.[11]

One of the Social Gospel's most influential leaders was Washington Gladden (1836–1918), who for thirty-six years was a Congregational pastor in Columbus, Ohio. He campaigned for applied Christianity. The best-known advocate of the Social Gospel was Walter Rauschenbusch (1861–1918). He was born in the USA of German ancestry. His parents had come as refugees to the USA after the defeat of liberalism in Germany in the revolutionary year of 1848. After some pastoral work in New York, Rauschenbusch returned as a teacher to Rochester Theological Seminary, where he had studied. His *Christianity and the Social Crisis* (1907) brought him nation-wide recognition.

In tune with the evolutionary mood of the age, the supporters of the Social Gospel hoped that society could be changed into a closer likeness of God's kingdom. The hymn 'God is working his purpose out' by A. C. Ainger (1814–1919), a teacher at Eton, sums up this mood of optimistic endeavour with its line, 'Nearer and nearer draws the time, the time that shall surely be . . .' The third verse continues:

What can we do to work God's work, to prosper and increase
the brotherhood of all mankind, the reign of the Prince of Peace?
What can we do to hasten the time, the time that shall surely be,
When the earth shall be filled with glory of God
as the waters cover the sea?[12]

Christian Pragmatism

Such confidence was shattered in Europe by the slaughter in the trenches during the First World War. The liberal optimism, which largely had abandoned the concept of sin and believed that the world could be put right by education and social and economic reform, was challenged by Karl Barth, Emil Brunner (1889–1966) and other continental European theologians. In the English-speaking world the writings of the American Reinhold Niebuhr (1892–1971), especially his *Moral Man and*

Immoral Society (1932), were more influential. He reinstated the doctrine of original sin and tried to expound a 'vital prophetic Christianity' or 'Christian pragmatism' also sometimes called 'Christian realism'. This was Christian in the sense that the law of love on the one hand and the Christian awareness of the law of self-love as an ubiquitous and persistent force describe the upper and lower limits of a social order in a sinful world. It was pragmatic in the sense that it becomes increasingly aware of the contingent circumstances of history which determine how much or how little it is necessary to emphasise' such regulative principles as justice, equality and liberty.

Life and Work

At the 1925 Stockholm Life and Work conference, there was a clear division between the British and American idealism and optimism that thought the church's task was to inspire humanity to build the kingdom of God – the Social Gospel approach – and the more pessimistic continental view which saw a clear distinction between the values of the world and the message of the gospel, which was as much a judgment on human sin as a message of God's grace. The Stockholm conference made a long list of social evils, but made no social or economic structural analysis.

The next Life and Work conference, which was held at Oxford in 1937, was dominated by the economic depression and the mass unemployment that it caused. Nearly three-quarters of the delegates were from the USA and the British Commonwealth. The conference, under the leadership of J. H. Oldham (1874–1969), who devoted much of his life to the ecumenical movement, had been well prepared for and the valuable papers were published as *The Church and Its Function in Society*. The general tone of the Oxford conference was 'Christian realism', although perhaps not enough attention was paid to the dangers of Hitler's Nazi Germany.

The World Council of Churches

The sufferings of the Second World War and the spread of communism served to accentuate the note of sober realism in the social attitudes of the ecumenical movement. There was an emphasis in Europe on rebuilding shattered societies and helping refugees and displaced persons. The first assembly of the World Council of Churches, with representatives from 147 churches (there are now over 300 member churches) was held at Amsterdam in 1948. It was overshadowed by the Cold War, although it avoided lining up behind either capitalism or communism as an economic system.

The second assembly was held at Evanston, Illinois, in 1954 and was notable for a report on 'The Church amid Racial and Ethnic Tensions'. Following the meeting a study of Rapid Social Change was initiated, which continued until the next assembly held in New Delhi in 1961.

In the 1960s there was a new mood of optimism, although this was soon dispelled by the growing threat of nuclear war and by economic instability. As African and Asian Christians came to share the leadership of the world church, the concerns of the developing world and the call for economic justice rather than relief came to the fore. The Papal Encyclical *Populorum Progressio* of 1967 had spoken of economic development as the new name for peace. The 1968 Uppsala assembly regarded this as too optimistic and felt that social transformation within Third World countries was more important than the transfer of resources from the industrialised world to the developing world. Racist issues also were prominent and following the assembly the controversial Programme to Combat Racism was established. The Uppsala assembly was also the prelude to the development of contextual theologies, such as black, feminist and liberation theologies, which have been influential in WCC circles. After 1968, there were also changes to the Churches' Commission on International Affairs, which now came to express a radical Third World perspective, often non-aligned or 'anti-Western' on international issues and with a pacifist tendency.

Love Your Neighbour

Following the 1975 Nairobi assembly, at which there were sharp disagreements about the Christian attitude to people of other faiths, the phrase 'A Just Participatory and Sustainable Society' provided the framework for discussion of social ethics. At other conferences in Bucharest and Massachusetts, attention focused on scientific and technological developments. Criticism was voiced of transnational companies and their effects on developing economies.

The 1983 Vancouver assembly is remembered for the high quality of its worship, but the reports were thin and showed a certain utopian naivety. The same could be said of the 1991 Canberra assembly which was overshadowed by the Gulf War.

In the 1990s, the threat of nuclear war has receded, but horrific violence is still evident in many parts of the world – indeed it is reckoned that some eighteen million people have died in wars and civil wars from 1945 to 1995. The west European churches have been concerned to re-establish links with the churches of eastern Europe. Feminist and ecological issues have gained prominence, as well the injustice of continuing Western economic dominance and cultural imperialism. The World Council of Churches has had serious financial difficulties that have led to cut-backs in its work. It is probable that few members of local congregations feel involved in the life of the WCC. Many Christians in North America and Europe feel alienated from the Third World ideology that seems to dominate WCC thinking, although perhaps this reflects the failure of those Christians to acknowledge the economic exploitation and racism of Europe and North America.

There have been a variety of criticisms of the World Council of Churches' social teaching and programmes. In part this is inevitable given the varied make up of the WCC. Ronald Preston, for many years Professor of Social and Pastoral Theology at Manchester University, has identified five main forms of criticism.

The first is that the World Council of Churches is unrepresentative and, while quick to criticise the 'First World', excuses abuses of human rights in the 'Third World'. The second criticism, from the so-called 'New Right', defends free market forces and objects to the church meddling with politics. Similar attacks were made on the Church of England's report *Faith in the City* (1985), which was criticised by some for blaming crime and delinquency on bad social and economic conditions, rather than on the individual's moral failure. Other criticisms of the WCC come from those who uphold a separation of church and state, whereas a fourth group is utopian and regards the WCC as too ready to compromise with political powers. The fifth criticism, which is Preston's own, is that the WCC is not realistic enough and does not sufficiently analyse the complexities of social and political decisions.[13] Preston's criticism may be fair, but it highlights the difficult question of how religious bodies can influence world affairs.

Roman Catholic Social Teaching

Throughout the nineteenth century, the Roman Catholic church seemed like an embattled fortress, trying to resist the acids of the French Revolution, nationalism and industrialisation. Leo XII's encyclical *Rerum Novarum* (1891) caused a surprise by backing trade unions. The encyclical also stressed the Natural Law. *Quadragesimo Anno* (1931) introduced the notion of subsidiarity, which implies that decisions should be made at the lowest possible level. This has recently been the subject of discussion in the European Community. The encyclical also distinguished 'moderate' socialism from communism.

Vatican II and subsequent documents have addressed social issues in a greater spirit of dialogue with the modern world. *Pacem in Terris* (1963) allowed for the possibility of Marxism containing elements that are positive and deserving of approval. *Populorum Progressio* (1967) emphasised the urgent need for economic development in the Third World. Pope John Paul II's *Laborem Exercens* (1981) endorsed the Marxist emphasis on the primacy of labour among the factors of production and encouraged schemes whereby workers became part-owners of the places where they work. *Sollicitudo Rei Socialis* (1987) recognised that structural sin, that is to say, the structures of society, as well as individual decisions, can be wrong. *Quadragesimo Anno* for the first time mentioned ecological issues. The Pope has repeatedly also called for peace and disarmament.

Although Pope John Paul II has made clear his disagreement with the revolutionary approach of liberation theologians, Catholic social teaching is more radical than the popular opinion of the present Pope, based on his views about birth control and sexual morality, might suggest. They are a challenge to many of the presuppositions of those in the West, and indeed to members of Catholic parties in Europe and Latin America, which tend to be right wing. Again, however, the question is, how does the church exercise an influence? There are deeper questions about the possibility of the application of ethical values to political and economic decisions and about how Christians should interpret the prayer 'Thy kingdom come on earth as it is in heaven'.

A Global Ethic

Gradually Christians are recognising that ethical concern about world society is not a monopoly of the churches. Indeed, if the critical issues of today are to be tackled, then all people of faith and good will need to act together.

There continues, however, to be some pessimism as to whether ethical values can be applied to political life. In his recent *A Global Ethic for Global Politics and Economics* (1997), Hans Küng argues for the relevance of ethical considerations. Further, in his advocacy of *The Declaration Towards a Global Ethic*, of which he was the main author and which was adopted at the Parliament of the World's Religions in Chicago in 1993, Küng has stressed the need for the world religions to articulate the ethical values which they share. There will, Küng has said, be 'no human life together without a world ethic for the nations',[14] and that requires peace among the religions, which itself requires dialogue among the religions.

My own hope is that the religions of the world will come

together to affirm the spiritual and moral values on which a new world society needs to be based. Unless people and nations can learn to co-operate, there will be repetitions of the bitter violence witnessed in former Yugoslavia. The great issues that face world society, such as the poverty and hunger of millions, the endemic violence, the drug trade, or the abuse of the environment – to name only a selection of key concerns – all have a spiritual and moral dimension. Together with the technical issues, the key question is one of a will to act which depends upon the recognition of human responsibility for one another. The ecumenical and interfaith movements are not to be seen as ends in themselves, but as a way by which people of faith and good will can work together for a society based on ethical values. People of faith can help to shape public opinion and so influence political decisions. Perhaps most important of all, they affirm the hope that change is possible and that 'God's will' is to be done on earth.

An attractive book on the Christian way of life is Donald Nicholl, *Holiness* (Darton, Longman and Todd, 1981).
Robert Bruce McLaren, *Christian Ethics* (Prentice-Hall, 1994), is a good introductory guide to the subject.
On Christian responsibility in society, a classic is Reinhold Niebuhr, *Moral Man and Immoral Society* (1932). Hans Küng's *Global Responsibility* (SCM Press, 1991), deals with similar issues in a world context.

9

'Go, Post a Lookout'

The prophet Isaiah was told by the Lord to post a lookout and when he asked the watchman what he saw, the reply was, 'Morning is coming, but also the night' (Isa. 21:6, 11).

Looking into the future is a risky business and the watchman was sensible to hedge his bets! There are many predictions of environmental disaster, increasing famines, further violence and ethnic cleansing, not unlike the warnings of Jesus that 'Nation will rise against nation, and kingdom against kingdom. There will be earthquakes in various places, and famines. These are the beginning of birth-pains' (Mark 13:8). There are also signs of a new dawn, as people of faith are renewed in their spiritual life and engage more actively with the problems and suffering of the world. This will be the focus of this final chapter.

This, however, should not obscure the personal strength and encouragement that the individual believer finds in following Christ. Discipleship is costly but the new life, which has the quality of eternity, gives meaning and inner peace to daily life. Jesus said, 'If anyone would come after me, he must deny himself and take up his cross daily and follow me. For whoever wants to save his life will lose it, but whoever loses his life for me will save it' (Luke 9:23). The 'daily', which is only in Luke, is significant. I have stressed the disciple's personal trust in God's forgiving love which may come as an unforgettable experience, but the knowledge of this and the commitment that flows from it needs to be renewed each day.

Is Church Membership Declining?

'The British believe in . . . not putting bums on pews' was the headline of a recent article in a Sunday newspaper in 1997.[1] Based on a comprehensive survey, the article suggested that in the past twenty years, regular adult attendance at church had fallen from nearly eleven per cent to just over eight per cent of the population – a drop of about one million people. The Blyth Valley in Northumberland had the lowest figure for church attendance. There, ninety-seven per cent of the population do not attend church regularly, whereas in the Ribble Valley in Lancashire twenty-six per cent of the population do attend regularly.

In contrast to the message that the newspaper draws from the figures, it has been argued in some quarters that in fact more people attend church than did twenty years ago, but that they attend less regularly. This is because the pattern of life on a Sunday has changed. Church services now have to compete with a wider range of activities. Many shops are open, professional and amateur sport takes place on a large scale, and families travel to see relations or for recreational purposes. In the small villages in Oxfordshire where I am vicar, I count regular attendees as those who come at least once a month.

The situation may not be as grim as the newspaper article suggests. Even so, there is much to suggest a decline in participation in the institutional church across much of Europe, although in other areas of the world, such as Africa, South Korea or China, church membership is growing. Several commentators, however, note that even where there is a decline in church attendance, the number of people who say they believe in God remains high.

Is the problem then with the way the churches articulate their beliefs, or with the patterns of church worship, or are the reasons sociological? Some people complain that the churches seem uncertain about their beliefs and moral teaching and seem to adapt them to current fashions, whereas others think there is a need for radical rethinking. A lot of changes to the forms of worship have taken place. Liturgies have become more

imaginative and relaxed. Many new hymns have been written
and the style of music in several churches is more contemporary. Yet, others deplore these changes and suggest that the
beauty and awe of traditional worship has been thrown away.
Perhaps the decline is because the pattern of life has changed.
People are more mobile. In a village the church may still be
one of the centres of community life, whereas in urban areas
when people move, they may find it hard to relate to a new
church.

My Hopes for the Church

I sometimes reflect on my dreams for the church into which I
was ordained in the 1960s. It was to be a more united, more
open and more compassionate body, less interested in church
membership and institutional preservation, and more concerned to struggle for peace and to speak for and to bring
comfort to the marginalised. My disappointment is that the
church has been slow to change, reluctant to seek unity, afraid
to identify with the poor and hesitant about opening its doors
to spiritual explorers who may have questions about traditional
beliefs. Many in the Roman Catholic church, who have witnessed the retreat from the openness of the Second Vatican
Council, would echo my sense of disappointment.

After having spent a year with the Church of South India,
which had united Anglicans and Protestants of several denominations, I was enthusiastic about church unity. At the time of
my ordination discussions to unite the Church of England and
the Methodist Church were well advanced – even so, as I was
marrying a Methodist, the diocesan bishop refused permission
for us to have Communion at our wedding service. The plan to
unite the two churches failed to secure the support of two-thirds
of the members of the Church of England's ruling body.
Another attempt a few years later was also frustrated. A coming
together of those two churches might have encouraged further
union: it would have been a powerful witness and could have
stimulated many other necessary changes. In fact, for nearly

forty years the traditional elements in the Church of England have delayed progress on unity and the ordination of women and other matters. As a result an enormous amount of the church's energy, at least at the level of institutional decision-making, has been taken up by internal wrangles, rather than by active service of the community.

Having seen a little of the abject poverty of some people in India, on my return I quickly became involved in the work of Christian Aid and the beginnings of the World Development Movement, which campaigned on political matters relating to aid and trade. My hope was that the church would become a leading voice for economic and racial justice as well as for disarmament. The Church of England in its report *Faith in the City* and in other reports has shown considerable awareness of social problems and some Christians have taken effective and imaginative action to help those in need in Britain and abroad, through bodies such as Shelter, Crisis or Christian Aid. Yet the churches have hesitated really to identify with the poor or to release their accumulated wealth for the service of the needy. There have been several reports about the Christian attitude to nuclear weapons, but although some Christians were very active in the Campaign for Nuclear Disarmament, the churches remained at a distance from the campaign. The Church of England has not taken as radical a political and social stance as the Episcopal church in the USA. Again, whilst the church has been vocal in its opposition to legislation to restrict the rights of aliens who seek asylum in Britain, there was considerable opposition to the World Council of Churches Fund to Combat Racism. Uncertainty about the appropriate Christian attitude to other faiths has also meant that the church's welcome to members of other faiths who have settled in Britain has been hesitant. At times, the church has seemed defensively to want to hold on to its special role in British life.

John Robinson's provocative book *Honest to God* was published in 1963. It struck a chord with many thoughtful Christians, but although some academic theologians, who have become increasingly detached from parish life, have pursued this radical agenda, the churches to my mind have lacked the courage sufficiently to relate the gospel to contemporary thought. Laity keep their thoughts to themselves lest they upset the clergy and the clergy keep their doubts to themselves lest they disturb the laity. Despite the efforts of the Modern Church People's Union and 'Sea of Faith' conferences and other theologically radical groups, many questioning followers of Jesus have drifted away from church life, or at least from partici-pation in the church's decision-making forums, thus allowing undue influence to more traditional positions.

Despite the hopes I have had for the churches in Britain, I have to admit that the areas of church growth have in most cases been amongst the more conservative churches. This is seen in the growing strength of Evangelical churches and of the house church movement. There are perhaps several reasons for this growth. Evangelical churches emphasise personal experience of Jesus' forgiveness and of the presence of the Risen Christ in daily life. Usually, Evangelical churches are charac-terised by warm and close fellowship. Their teachings are clear and based on an uncritical and therefore apparently straight-forward way of reading the Bible. On most issues of personal morality, they uphold a strict and traditional pattern of behaviour.

The question, however, is whether despite the growth of conservative churches both in Europe and North America and in other parts of the world, and the likelihood that they will remain strong, they offer the key to the future in a world that is changing very quickly. I still hope that the church will become more open to intellectual enquiry, more willing to seek not only Christian unity but fellowship with other faiths and more closely engaged with the critical issues of today's world. I recognise that other Christians feel just as strongly that the opposite path is the one to follow. Indeed, the real division in the church of the future is likely to be not so much along denominational lines, but between so-called 'liberal' and 'conservative' Christ-ians. Before, however, we look at the questions of intellectual openness, fellowship with other faiths and social engagement, it will help to see why many thinkers picture the new century – it seems presumptuous to speculate about the new millennium

– as very different from the century that is drawing to a close.

A Changing World

There is a story that as Adam and Eve were driven from the Garden of Eden, Adam turned to his wife and said, 'Dear, we live in an age of transition.' Change is nothing new, but perhaps the speed of change is faster than ever before.

Father Bede Griffiths (1906–94), who established a Christian *ashram* in South India, in one of his last books wrote, 'The world today is on the verge of a new age and a new culture.'[2] He suggested that scientists are moving away from a mechanistic model of the universe which has dominated their thinking for more than two hundred years. Like those who advocate a creation-centred spirituality, Bede Griffiths welcomes a more holistic approach, which sees the universe as a co-ordinated and integrated whole. Indeed, the *Gaia* (Greek for the earth) theory sees the planet as a living entity in which all life is interdependent. Some psychological studies are also moving beyond a concentration on the ego and discovering a new spiritual depth.

Other writers draw attention to a new understanding of human knowledge. It is never absolute but conditioned historically by the context of the person who knows. Further, our knowledge is interpreted knowledge. Reality speaks to each person with the language he or she gives it. We are not in a position to make ultimate or unconditioned statements. The questions that we ask and how we pose them partly determine the answers at which we arrive. All reality is perceived and spoken of from a cultural, class or sexual perspective. Any statement is from a particular point of view. This does not, however, mean, in my view, that there is no reality and that all so-called 'knowledge' is only a human construct. But it calls in question any claim to absolute and eternal, divinely revealed truths.

Politically and economically the world is moving on from its domination by European powers and more recently by the USA. At the same time, nation states are slowly recognising their interdependence and that great issues, such as global warming, poverty, drug abuse and international terrorism cannot be dealt with by one country on its own. Global companies and global communications are also limiting the power of nation states. There has also been large-scale human migration, so that now more societies are multi-ethnic and multi-faith.

The Nature of Belief

New understandings of the nature of human knowledge question the possibility of making statements that are absolutely true. Whereas up to the nineteenth century, and still in some quarters today, statements about reality were thought of as absolute, static and exclusively true or false, today it is recognised that they are always partial and historically conditioned. The idea that there are absolute or unchanging beliefs, on which the religious certainty of conservative Christians is based, is open to question. We have seen that most New Testament scholars recognise that the gospels are documents shaped by their historical context. They reflect the concerns of the evangelists and the Christian communities to which they belonged as well as the interests of those who handed on the traditions about what Jesus said and did. The same is true of the creeds of the church. Although their use in worship can seem to give them a pre-eminent status, they too, as we have seen, are historically conditioned. Their production, for example, was partly occasioned by the wish of emperors that Christianity could bind together the peoples over whom they reigned.

The creeds, or other doctrinal formulae, should not be used as a test to determine whether a person can belong to the church. As long ago as 1938, the report *Doctrine in the Church of England* said:

The general acceptance of formulations drawn up in another age and another context of thought gives rise to special problems, especially when some of the phrases used are indisputably symbolic and no clear distinction is drawn, or (perhaps) can be drawn, between these and others . . . The word 'symbolic' is ambiguous. Statements affirming particular facts may be found to have value as pictorial expressions of spiritual truths, even though the supposed facts themselves did not actually happen.

The Report also says that 'assent to formularies and the use of liturgical language in public worship should be understood as signifying general acceptance without implying detailed assent to every phrase or proposition thus employed'.[3]

Further, truth is limited by language. Every description of reality is partial, because although reality may be observed from many perspectives, language can express only one thing at a time. This suggests, for example, that there is never one right reading of a text. It is more like a work of art, perhaps particularly a statue which can be observed from different perspectives. Even more is this the case in our thought about God. The recognition of the limits of language and human knowledge when we speak about the divine is at the same time an affirmation of the mystery of God. It is, as the Indian theologian Stanley Samartha says, 'the homage which the finite mind pays to the inexhaustibility of the infinite'.[4]

In the fourth century, the Greek father St Gregory of Nazianzus wrote a poem which expresses the limitations of language before the Mystery of God:

By what name shall I call upon you,
who are beyond all name!
You, the Beyond-all, what name shall I give you?
What hymn can sing your praises, what word tell of you?
No mind can probe your secret, nor intelligence comprehend
you.

From you proceeds all that is spoken: but you are beyond all
speech.
From you stems all that is thought, but you are beyond all
thought.

All things proclaim you – the mute and those with power of

speech.
All things join to celebrate you, the unconscious and that
which is conscious.

You are the end of all longings and of all silent aspiration
You are the end of the groanings of your entire creation.
Those who know to interpret your world unite to sing your
praises.

You are both all things and none: not a part yet not the
whole.
All names are given to you and yet none can comprehend you.
How shall I name you then, O you, the Beyond-all name?[5]

The Experience of God

The experience of God is always greater than human understanding. Confidence rests in that experience, not in attempted human descriptions of it. This is why those who value a mystical approach can combine the deep assurance of faith with intellectual openness. The Bible, in a similar way, as the Word of God is secondary to the Word or Logos who became flesh in Jesus Christ. The Bible, like the creeds, points beyond itself to a living relationship with God in Christ. This is why I began this book with some account of personal spiritual journeys.

There is probably no way to argue for the truth of spiritual experience, except perhaps in the change that such experience may effect in a person's life. There are those who think that a major shift in human consciousness is taking place, one aspect of which is an emphasis on spiritual experience rather than intellectual truths about religion. To some, the church may seem to purvey doctrines and dogmas rather than the path to authentic encounter with the divine. This may be why belief in God remains high whilst active participation in the life of the church declines. This may also be one reason for the interest in Western societies in new religious and spiritual movements. They claim to teach a way to experience the divine. In the churches also the renewed emphasis on contemplative meditation or 'centring prayer' reflects the desire to discover and set free the Spiritual Power which dwells in the heart of every person.

The emphasis on spiritual experience is not without its difficulties and there can be dangerous aberrations, especially when the spiritual is confused with the psychic. Personal spiritual experience should be balanced by reference to a community of faith and its traditions and to scripture. Its authenticity is seen in a life of love and service.

My immediate point, however, is that the emphasis on spiritual experience allows both confidence and openness. The danger of fundamentalism is that it rejects the view that all truths are historically conditioned and gives an absolute authority to a particular truth. It cannot allow for other truths. Similarly, fundamentalism rejects the idea of symbolism and myth and sees a particular religious story as true in an absolute sense. Such a position allows for no compromise or willingness to accept the validity of other spiritual traditions. Fundamentalists cannot theoretically accept a pluralist society in which equal status is accorded to people who belong to different religions. Fundamentalists are committed, by the logic of their belief, to work for the victory of their views. Many do so by honest democratic persuasion, but others seek to coerce those who disagree with them. This is why fundamentalism is so dangerous in a world where both many national societies are becoming multi-ethnic and multi-faith and the lives of all people are becoming increasingly interdependent.

A faith community in which spiritual experience is central can be open to those who are questioning or who have doubts. It becomes a pilgrim community in which people grow by sharing their experiences and insights.

Such a community can also relate to other communities of faith. Rabindranath Tagore (1861–1941), the Indian poet and writer, said on one occasion that 'to reject any part of humanity's religious experience is to reject truth'.[6] This is not to say that all religious claims are the same nor equally valid. People may have a true experience of the divine but may misinterpret its significance. Interfaith dialogue is not just a matter of understanding the other, it is a grappling together towards a deeper apprehension of the divine, in which different insights correct and enrich each other.

The assumption, however, is that other traditions of faiths are genuine responses to the reality of the Transcendent. Yet this is an assumption that many Christians are still reluctant to make. They may be willing to work with people of other faiths on practical matters and to ensure good religious community relations, but because they do not accept the spiritual authenticity of other traditions they are unwilling to come together with them in prayer. This, however, is to impoverish attempts to bring spiritual and moral values to bear on both national and world society, because practical action needs to flow from the life of the spirit.

Prayer and Action

In the twentieth century, several religious teachers have stressed the interconnectedness of the life of prayer and contemplation and that of practical action. Mahatma Gandhi (1869–1948) said that 'the only way to find God is to see him in his creation and to be one with it. This can only be done by the service of all, *sarvodaya*. I am part and parcel of the whole and I cannot find him apart from the rest of humanity . . . If I could persuade myself that I could find him in a Himalayan cave, I would proceed there immediately. But I know that I cannot find him apart from humanity.'[7] The Catholic contemplative Thomas Merton (1915–68) also saw the inextricable link between prayer and action. The practice of solitude, he wrote, brought 'a deepening awareness that the world needs to struggle against alienation. True solitude is deeply aware of the world's needs. It does not hold the world at arm's length.'[8] In a paper given at Bangkok, on the day of his death, Merton said that 'the monk is essentially someone who takes up a critical attitude towards the contemporary world and its structures'.[9]

It is in waiting in the presence of God that the evil and cruelty of the world becomes clear. The vision of the world as God intends it to be and the reality of suffering in so many people's lives should result in commitment to serve the poor and to struggle for justice. Equally, the person who immerses himself or herself in such action and struggle needs the inner resources of a spiritual life.

Spiritual life and concerned action belong together. Both can help Christians into a closer relationship with people of other faiths and of good will. Just as the emphasis on spiritual experience moves a person beyond differences of ritual and belief, so the urgency of the need to end war and violence and injustice, to bring relief to the hungry, to stand with those who are exploited and to seek to protect the environment unites Christians with people of other faiths. The American theologian Paul Knitter has said that 'concern for the widespread suffering that grips humanity and threatens the planet can and must be the "common cause" for all religions'.[10]

Identification with the Poor

Where the church is identified with the poor, and is active in the struggle for peace and justice, it does not have to worry about questions of relevance. It may attract opposition, especially for supposedly 'meddling in politics', but it is certainly not on the margin.

Don Samuel

The work of Bishop Samuel Ruiz Garcia, Bishop of San Cristóbal de Las Casas in Chiapas in Mexico may be taken as an example of this involvement. Don Samuel, as he is known to everyone, was the first of five children of a family of modest means from Irapuato in the state of Guanajuato. He was ordained in 1949 and was made a bishop by Pope John XXIII who sent him to San Cristóbal. His training gave no hint of the identification with the poor that has been the hallmark of his ministry. His first pastoral letter was a denunciation of communism.

Early on, however, he made a decision to visit every town and village in his vast diocese, which encompassed the whole state of Chiapas – some 29,000 square miles. What shocked him most, as he travelled through the forests and up and down the mountains, was the poverty and abandonment in which the indigenous people lived. He tried to provide assistance, but came to see that this help was destructive of the indigenous culture. As he wrote later, 'We had only our own – ethnocentric and moralistic – criteria to judge customs. Without realising it, we were on the side of those who oppressed the indigenous.'[11]

The Second Vatican Council was a turning point for him as for so many other Catholics. By 1968, the bishops of Latin America were denouncing 'the institutionalised violence of the international monopolies and the international imperialism of money'.[12] At first the bishop had stayed in the big house when he visited a village, but later he stayed in the shacks of the poor. He became more and more aware of the oppression and exploitation of the indigenous people.

Don Samuel set out to incarnate the gospel in the cultures of the various communities. This meant that instead of using Spanish for everyone, each of five language groups had to be addressed in its own mother tongue. The number of catechists, who were now chosen by the local community, increased. Readings from the book of Exodus helped to make the people aware both of their oppression and of a desire for liberation. The diocese committed itself to accompany the people in their search for integral liberation and soon peasant organisations proliferated.

Don Samuel's concern for the poor was quickly met by the hostility of the rich landowners and of the government. The Vatican, which was seeking to improve the relations of the Catholic church with the Mexican government, was also critical. But Don Samuel was good at enlisting the support of international human rights bodies.

When, on New Year's day 1994, the Zapatista National Liberation Army's uprising took place, it was Don Samuel who became the mediator.

The problems of the Chiapas people, and indeed of Mexico,

are by no means solved, but it was clear to my wife Mary and me, when as part of the Peace Council we visited San Cristóbal in 1996, with what enormous respect and affection Don Samuel is regarded. The meeting of the Peace Council ended with the first interfaith service in the cathedral, which was crowded for the occasion. After the blessing, the Peace Councillors mingled with the congregation to light the candles which everyone had been given.

This is but one example. Better known is the struggle of Martin Luther King (1929–68) against racial discrimination in the USA, or Bishop Desmond Tutu's (b. 1931) vocal opposition to apartheid in South Africa. The respect that Desmond Tutu has gained is evident in his appointment to chair the Truth and Reconciliation Commission.

Where the church has a feeling of being out of touch and irrelevant, it is because it has not identified with crucial issues of the moment. Many individual Christians and Christian groups have been active in the search for peace, for equality of the sexes and for protection of the environment, yet it seems that seldom has the church, as a body, been the leader in these campaigns.

What Should be the Priorities for the Church?

What then seem to be the key issues on which one may hope to look to the church for a spiritual and moral lead? The Four Irrevocable Directives identified in the Declaration Toward A Global Ethic, which was drawn up at the 1993 Parliament of the World's Religions, may serve as a guide to this discussion. At the end of the Parliament, most members of the Assembly added their names to the Declaration. Leading Christians of many denominations were amongst those who signed, including Cardinal Joseph Bernardin of Chicago and the Rev Wesley Ariarajah, Assistant Secretary-General of the World Council of Churches. Christian contributors to the book *Yes to a Global Ethic* (1966) include Cardinal König, who was Archbishop of Vienna from 1956 to 1985; Dr Konrad Raiser,

General Secretary of the World Council of Churches; Patriarch Bartholomew I, the Ecumenical Patriarch of Constantinople; Dr George Carey, Archbishop of Canterbury; Cardinal Paulo Evaristo Arns, Archbishop of São Paulo; Bishop Desmond Tutu of Cape Town, who is a Nobel Peace Prize Winner; and Cardinal Bernadin.

The Declaration in its fuller form affirms that every human being should be treated humanely. The four directives are:

> *Commitment to a culture of non-violence and respect for life.*
> *Commitment to a culture of solidarity and a just economic order*
> *Commitment to a culture of tolerance and a life of truthfulness*
> *Commitment to a culture of equal rights and partnership between men and women.*

Non-Violence

The first directive is controversial, as the dominant tradition in the church has not been pacifist. As we have seen[13] arguments were developed that allowed Christians to take part in a just war. Many Christians, however, who were not pacifist, opposed the possible use of nuclear weapons and also opposed threats to use such weapons. It was argued that the devastation such weapons would cause outweighed the dangers of a cruel dictatorship, which they might prevent. Many Christians were active in campaigns to oppose nuclear weapons, although I personally was sad that this never became the position adopted by the Church of England.

The statement of the Global Ethic seemed to go too far for some Christians. Did it rule out the use of force by a United Nations peace-keeping body? The Declaration was in fact carefully nuanced. It recognised that 'wherever there are humans there will be conflicts'.

Such conflicts, however, should be resolved without violence within a framework of justice. This is true for states as well as for individuals. Persons who hold political power must work within the framework of a just order and commit themselves to the most non-violent, peaceful solutions possible. And they should work for this within an international order of peace which itself has need of protection and defence against perpetrators of violence.[14]

The use of force is not ruled out. The commitment is to the most 'non-violent, peaceful solution possible' as well as to the establishment of an effective international order. Violence is not just the use of armed force. Economic exploitation is a form of oppression. The Declaration recognises the importance of justice and does not rule out resistance to tyranny, even in the last resort by violence. It is said, 'Wherever those ruling threaten to repress those ruled, wherever institutions threaten persons, and wherever might oppresses right, we are obliged to resist – whenever possible non-violently'.[15] It is also true that boycotts and economic embargoes are a form of violence and can cause considerable suffering.

Even if the commitment of the Declaration is not to complete pacifism, it is a major challenge to the behaviour of many nations. At present some forty wars are raging in the world and violence seems to be endemic. Major Western powers such as the USA and Great Britain have been willing in recent years to resort to war, although many Christians in the USA opposed the Gulf War. If the churches are to be outspoken in their call for non-violence and an international order, they may expect opposition, especially from those who want to hold on to the full sovereignty of the nation state.

Economic Justice

The commitment to a culture of solidarity and a just economic order may be even more challenging as it questions the standard of living to which many Christians in the West have grown accustomed. If the poorer nations are to improve their standard of living does this mean at least slower growth in the richer nations? If not, the strain on natural resources and the increasing pollution may be catastrophic. Another issue is 'Third World debt', and many Christians with others are campaigning through the Jubilee 2000 Coalition for the cancellation of unpayable debts by the poorest nations. Christians are also campaigning about intolerable working conditions in many developing nations. One of the worst forms of exploitation is the growing sex-tourism in some Asian countries.

Archbishop Paulo Evaristo Arns

In some parts of the world, the church is helping the poor to take control of their own future. In 1971, Archbishop Paulo Evaristo Arns of São Paulo launched a programme called 'Operation Periphery', which involved many people in helping to solve the problems of those who lived on the outskirts, 'the periphery', of the city. It led the Christians of São Paulo to get to know the millions of inhabitants who lived in poor housing and who had to travel perhaps five or more hours a day to get to their work. Those who lived on the periphery were helped to organise themselves into communities which could press for better education, better transportation and better health conditions, which meant provision of clean water, sewerage and garbage collections. This, says Paulo Evaristo Arns, led the inhabitants of these poor areas to see other needs of which they had not been conscious before.

> It soon became clear to all those involved that it was very dangerous to be poor. Not only were the poor more liable to disease and to the destruction of their homes by floods, but they were looked upon by society as being potential criminals. If something was stolen, the police arrested the poorest person in the vicinity. If there was a riot at a football game, the police beat the worst-dressed of the men. For this reason, the communities founded, in each neighbourhood, a centre for the Defence of Human Rights.[16]

The search for a just economic order is not only a matter of relief, it needs 'conscientisation', or making people aware of the oppression that they suffer or cause. It also requires political struggle.

Unemployment

The commitment to a culture of solidarity and economic justice is equally important in the so-called 'developed nations', where in many of them there is a growing gap between those who have a comfortable lifestyle and those who are deprived and marginalised. Patriarch Bartholomew I, in his response to the Global Ethic, underlined 'the tragedy of unemployment which plagues Europe today'. He wrote:

> It is obvious that neither moral counsel nor fragmented measures of socio-economic policies are enough to confront rising unemployment. The problem of unemployment compels us to re-examine the self-evident priorities in our society . . . We are trapped in the tyrannical need continually to increase productivity . . . Thus, the economy becomes independent of the needs of society.

The demand for profit, the Patriarch suggests, is at the expense of the quality of human life and relationships. An example of this is the reluctance of firms to encourage job-sharing. 'What', he asks, 'will be the political mandate that will convince humankind willingly and joyfully to sacrifice its impetuous need for consumption and its limitless demands for unquenchable productivity in order to rediscover the communion of life within the community of persons?'[17]

There needs to be a moral change which will demand new political and economic policies. Christian conviction has to be expressed in the struggle for a new pattern of society.

The Environment

The Patriarch also highlights the urgency of ecological issues. Much of the discussion of the first directive has concentrated on the issue of non-violence, but it also says that 'the lives of animals and plants . . . deserve protection, preservation and care'.[18] The church's record on this issue has been subject to criticism, and certainly modern European society has tended to exploit the natural world and to emphasise the gap between human and other forms of life. Some of this, however, is more a reflection of the Enlightenment than of biblical thinking. When, according to Genesis, God gave human beings dominion over the natural world, they were expected to exercise their rule in a way that reflects God's loving rule and care. Increasingly, Christians are giving attention to ecological issues. The Orthodox church, for example, has established the first day of September as a day of meditation and prayer to focus on the continuing ecological destruction of the planet. The church also convened an international conference in Crete, but as Patriarch Bartholomew says, 'our efforts will be meaningless if they remain fragmented'.[19] The demands of the world call upon Christians not only to act ecumenically but together with all people of faith and good will.

A Partnership Between Men and Women

The church's record on the fourth directive which calls for a commitment to a culture of equal rights and partnership between men and women has also been criticised. Much of the discussion in the Anglican communion has concentrated on the question of whether women should be ordained. As yet, the issue has hardly been publicly debated in the Roman Catholic and Orthodox churches.

Women theologians, especially in Asia and Africa, have drawn attention to Jesus' own willingness, despite the conventions of the time, to meet freely with women and to identify himself with the deprived. There is a call to the churches to put their own houses in order, but perhaps even more important to join with those who struggle for an equal partnership of men and women.

In many parts of the world, women are still oppressed, and in Western society sexism is still rampant. The contemporary American theologian Charlene Spretnak quotes figures which indicate that one in every three women in the USA will be raped during her lifetime, and that one woman is physically beaten every fourteen seconds in the USA. She also says that a

261

random survey of women in Los Angeles in 1986 found that sixty-two per cent had been sexually abused as children.[20] The churches have to challenge this abuse and the culture that underlies it.

The question of homosexuality is even more controversial. Yet despite the churches' traditional teaching on the subject, the demand to reject all forms of discrimination seems likely to lead to growing acceptance of different lifestyles and patterns of relationship, although this is already a divisive matter between conservative and more liberal Christians.

A new awareness of the feminine will also change ways of thinking and perhaps help a rediscovery of the inner life. There are questions about traditional language used in worship. Many churches now avoid the use of the word 'man' when human being is meant. I try to avoid the male personal pronoun in writing of God, but sometimes to do this makes a sentence rather clumsy.

The issues go deeper. Charlene Spretnak says that 'efforts radically to transform all institutions in a society must necessarily fall short if the deepest informing assumptions go unexamined'.[21] This she tries to do. She says:

> [The] social structures and attitudes in our society draw legitimacy from the central assumptions of Western religion and philosophy. Creativity in the universe, ultimate mystery, the divine – all are symbolised by the distant father-god, ruling in transcendence far above Earth's realm of blood, mud, birth and death. The goal of most Western spirituality has been to transcend nature and the flesh (which meant primarily man's escaping the 'lure' of woman's flesh). Western philosophy, following the Pythagoreans, identified man with mind, subjectivity, determinate form (substance) and potential transcendence. It has identified woman with body, passivity, indeterminate and disorderly form (process) and 'dumb' matter. Throughout the history of Western philosophy, three vital concerns of men raised in patriarchal culture continually appear: separateness, reactive (defensive) autonomy, and control.[22]

* * *

Since the mid-seventies, Charlene Spretnak says, a movement of spiritual renewal that honours nature, the female and the body has flourished. This 'Goddess spirituality', as it is often called, is evident in some New Age movements. Some Christians strongly object to talk about Mother Earth or calling God 'she', but others believe that this tradition, present in Celtic Christianity, needs to be rediscovered. It should help a recovery of the importance of ritual and symbolism, an embodied way of knowing the world, and a more intuitive approach to religious teaching. It will also foster a greater sense of the unity of all life and of our dependence on and relationship to the Earth.

Truthfulness

The third directive is a commitment to a culture of tolerance and a life of truthfulness. Discussion of this tends to concentrate on the media and the power of the mass media, which as it becomes increasingly global in its coverage, is becoming immense. Control of the media is concentrated in too few hands. There are other issues, such as the ethical dimension of scientific and medical advances, and issues of integrity in political and business life.

There are also significant questions for the churches about their own integrity. In some church circles, Christians are hesitant to raise difficult questions or to express their doubts. Many Christians have been 'shielded' from the fruits of biblical criticism. The question of integrity is also one about authority, power and control. The 1938 report *Doctrine in the Church of England* says that 'every individual ought to test his or her belief in practice and, so far as his or her ability and training allow, to think out his or her own belief and to distinguish between what has been accepted on authority only and what has been appropriated in thought or experience'.[23] Such an emphasis has to allow for variety of belief and view within the community.

Another test for the church is how far it can build an accepting fellowship where people can articulate their own experience of God in Christ. This again raises questions about the future organisation of the institutional church and whether it can or should maintain its present hierarchical structure where authority seems to come down from on high. At the Reformation some churches rejected this and many theologians acknowledge that the local church is a true church, but doctrines of authority and the adoption of some modern centralised styles of administration seem to give the lie to this.

Is the church a body with agreed beliefs guarded and maybe adjusted by a self-perpetuating hierarchy? This has been the dominant pattern in the largest churches, since, following the conversion of Constantine, Christianity became the religion of the Empire. If, however, instead of correct belief about God's self-revelation in Christ, experience of the living God present by the power of the Spirit in Jesus Christ is at the heart of Christian fellowship, then the Christian community becomes a circle of friends who strengthen each other in their search for deeper awareness of divine reality and love. In that search, the individual and the community are open to inspiration from many quarters, but inspiration that is tested by the mind of Christ and the common experience of the group. Leadership in such a community is shared.

The test of the authenticity of faith is the caring and loving quality of the life of the community, its service to others and its commitment to the struggle for justice and integrity of the whole creation.

To those who follow Christ in this way, the fortunes of the institutional church are of limited interest. What matters most is so to abide in Christ and for Christ to abide in the believer that the divine love may radiate the fellowship of believers and bring light to the world.

O Lord, let the Church be truly your collective body in the world today, the Christ-Community, guided by You, filled with your Spirit, loving and serving men and women as you did when you lived our human life.

Help the Church to give itself for the world so that men and women may have the priceless treasure of your grace and love, O Lord of the Church, O Saviour of the world.[24]

Books which give a sense of a new age include Bede Griffiths, *A New Vision of Reality* (Collins, 1989); Leonard Swidler, *The Meaning of Life at the Edge of the Third Millennium* (Paulist Press, 1992); Charlene Spretnak, *States of Grace* (HarperCollins, 1991); Keith Ward, *A Vision to Pursue* (SCM Press, 1991); and Hans Küng, *Theology for the Third Millennium* (HarperCollins, 1991), and *Global Responsibility*, to which reference has already been made.

Notes

Chapter 1 A Life-Changing Encounter

1. Christian Aid Leaflet.
2. *The Oxford Book of Prayer*, ed. George Appleton (Oxford University Press, 1985), pp. 296–7.
3. Ibid. p. 175.
4. Augustine, *Confessions*, English trans. Henry Chadwick (Oxford, 1991), p. 73.
5. Ibid. pp. 152–53.
6. Quoted from *Encyclopaedia Britannica*, 15th edn, vol. 11, p. 89.
7. *Hymns and Psalms*, 706.
8. Ibid., 744.
9. Quoted from B. H. Streeter and A. J. Appasamy, *The Sadhu* (Macmillan, 1922), pp. 4–6.
10. *With Passion and Compassion*, eds. Virginia Fabella and Mercy Amba Oduyoye (Orbis, 1988), p. 22.
11. Chung Hyun Kyung, *Struggle to be the Sun Again* (Orbis, 1990; SCM Press, 1991), p. 56.
12. See below, p. 75.
13. See below, p. 78.
14. Karl Barth, *Theologische Fragen und Antworten* (Evangelischer Verlag, 1957), pp. 10ff., quoted by John Macquarrie, *Twentieth-century Religious Thought* (SCM Press, 1963), p. 321.

15. Paul Tillich, *The Shaking of the Foundations* (Penguin, 1962 edn), p. 163.
16. R. Gombrich, 'What Kind of Thing is Religion?', in *Shap Handbook on World Religions in Education* (Commission for Racial Equality, 1987).
17. From the hymn 'Teach me, my God and King', *Hymns and Psalms*, 803.

Chapter 2   Who is Jesus?

1. See Acts 10–11 and 15.
2. Mark 1:41, in the older manuscripts, says that Jesus was 'moved with anger' when he saw the man with leprosy – perhaps because of the ravages of the illness. Matthew and Luke omit the word and most translations follow those manuscripts which have 'moved with pity'. John 11:35 says that Jesus wept at the grave of his friend Lazarus.
3. *John Betjeman's Collected Poems*, ed. The Earl of Birkenhead (Guild Publishing, 1958; 4th edn, 1980), pp. 188–90.
4. For example, in the well-known hymn 'Rock of Ages' (*Hymns and Psalms*, 273), there are the lines: 'Not the labours of my hands/Can fulfil thy law's demands.'
5. *Antiquities* XIII. 10.6 (293).
6. E. P. Sanders, *Jesus and Judaism* (SCM Press, 1985), p. 292.
7. The dates of both Hillel and Philo are uncertain. Hillel flourished in the last half of the first century BCE and the first quarter of the first century CE. Philo was born between 15 and 10 BCE and died in the middle of the first century CE.
8. In Matthew and Luke, Jesus' reply is evasive.
9. From the hymn 'Ah, holy Jesus', by Robert Bridges: *Hymns and Psalms*, 164.
10. C. K. Barrett, *The Gospel According to St John* (SPCK, 1962), p. 460.

Notes

Chapter 3 Is He the Christ, the Son of God?

1. Alan F. Segal in *Jews and Christians Speak of Jesus*, ed. Arthur E Zannoni (Fortress Press, 1994), pp. 131–32.
2. Norman Solomon, *Judaism and World Religion* (Macmillan, 1991), pp. 131–69.
3. The references are Mark 1:1; 1:11; 5:8; 9:8; 14:62; and 15:39.
4. See also Romans 5:19.
5. Larry W. Hurtado, *One God One Lord* (SCM Press, 1988).
6. James G. Dunn, *The Parting of the Ways* (SCM Press, 1991), especially chapters 9–11.
7. Gregory of Nyssa, *On Not Three Gods*, 375 AD, in *The Christology of the Later Fathers* (SCM Press, 1954), p. 265.
8. Quoted by Geoffrey Parrinder in *Jesus in the Qur'an* (Sheldon Press, 1965), pp. 130–31.
9. Maimonides, *Commentary on the Mishnah* (1965), vol. 2, p. 225.
10. Maimonides, *The Guide for the Perplexed*, trans. S. Pines (Chicago, 1963), p. 111.
11. See further Daniel Cohn-Sherbok, *Judaism and Other Faiths* (St Martin's Press, New York, 1994) pp. 32–42; and David Novak, *The Image of the Non-Jew in Judaism* (Edwin Mellen Press, 1983); and chapter 1 of *Jewish-Christian Dialogue*, (Oxford University Press, 1989).
12. Hans Küng and Pinchas Lapide, *Brother or Lord* (Font/Collins, 1977), pp. 1–2.
13. Tony Bayfield in *Dialogue With A Difference*, eds. Tony Bayfield and Marcus Braybrooke (SCM Press, 1992), p. 27.
14. Raimundo Panikkar, 'Toward an Ecumenical Theandric Spirituality', *Journal of Ecumenical Studies*, vol. 5, 1968, pp. 522–33.
15. HB Archbishop Anastasios of Tirana in *Current Dialogue*, World Council of Churches, no. 26, June 1994, p. 46.
16. J. M. Creed, *The Divinity of Jesus Christ* (Cambridge University Press, 1938; Fontana/Collins 1964), p. 59.
17. H. P. Liddon, *The Divinity of Our Lord*, p. 466.
18. 'The great God of heaven is come down to earth' by H. E. Bramley (1833–1917), *English Hymnal* (Oxford University Press, 1906), 29.

19. See above, p. 34.
20. See above, p. 11.
21. Albert Schweitzer, *The Quest of the Historical Jesus* (1921), p. 63.
22. Ibid., 3rd edn, 1954, p. 401.
23. D. M. Baillie, *God Was in Christ* (1947, Faber and Faber, 1961 edn), p. 114.
24. *English Hymnal,* 157.
25. Baillie, *God Was in Christ,* p. 117.
26. John Robinson, *Honest to God* (SCM Press, 1963), pp. 74–75.
27. Paul Tillich, *Systematic Theology* (1951–63), vol. 2, p. 99.
28. M. K. Gandhi, *Christian Missions* (1941), p. 112.
29. The quotations are from the *Concise Oxford Dictionary,* 1991. Two well-known collections of essays which take this approach are *The Myth of God Incarnate,* ed. John Hick (SCM Press, 1977); and *The Myth of Christian Uniquenss,* eds. John Hick and Paul F. Knitter (SCM Press, 1987).
30. 'O Sacred head sore wounded', *Hymns and Psalms,* 176.
31. 'O sinner, raise the eye of faith', *English Hymnal,* 103.
32. In *With Passion and Compassion,* eds. Virginia Fabella and Mercy Amba Oduyoye (Orbis, 1988), p. 38.
33. 'Servant of God, remember', *English Hymnal,* 104.
34. P. Wernle, *The Beginnings of Christianity,* vol. 1, p. 109, quoted by Baillie, *God Was in Christ,* p. 172.
35. *Hymns and Psalms,* 180.
36. Ibid., p. 424.
37. *New Life* (Galliard, 1971), p. 27.
38. Robinson, *Honest to God,* p. 76.
39. Fabella and Oduyoye, *With Passion and Compassion,* p. 23.
40. Ibid. p. 31.
41. Ibid. p. 121.
42. Ibid. p. 186.
43. Ibid. p. 188.

Chapter 4   God

1. The traditional date of the creation in Jewish tradition is 5753 BCE. Older annotated editions of the Authorized Version of the Bible had the date 4004 BCE, which was a result of calculations by Archbishop Ussher (1581–1656), a seventeenth-century bishop of Armagh.

2. Zoroastrians often date Zoroaster, who is sometimes known as Zarathustra, to about 6000 BCE. Until recently critical scholars dated him to the sixth century BCE, but some scholars now put his date earlier to around 1200 BCE.

3. W. R. Matthews, *God in Christian Thought and Experience* (Nisbet, 1930), p. 41 referring to *Republic*, 378 BCE; *Timaeus*, 28a.

4. John Ferguson in *Man and his Gods*, ed. Geoffrey Parrinder (Hamlyn, 1971), p. 132.

5. Matthews, *God in Christian Thought and Experience*, p. 41.

6. See p. 1.

7. *In Memoriam A H H*, 1850, canto 56.

8. Charles Darwin, *The Origin of the Species by Means of Natural Selection* (1859; Penguin edn, 1985), p. 153.

9. Keith Ward, *God, Change and Necessity* (Oneworld Publications, 1996), pp. 87–88.

10. J. H. Newman, *Apologia* (1864; 1892 edn.), p. 335.

11. Oliver Quick, *Doctrines of the Creed* (Fontana/Collins, 1963), p. 46.

12. Elie Wiesel, *Night* (Orbis, 1987; SCM Press, 1988).

13. Johann-Baptist Metz, *Christen und Juden nach Auschwitz,* 1980).

14. Hans Jonas, 'The Concept of God', in *Out of the Whirlwind,* ed. A. H. Friedlander (Schocken, 1976), p. 475.

15. Arthur A. Cohen, *The Tremedum* (Crossroad Publishing, 1988), pp. 6–7.

16. Choan-Seng Song, *The Compassionate God* (SCM Press, 1982), p. 249.

17. Phillip Berryman, *Liberation Theology* (I. B. Tauris, 1987), p. 156.

18. Dorothee Sölle, 'God's Pain and Our Pain: How Theology has to Change after Auschwitz', in *Remembering for the Future* (Pergamon Press, 1988).

19. Chung Hyun Kyung, 'Come Holy Spirit, Renew the Whole Creation' (WCC Seventh Assembly, document PL 3.3).

20. Chung Hyun Kyung, *Struggle to be the Sun Again* (Orbis 1990; SCM Press, 1991), pp. 39, 47.

21. Quick, *Doctrines of the Creed*, p. 75.

22. W. H. Vanstone, *Love's Endeavour, Love's Expense* (Darton, Longman and Todd, 1977), pp. 119–20.

23. Richard Harries in *Dialogue With A Difference*, eds. Bayfield and Braybrooke, pp. 107–8.

24. *English Hymnal* (Oxford University Press, 1906), 80.

25. Rabi'a. Quoted by Margaret Smith in *An Introduction to Mysticism* (Sheldon Press, 1977), p. 66.

26. F. M. Dostoevsky, *The Brothers Karamazov* (Penguin, 1976), bk 5, ch. 4 pp. 284ff.

Chapter 5   Many Mansions

1. Justin Martyr, *Dialogue with Trypho*, 47:1–4.

2. Augustine, *Epistle* 82 quoted by John G. Gager, *The Origins of Anti-Semitism* (Oxford University Press, 1983), p. 189.

3. Pliny, *Epistles* X.96, quoted in *A New Eusebius*, ed. J. Stevenson (SPCK, 1957), p. 13.

4. Pliny, *Epistles* X.97. Ibid., p. 16.

5. *The Martyrdom of Polycarp*. Ibid., p. 21

6. See Bede, *Historia Ecclesiastica*, bk 2, sect. 1.

7. See p. 73.

8. Quoted by J. W. Bowden, *The Life and Pontificate of Gregory VII* (1840), vol. 2, bk 3, ch. 20.

9. Julian of Norwich, *Revelations of Divine Love* (the long text), ch. 86, Revelation 16.

10. Ibid., ch. 27, Revelation 13.

Chapter 6 A Changing Church in a Changing World

1. Quoted in *Encyclopaedia Britannica*, 15th edn, vol. 6, p. 953.
2. Ibid. p. 954.
3. See Luther's *Sermon of the Threefold Righteousness* (1518), and his statements during the Heidelberg Disputation.
4. Speech at the Diet of Worms, 18.4., 1521.
5. *Assertio septem sacramentorum adversus Martinum Lutherum.*
6. J. Foxe, *Acts and Monuments* (1877) vii, p. 550.
7. J. Strype, *Memorials of Thomas Cranmer* (1812 edn), vol. 1, p. 558.
8. J. Bunyan, *The Pilgrim's Progress* (pt 1, 1678; pt 2, 1684), 3rd edn. 1811, p. 424.
9. Appleton, *The Oxford Book of Prayer*, 237, p. 81.
10. Ibid. 254, p. 86.
11. Quoted by Kenneth Scott Latourette, *A History of Christianity* (Eyre and Spottiswoode, n.d.), p. 837.
12. From the Prayer of Humble Access in the *Book of Common Prayer*.
13. *The Works of Mr Richard Hooker*, eds. Keble, Church and Paget (1888), ii, p. 362.
14. Karl Marx, *A Contribution to the Critique of Hegel's Philosophy of Right* (1843–44), Introduction.
15. See below p. 233.
16. Latourette, *A History of Christianity*, p. 1308.
17. See further, Kenneth Cracknell, *Justice, Courtesy and Love* (Epworth Press, 1995).
18. See below, p. 237.
19. See below, p. 238.
20. See above, p. 16.
21. 'Declaration on the Relationship of the Church to Non-Christian Religions' in *The Documents of Vatican II*, ed. W. M. Abott SJ (Geoffrey Chapman, 1966), p. 660.
22. Quoted by Richard Hughes Seager, *The World's Parliament of Religions* (1995), p. 132.
23. Quoted in *The World's Parliament of Religions*, ed. John Henry Barrows (1893), p. 67.
24. See page p. 175.

Chapter 7   Love God

1. *Hymns and Praise*, 697.
2. Quoted in Appleton, *The Oxford Book of Prayer*, p. 231.
3. *The Alternative Service Book* (1980), p. 136.
4. *Book of Common Prayer 1662.*
5. *Songs of Praise* (Oxford University Press, 1931), p. 329.
6. See p. 108.
7. Gregory Dix, *The Shape of the Liturgy* (Dacre Press, 1945).
8. *Hymns and Praise*, 608.
9. *Hymns and Praise*, 593.
10. *New Oxford Book of Christian Verse*, ed. Donald Davie (Oxford University Press, 1981), p. 81.
11. *Songs of God's People* (Oxford University Press, 1988), 13.
12. *Hymns and Praise*, 626.
13. *Hymns and Praise*, 106.
14. The Trinitarian formula, in the opinion of many scholars, suggests that these are not the actual words of Jesus, but reflect the practice of the Church.
15. In *The Pastoral Care of Homosexual Persons*, 1986
16. See page 147.
17. *New Life* (Galliard, 1971), 85.

Chapter 8 Love Your Neighbour

1. In *Epistolam Joannis ad Parthos* (413 CE), tract. 7, sect. 8.
2. Quoted in *The Oxford Dictionary of World Religions*, ed. J. Bowker (Oxford University Press, 1997), p. 322.
3. Quoted by Lewis G. Regenstein in *Replenish the Earth* (SCM Press, 1991), p. 178.
4. Quoted in *The Oxford Dictionary of Quotations* (4th edn, 1992), with reference to the *Dictionary of National Biography.*
5. *Encyclopaedia Britannica*, 15th edn, vol. 6, p. 334.
6. Capitualry of 789 CE.
7. *The Fourth R: The Durham Report on Religious Education* (National Society and SPCK, 1970), pp. 67–72.
8. Janet Lacey, *A Cup Of Water: The Story of Christian Aid*

(Hodder and Stoughton, 1970), p. 128.
9. Ibid., p. 182.
10. R. Coupled, *Wilberforce* (new edn., 1945), p. 104.
11. See above, p. 75.
12. *Hymns and Praise*, 769.
13. Ronald H. Preston, *Confusions in Christian Social Ethics* (Eerdmans, 1994).
14. Hans Küng, *Global Responsibility* (Continuum, New York, and SCM Press, 1991). See also *A Global Ethic*, eds. Hans Küng and Karl-Josef Kuschel (SCM Press, 1993).

Chapter 9 'Go, Post a Lookout'

1. *The Observer*, 9 November 1997, p. 19, referring to *UK Religious Trends* (Christian Research/Paternoster Press, 1997).
2. Bede Griffiths, *A New Vision of Reality* (Collins, 1989), p. 9.
3. *Doctrine in the Church of England* (SPCK, 1938), pp. 37–39.
4. Stanley Samartha, *One Christ, Many Religions* (Orbis, 1991), p. 4.
5. The English trans. from the Greek is by Mary Rogers. The poem was quoted by Fr Murray Rogers in 'My Gift From Hindu Friends', in *World Faiths*, no. 99 (summer, 1976, p. 20).
6. Quoted in *Theologizing in India* (1981).
7. Quoted from *Harijan* by Bede Griffiths, in *Christian Ashram* (Darton, Longman and Todd, 1966), p. 127.
8. T. Merton, *Conjectures of a Guilty Bystander* (Sheldon Press, 1977), p. 58.
9. T. Merton, *The Asian Journal of Thomas Merton* (Sheldon Press, 1974), p. 329.
10. Paul Knitter, *One Earth, Many Religions* (Orbis, 1995), p. 21.
11. Quoted by Gary MacEoin, *The People's Church* (Crossroad Publishing, 1996), p. 23.
12. Ibid. p. 25.
13. See above p. 220.
14. *A Global Ethic*, eds. Küng and Kuschel, p. 25.

15. Ibid. p. 28.
16. *Yes to a Global Ethic*, ed. Hans Küng (SCM Press, 1996), pp. 158–59.
17. Ibid. p. 129.
18. Küng and Kuschel, *A Global Ethic*, p. 26.
19. Küng, *Yes to a Global Ethic*, p. 130.
20. Charlene Spretnak, *States of Grace* (HarperCollins, 1993), p. 117.
21. Ibid. p. 133.
22. Ibid. p. 119.
23. *Doctrine in the Church of England* (SPCK, 1938), p. 36 (Slightly altered to avoid sexist language!).
24. George Appleton, *Jerusalem Prayers* (SPCK, 1974), p. 77.

Index

Index

Index

Index

Index

Index